ADVANCED
ROWING

ADVANCED ROWING

International Perspectives on High
Performance Rowing

CHARLES SIMPSON AND JIM FLOOD

B L O O M S B U R Y

LONDON • OXFORD • NEW YORK • NEW DELHI • SYDNEY

Bloomsbury Sport
An imprint of Bloomsbury Publishing Plc
50 Bedford Square, London, WC1B 3DP, UK
29 Earlsfort Terrace, Dublin 2, Ireland

www.bloomsbury.com

BLOOMSBURY and the Diana logo are trademarks of Bloomsbury Publishing Plc

First published 2017

© Charles Simpson and Jim Flood, 2017
For photo copyright please see page 231

British Library Cataloguing-in-Publication Data
A catalogue record for this book is available from the British Library.

Library of Congress Cataloguing-in-Publication data has been applied for.

ISBN: Print: 978-1-4729-1233-6
ePDF: 978-1-4729-2151-2
ePub: 978-1-4729-2150-5

4 6 8 10 9 7 5

Typeset in FBCalifornian by Deanta Global Publishing Services, Chennai, India
Printed and bound in Great Britain by CPI Group (UK) Ltd. Croydon, CR0 4YY

To find out more about our authors and books visit www.bloomsbury.com. Here you will find extracts,
author interviews, details of forthcoming events and the option to sign up for our newsletters.

Contents

Introduction

The motivation for this book evolved gradually over many years of intense discussion about what features help to develop an advanced level of rowing performance. We were well aware that national and international coaching conferences included presentations from many top-level coaches about their strategies for success, but much of this information was interesting without being sufficiently detailed to help develop the performance of other rowers. It was also difficult to evaluate how much of the information on international level rowing was applicable to the majority of rowers worldwide who compete at the national level. Nevertheless, those with ideas and knowledge to share had a growing audience of rowers and coaches ready to hear it. Thus, we have assembled a range of expert contributors who each have extensive experience of rowing as athletes, coaches, scientists and commentators in order to share their insights about rowing at the national and international level.

Our intended audience includes rowers and coaches who will have a good working knowledge of the sport. Some of the material in this book may still be useful to individuals who compete in junior, master or Para-rowing competitions, however, we have purposely excluded these groups in order to avoid making the text too general and non-specific. The first two sections of the book consider the opinions and experiences of high performance coaches who work with international standard athletes (Part 1) or national standard athletes who compete in club and university teams (Part 2). We asked these contributors to begin with an overview of their training facilities and then to discuss their thoughts about training, testing, team selection, interpersonal relations between athlete and coach as well as their comments on technical development, specific race preparation and the use of support services and other experts.

Essentially, we hope that these chapters give good insight into the day-to-day practices of top coaches across three continents. Readers will certainly find considerable overlap. One of the strong commonalities that we noted was an enthusiastic level of curiosity. These top coaches are still reading avidly about the latest research and developments in rowing; they often work with research establishments to analyse data about the effectiveness of their training methods; they describe themselves as 'still learning', 'still experimenting', 'still trying out new ideas'. Above all, they talk about building a relationship with their athletes so that they get to know 'what makes them tick'. Many of these coaches talk about their own formative experiences as a rower or cox, and the way in which their coaches involved them in decision making – and how this has become part of their own practice. Another commonality that many of these coaches refer to is the 'X factor' – that is the rower who defies conventional wisdom in respect of physical attributes – and yet with that person in a crew the coach knows, intuitively, that boat will eventually go faster.

There are also differences between coaches both within each competitive level (national or international) and between levels. Some of these differences are highly revealing. For example, the differences in training methods, facilities and training volume can be substantial – as is the size of the pool of rowers from which different countries select their teams. What is remarkable is that some countries can win World Championships and Olympic events with a national team of rowers who also work or study, with facilities and a budget not much larger than that of a metropolitan rowing club. Hopefully, this will provide inspiration for any club or university coach working at the national level.

We also anticipated that there would be specific mention by our coach contributors of many specialised aspects of preparing rowers for competition that would either have required more detail than we could reasonably expect within the chapter, or where the details of the topic were beyond the technical expertise of the contributor. Thus, Part 3 contains further details of selected topics of relevance to advanced rowers that we thought useful to include. These chapters combine aspects of scientific research with applied practice, underlining that the development of competitive rowers at the advanced level is part science and part art.

We hope that this book will give all readers useful insights into the features that are important for creating high performance rowing programmes. We also hope that it can help demystify much of what makes teams successful. Understandably, aspiring rowers and coaches often seek to understand what the most successful teams do in order to improve their own practices and subsequent performances. However, when the quality of this information is poor, it can give rise to misinformation and excessive speculation that may waste time, resources and opportunity. We would encourage readers to keep an open mind to the reality that success in rowing is multifaceted and not likely to be understood through brief and simple answers. We hope that readers will find the content within all three sections interesting and enjoyable as well as valuable for the purposes of advancing their own rowing performances.

Charles Simpson and Jim Flood

Part 1

Senior International Rowing

Noel Donaldson Head Coach, Rowing New Zealand

Noel Donaldson rowed at high school and then became a very accomplished cox, steering the Australian men's eight at the 1979 World Rowing Championships. He began coaching at high school level, before his appointment as Rowing Australia's Elite Development Manager for the under-21s and under-23s. He coached the team's 'Oarsome Foursome' to back-to-back Olympic golds in 1992 and 1996, following this with a bronze medal in M2- in 2000. As the men's head coach he led the Australian team to gold, silver and bronze in Athens in 2004. From 2004 to 2008 he was Rowing Australia's High Performance Director and from 2008 to 2013 their men's head coach. In 2013 Noel accepted the post as Lead Coach for men's sweep with Rowing New Zealand, where he has coached the outstanding pair of Hamish Bond and Eric Murray to three consecutive gold medals including a double gold in 2014 in the M2- and M2+, and gold again in the M2- at the Rio Olympics.

My interest in rowing started in 1968 when I became a cox for my school rowing team in Melbourne, Australia. My older brother had been coxing there for a while and rowing seemed a cool thing to do, so I spent five years developing as a cox. After finishing my schooling, I progressed my coxing at club and state levels before gaining selection for the Australian national team. Coxing is probably the best preparation to become a coach and in 1974 I started my first coaching role, which was working with the under-15s group back at my school. I did that for a few years before taking a break from coaching to complete a degree in hospitality management. Not long after I finished my studies, I received a call from my old rowing master asking if I was available to coach the following year. My cheeky response was 'Only if you offer me a full-time job', which he took seriously and came back with an offer. At this time, I had been trying to keep up with my rowing but the unsociable hours of the hospitality industry made this difficult, so I accepted the coaching job. At the same time, I enrolled on a degree course in physical education, and within a short time I was studying full-time, working full-time and coxing for the Australian national team. Despite the complexities and the hectic nature of my schedule, however, the experience of competing at a high level, together with my later studies of sports science, provided a very strong basis for my development as a coach.

My interest in the process of coaching began at school when my coach Rob Stewart, a former national lightweight rower and a very good coach, began to involve me in discussions about how the boat was travelling. He also gave me a sense of 'ownership' of the crew and developed my confidence in giving feedback to both him and the crew. This was a time of wooden boats and oars so 'feel' was a key factor in the successes we had with a relatively light crew. A further spur to success was that in the second year of coxing this crew we did not get the result we worked for, despite making every effort. I learned a lot from that experience. By this time, I was developing an understanding of some of the factors that make a boat move well, and also realising that coaching was something I could aspire to.

This curiosity about how to move a boat was developed further when I was coxing the national team with Brian Richardson in the stroke seat. Brian went on to become head coach of Canada, Australia and more recently has been coaching in Denmark. He would say to me things like, 'Tell three to stop wobbling in his seat'. I sat there thinking, 'how does he know that?' Later I worked out that he could feel a slight wobble and, knowing the idiosyncrasies of each of the crew, he could pick out the one responsible. On occasion, I still get into the cox seat to get a feel for what is going on with the crew.

Over the years, I have had a variety of different senior coaching roles in Australia, mostly in Melbourne and then at the Australian Institute of Sport in Canberra. I had great success in coaching the Australian men's coxless four to golds in the 1992 and 1996 Olympics and held various coaching and administrative roles with Rowing Australia, including head coach. However, at the beginning of 2013, I was appointed lead coach for the New Zealand men's sweep team. At the time, New Zealand's rowing teams were doing extremely well, especially in small boats, and part of my role has been to expand the depth of talent and build towards success in the larger boat classes. This has required the support of a range of other coaches and support staff to cope with the growing number of high-performance athletes in our hands. Trust is clearly important to making these relationships work and I was lucky in this respect that part of my role was to encourage the other staff in our team to take greater ownership of their area. As a team, we have been able to focus on making boats go faster rather than on internal politics.

TRAINING ENVIRONMENT

Rowing New Zealand has an international regatta course at Lake Karapiro on the North Island, which was the venue for the 2010 World Championships. As the main hub of rowing in New Zealand the training centre at Karapiro is also home to a large number of support and administration staff. There are also four regional performance centres around the country that have the aim of developing athletes capable of representing New Zealand at international events.

Lake Karapiro is an impressive body of water. It was created in the mid-20th century when a dam was built across the Waikato River as part of a hydroelectric project. This is essentially where we do all our water-based training when we are in New Zealand. Our athletes spend about three months each year training and racing

View of Lake Karapiro. *Credit: Don Somner*

overseas, mostly in Europe, so we appreciate the stability in day-to-day experience that comes from using the same body of water. Our training centre has all the essential components necessary for a rowing team including a fully buoyed eight-lane 2000-metre racecourse, which is available during most of the year, including the New Zealand club racing season (September to April).

The lake measures 11km in length by approximately 1km at the widest point. It has some twists and turns but nothing that becomes irritating or an impediment to good rowing. Of course, the water can get rough on such a large reservoir, but we rarely lose water time due to poor weather. This part of New Zealand has a pretty mild climate, with an average daily temperature of 10°C in winter (June to August) and about 25°C in summer (December to February), so we don't have much to complain about.

The lake has a large dam at one end and a road bridge at the other where the lake becomes a river again. If we want, we can row under the bridge and do another 4km of rowing before the river narrows, even then you can go on for another 10km, but we mostly stay on the lake. We share the water with many other users including various rowing programmes as well as canoe and water ski clubs. There is even the occasional hydroplane motorboat racing competition. Regular lake users are respectful of other groups and give us plenty of space for our training and racing. It is also spectacularly scenic with very clean, clear water and lots of surrounding green spaces.

Overall, Lake Karipiro is a fantastic and inspiring place to do our training and although our athletes row in many spectacular locations overseas, we all enjoy coming back to do quality training and preparation here.

The boathouse at Karipiro is about 7km from the small town of Cambridge and it's another 20km further to the city of Hamilton. Most of the team cycle to practice along a pretty flat cycle track that runs alongside the lake and that is mostly protected from motor vehicles. The boathouse accommodates offices for the various Rowing New Zealand staff, including the seven full-time rowing coaches. We also have facilities for strength training and a rowing ergometer section. There are dedicated areas for massage therapy, sports medicine and meeting rooms. There is lots of storage on the ground floor for boats and there is also an athlete lounge where the rowers can relax and watch videos or use computers. We don't yet have any catering services on site, but if the athletes want food, they can help themselves to the well-stocked kitchen that usually has plenty of fresh fruit, vegetables, dairy produce, bread, cereals and snacks. There are microwaves and other essential kitchen supplies if athletes want to get more creative. We don't have any overnight accommodation in the boathouse – it's really not needed since all the senior athletes live nearby – but we do have arrangements with a local chalet company so we can offer short-term accommodation to team members where necessary.

Perhaps the hardest aspect of our training environment to describe is the atmosphere. We currently have an incredible number of the world's best rowers training in one central location. Unsurprisingly, everyone who trains in this facility is extremely competitive. The athletes find ways to compete with each other both on and off the water with no regard to whether an athlete is male or female or whether they are in the sweep or sculling programme. Everyone is watching everyone else, even if some

Indoor training facilities in the Karipiro boathouse. *Credit: Steve McArthur*

The boathouse at Lake Karipiro. *Credit: Steve McArthur*

are better at hiding it than others. This competitiveness, which reaches through the entire team, is especially useful. The geographical isolation of New Zealand prevents us from gaining the kind of racing experience afforded to rowers in Europe. So, we have learned to embrace this competitiveness and use it to create a fun environment. For example, we created a squad triathlon to let all the athletes compete against each other in an unfamiliar event. This upsets the usual rowing-determined pecking order, creates many surprising results and gives everyone a chance to channel their competitiveness into something unusual. We have fun gym sessions, pushing cars uphill and other competitive team activities. Personally, I don't know the point at which competitiveness can become harmful, but I don't think there needs to be a limit on how much fun and enjoyment athletes should get from training, both on and off the water.

TRAINING AND CONDITIONING

As a lead coach one of my responsibilities, together with our lead physiologist, is the design of a national training programme based on the principles of periodised planning. We plan backwards from international to domestic competitions. This does not include every single session but it does have weekly flows and includes the loadings, the testing activities and the competitions. Some head coaches would recommend more detail with no room for negotiation, but many of the good coaches we work with like to have some control over the process so they can interpret it in their own way – and this is the model we operate.

Our training programme is reasonably similar to what is typically prescribed to many other international rowing teams. It is a polarised programme where the majority of our training (80 per cent or more) is performed at relatively low intensities (approximately 70 per cent maximum heart rate) and athletes spend between 20 and 30 hours each week actively engaged in the training. Fortunately, most of the athletes that I coach on a day-to-day basis, which is about 15, are able to commit to full-time rowing. Several of my current group are registered for university courses but much of their part-time academic workload is completed online. A few athletes also have obligations to corporate sponsors, such as giving occasional talks or performing ambassadorial roles, but this is usually no more than half a day per week and training is rarely compromised.

We have the facilities to capture the volume of training that our athletes perform using our GPS systems and daily activity logging. In a typical week, I know exactly how much training each of my athletes has actually done. In spite of rumours to the contrary, the total weekly volume of rowing activity (on-water and ergometer) rarely exceeds 200km and is more usually between 150 and 180km per week, most of which is on-water rowing. For instance, we perform our highest training volumes in March and April when our men's eight undertake between 160 and 180km of actual rowing, and this drops back every fourth week to somewhere between 120 and 140km in order to give the athletes' bodies a chance to recover and adapt to the schedule. Table 1 on the following page shows one of our hard training weeks (May).

We also do a sizable amount of non-rowing activity. Cycling, for example, constitutes a regular part of our aerobic training base and is included throughout the

Most of the New Zealand rowers complete between 50–200 miles per week. *Credit: Steve McArthur*

Table 1: Example Training Week: May (Senior Men's Eight)

Day	Time	Training	Rest	Stroke rate (strokes/min)	Intensity	Distance (km)	Training time (hours:min)
Monday	am 1	Rowing: Steady state paddle in Eight and stretching	n/a	21	U2	14	[Monday: 3:10]
	am 2	Weight training: Standard session (and download heart-rate monitors today)	n/a				
	pm 1	Rowing ergometer: Intervals 3 x 30 sec Max Power and 6 x 4 min at 100% VO2	3 min + 2 min	free rate	AN/TR		
Tuesday	am 1	Rowing: Row in Eight including rate switches every 5 min	n/a	18 + 24 + 18 etc…	U2/U1	26	[Tuesday: 4:10]
	am 2	Meeting with Sport Psychologist					
	pm 1	Rowing: Steady state paddle in Eight	n/a	21	U2	22	
Wednesday	am 1	Rowing: Team workout 3 x 3 km in Eight	back-to-back	30, 32, 34	TR	16	[Wednesday: 3:45]
	am 2	Rowing: Steady state paddle in Eight and easy 45 min bike ride home	n/a	21	U2	16	
	pm 1	Weights: Circuit style session	n/a				
Thursday	am 1	Rest					[Thursday: 3:40]
	am 2	Cycling: 45 min - Rowing: 30 min 'tank emptier' to exhaustion in Eight	n/a	18, 20, 22 … 40, max	U2 to AN	31	
		Cycling: easy 45-min bike ride home	n/a		U3		
Friday	am 1	Rowing: Bungee cords (1 x 3 min; 4 x 4 min; 1 x 3 min) and racing starts; then 4 min at rate 32 without bungee cords	2 min + 3 min	26 + 26 + 28 + 30	U1 to AnT	18	[Friday: 3:40]
	pm 1	Weights: Standard session	n/a				
	pm 2	Rowing: Steady state paddle in Eight	n/a	21	U2	16	
Saturday	am 1	Rowing: Team workout 2 x 4 km rate 28 to 30 in Eight	row back	28 + 30	TR	22	[Saturday: 4:20]
	am 2	Rowing: Steady state paddle in Eight and 45 min easy bike ride home	n/a	21	U2	22	
		Make up any missed sessions from this week [otherwise rest]					
Sunday		Rest day					[Sunday: 0:00]
					Total	203	[Week: 22:45]

Table 2: Overview of training intensity zones used in example training week shown in Table 1

Training Zones	Description	Stroke Rate (per min)	Ergometer split*	Perceived Exertion	Critical Duration	% heart rate max	% VO$_2$ max	Blood Lactate Threshold Relationship	Lactate (mMol)
U3	Light Aerobic	<17	> TP+26	Very Light	>3 hours	60 - 75	<60	Below LT1	<2.0
U2	Moderate Aerobic	16 - 22	(TP+19) to (TP+25)	Light	1 - 3 hours	75 - 84	60 - 72	Lower half between LT1 & LT2	1.0 - 3.0
U1	Heavy Aerobic	18 - 26	(TP+13) to (TP+18)	Somewhat Hard	20 min - 1 hour	82 - 89	70 - 82	Upper half between LT1 & LT2	2.0 - 4.0
T4 (AnT)	Threshold	22 - 28	(TP+10) to (TP+12)	Hard	12 - 30 min	88 - 93	80 - 85	LT2	3.0 - 6.0
T5 (TR)	Maximal Aerobic	24 - 34	(TP+11) to TP	Very Hard	5 - 8 min	92 - 100	85 - 100	Above LT2	>5.0
T5 (RP)	Race Pace	28 -38	TP	as is	1:30 - 5 min	as is	as is		
AN	Anaerobic	36 - max	Max Speed, <TP	as is	10 sec - 1 min	as is	as is		

*TP is 2000-m race pace

Table 3: Gym based conditioning sessions for training week example shown in Table 1

Warm-up	STRENGTH (Mon & Fri):	CIRCUIT (Wed):
10x Overhead Squat (Broomstick)	Power Cleans (>80kg) or, Romanian dead lifts (>80kg)	3x Hang Power Cleans (70kg)
15x 4kg Dumbbell Shoulder Diagonals	Box Jump Ups (>60cm) or, Leg Press (>250kg)	7x (Floor) Power Cleans (70kg)
30x Sumo Stance, Squat	Squat (>120kg) or, Barbell Hip Thrusts (>160kg)	10x Seated Cable Row (70kg)
10x Thoracic-spine Rotations	Bench Press (>75kg) or, Clap Push Ups	**As many rounds as possible for 6 mins**
5x Cat/Camel Stretch	1-arm Dumbbell Rows (>40kg)	15x Kettlebell Swings (20kg)
60s Wide-kneeling Groin Stretch	PLUS, INDIVIDUAL "WORK-ONS", examples:	5x 60cm Box Jump-Ups with Burpee
100x Skips	*eyes closed, 1-leg balance (4x30s)	**6 Rounds for time**
15x Burpees or, Push-ups	*kneeling, alternate arm/leg raise (4x10)	5x Chin Ups
10x Overhead Squat	*side hold, with leg lift (2x10 each side)	5x "Clap" Press-Ups
	MON - HEAVY: 5 sets x 6 reps (increase weight each set)	10x "Jump" Squats
	FRI - LOW: 3 sets x 10 reps (using 85% 1RM - HEAVY)	**As many rounds as possible for 6 mins**

year. Everyone does between 50 and 200km per week, though this includes travel to training and personal preference for their own cross-training time. This activity is so important that we include it as a separate feature in the weekly training reports for each athlete. There are obvious safety considerations with cycling, but we are fortunate to have very safe roads and dedicated cycling tracks around the lake as well as plenty of Wattbike cycle ergometers and wind trainers in the boathouse. There is a limit to how much rowing is beneficial before injuries and boredom become problematic, so the inclusion of regular cycling in our training has been helpful to improving the aerobic capabilities of our rowers.

Most of my athletes do regular weight training. However, there are exceptions, such as our Olympic champions in the coxless pair (Bond and Murray). Hamish and Eric have been in and out of weight training over their long careers – I have great respect for their approach and certainly they have found alternative ways to train, mostly by adding extra cycling and on-water rowing. However, most of our athletes do three sessions of weightlifting per week, and there is more detail about our approach to this provided by our strength and conditioning coach later in the book (see page 171).

The rowing ergometer is a regular feature of our weekly training up until the final weeks of the international rowing season. Most athletes use static Concept2 ergometers, although some athletes prefer the use of the Concept2 Dynamic erg and I also like the Rowperfect ergometers. So we can select different types of rowing machines to add variety to the training. Currently, we only use straight pull rowing machines and this reflects my belief that rowing machines, at least in our high-performance environment, are essentially a conditioning device. We get plenty of water time in sweep boats every month, so the key physiological and biomechanical adaptations for rowing success are already well catered for within our comprehensive training programme.

It is a major challenge to develop an effective training programme that can progress athletes towards their individual fitness goals and also ensures that collective team fitness reaches a peak that coincides with the World or Olympic championships. Of course, no coach knows exactly how to prescribe the ideal training programme for a given rower and even if we did, we still have to train athletes in crew boats. However, I am able to gain excellent insight into the progress of every athlete through the use of careful and detailed training logs. When a new athlete joins my group, we provide them with a Garmin watch that logs their GPS and heart-rate data. It is a strict requirement that all athletes use their watch at every training session, including any on-water or cycling activity. Our team physiologists work hard to ensure that the athletes know how to use these watches, including how to categorise their sessions (e.g. cycling, on-water rowing, ergometer etc.) as well as setting individual training zones for each athlete based on the results of our physiological profiling. All the data is uploaded at regular intervals and we use the Training Peaks software, which produces detailed reports of each athletes complete weekly training activity and performance.

The extensive data set of training information that we now have on each of our athletes, especially when incorporated with our on-water biomechanics data as

Rower with heart-rate monitor. *Credit: Steve McArthur*

well as our regular physiological profiling, helps inform decisions about training prescription. We also have a quantitative holistic measure of each athlete's 'readiness to train' which is rated on a 10-point scale and derived from a combination of physiological data (e.g. heart-rate variability) and the training load achieved (obtained from the Training Peaks output as 'Training Stress Balance'). All of this data, which could easily overwhelm a coach who was working in isolation without sport science support staff, is incredibly useful to help track each athlete's training achievements as well as to plan modifications for ongoing training sessions. Thanks to the cloud-based nature of the software and data capture, I can log in and review each athlete's training history as well as generating a tabulated or graphical overview of the squad's collective efforts. This allows me to make informed choices about when to offer the team (or an individual athlete) more recovery time or when to push the training load higher. These online records also keep me aware of what each athlete is doing even when I cannot see them training, such as when they take a two-hour bike ride in the hills around Cambridge.

Another benefit that we gain from our approach to recording training is that it helps to educate athletes about their own unique training progress and allows, indeed encourages, athletes to make their own choices. I have coached many highly successful rowers during my 40+ years of coaching and no two rowers have ever trained in exactly the same way. Moreover, all rowers respond in slightly different ways to a standard training programme, and years of trial and error have helped me to become much more comfortable letting athletes take greater ownership of their individual training. Of course, less experienced athletes such as junior and under-23 rowers, benefit from a strong-guided approach until they have enough confidence, experience and education to take greater independent control. Without the careful record keeping and accurate training load monitoring, it would be much harder to build the necessary level of trust and confidence between athlete and coach. Yet, once this trust and understanding has been achieved, we have a platform that allows our athletes to make greater training progress. I believe that much of what makes our training programme so successful is the extent to which we [coaches] are willing to adjust the training load based on the input of our sport science and strength and conditioning staff, in combination with the athlete's awareness of their own health and progress. The benefits that can be realised from this approach include, but are not limited: to a reduction in injury risk, optimisation of physiological and technical adaptations, improved athlete enjoyment and retention in addition to the welcome reduction in the number of decisions that I have to make each week.

I certainly do not want to mislead the reader about the scale and challenge of setting up a comprehensive training data capture approach. It is a massive project and requires a lot of co-operation and determination. We are fortunate to have excellent support staff that work with the athletes so that there is no burden on me to record the data. Instead, I can concentrate on using the weekly training reports to help support the progress of the team. I have been happy to publish accurate samples of our training in this chapter, but this only partly reveals why our athletes are successful. I think much of what makes training effective for high-performance rowers is knowing when to increase or decrease the training load and this requires a degree of flexible programming at the individual level. Fundamentally, these are not matters that can be made transparent, but I can at least highlight that data collection is at the heart of it. All athletes and coaches collect information without the need for formal records, simple or sophisticated – that's what we call 'experience'. However, in the demanding world of elite sport, there is much that can be gained from a building a systematic database of training information at the individual and team level. This has helped optimise our training approach and made it easier to educate our athletes and coaches about what training is required. A database that captures our athletes' training and performance gains has provided valuable insight into talent identification and athlete selection.

ATHLETE SELECTION AND TALENT DEVELOPMENT

In New Zealand, talent identification and development is a key part of our national strategy. We have regional performance centres that do the majority of the high-performance development and we have a very strong school system that is similar to the Australian system with its state programmes. As the national coaching team, we have great ideas about how to identify, retain and develop athletes, but in reality we can only have an impact at the top of the tree and not on the beginning of the talent pipeline. I would love to think that we could spend more time and energy in the schools and clubs, for example, to try to prevent the burn out that happens, but the reality is that we have very little control and not enough resources to do this.

We have much more influence on athletes after the age of 21 when they typically join the high-performance training groups with our national team coaches and support staff. We select these athletes through conventional methods including ergometer scores, laboratory testing and regatta performances. I also talk to the coaches at our regional performance centres about how athletes are progressing and, when all this information is combined with the objective tracking metrics, I am able to identify individuals who are suitable for fast tracking to the national team group. These are usually individuals who are making rapid and sustained progress. Once they are in our system, we can offer an enhanced level of support on a variety of important elements (e.g. strength and flexibility).

Rowing in New Zealand is still a minority sport and most of the participation base is in the high school system. For example, about 80 per cent of the rowers in New Zealand who hold a competition licence for official regattas are juniors. There are currently 65 rowing clubs as well as 155 high schools and nine universities that have established rowing teams. Rowing New Zealand has various development managers who work with regional and local coaches to develop athletes from schools and universities and this takes time and money. However, most of our senior rowing talent arrives through these pathways and many will have experience of competing at World Junior Championships by the time they come to us.

In terms of the attributes of potential champions, we look for the key anthropometric factors that provide good levers (e.g. standing height) and general athletic ability (e.g. strength). We then start to look at how effectively a person uses these attributes, and this is where we might consider their movement coordination in the boat. There are occasionally individuals with good athleticism but who lack effectiveness and efficiency in the boat. We have to allow these athletes time to develop and although we can fast track them into our system, it often doesn't succeed. Ultimately, our selection pool includes a range of athlete types. Some are brilliant technicians while others have a great kinaesthetic feel for the water. I hardly have to teach these individuals anything since they just know how to adjust to whatever boat they are allocated. Other athletes are mentally and physically very tough and resilient, so much so that they are prepared to really hurt themselves in ways that are difficult to comprehend. I think this is an often underappreciated aspect of international rowing success. Clearly, all the finalists in an Olympic regatta are willing to push towards the limit of what their body will allow, but there are some athletes who are willing to push their pain tolerance to unimaginable limits. These athletes are also able to use their personal determination to get even more benefit from the training and conditioning process. Some athletes display this willingness early in the selection and recruitment process, while others seem to acquire it through the process of development. Identifying such athletes is part of the 'art' of the coach.

All athletes have individual performance plans that include such things as ergometer score targets and the amount of weight they can lift. Ergometer scores are obviously an important part of high-performance rowing. We currently have an average 2000m personal best ergometer (stationary) score average in our men's pair of 5min 42sec and about 5:52 in the men's eight; everyone is 5:57 or better. This information is important for establishing the standards needed to win medals in senior international regattas and these help inform our targets for developing athletes. If we had a 21-year-old with a 2000m best of 6:15 at the start of a season, we would certainly expect the score to improve towards the range we see in our senior athletes, but our under-23 age group heavyweight rowers are more usually in the 6:00 to 6:12 area. All athletes have to participate in national team testing, which includes a 5000m test in November, 2000m in January and most importantly, our national selection trials, held each February, begin with a 2000m ergometer test. We also use the ergometer to create power continuums for each athlete. These are graphs that show a plot of each athlete's performance at 100m, 500m, 2000m, 5000m and 30 or 60 minutes. Ultimately, the rowing machine is one of the most important selection and talent identification tools that we have.

During my years of coaching, I have attempted to be more reliant on science to select crews, especially when working with crews at the Australian Institute of Sport where we had extensive input from biomechanists, physiologists and sport psychologists. However, the final results were not always as predicted on the basis of the individual capabilities, so I have found that it is important to consider other factors too, such as how well a crew get on and the collective effectiveness of their efforts. I think it was Aristotle who is often quoted as having said that, 'the whole is greater than the sum of the parts'; perhaps he had ancient Greek rowing crews in mind!

COACH AND ATHLETE RELATIONSHIP

It is important for athletes and coaches to have a good understanding of each other. That doesn't necessarily mean having a close personal understanding, though much is learned from the many hours spent together in training. However, there is no need for coaches and athletes to be on social terms, but I do think it is helpful for a coach to know a little about each athlete. This could simply include things about their family background and personal relationships as well as the important motivations they have. Much of this information is provided during the individual performance plan meeting we have before training begins.

These days we record how well athletes have slept and so on, but when looking at an individual I'm asking 'What's happening?', 'What's going through your mind?' If I know them well enough I will understand the ebbs and flows of their performance a lot better. It is unrealistic to expect to get the same performance out of an athlete every single day and they have various pressures from study, from home, from relationships and family. How relaxed a person are they, do they socialise, go out and have a drink? I need to know what makes them tick. On occasion, I have had the physiologists tell me that an athlete's scores are not good and the psychologist telling me that the same athlete is struggling with their training, and I say to them 'But do you know that their grandmother is suffering from terminal cancer?' As a coach, it is important to know more about each athlete especially so that you can be supportive on and off the water. I am aware that I can be pretty tough on athletes and I think this helps keep many athletes honest about their effort in training and competition. But, if I do not know something about their background and home life, then I would risk applying that same toughness for the wrong reasons. After all, I have a responsibility to help athletes find their best performance. I can't do that if I don't know who they are.

The need to provide motivation during training sessions varies according to the crew. For example, our men's pair (Bond and Murray) really understand how to push themselves and they know when sessions are going to be extremely hard. I try to work with them on that and try to understand what it feels like for them. Sometimes an element of wit or sarcasm can help get them into the right frame of mind. With younger, less experienced athletes, I might use different forms of extrinsic or intrinsic motivation. For example, I might raise my voice or remind them that the opposition is working as hard as they are, and this provides a spur so that they can get the most out of themselves. Sometimes, after an inadequate training session, I might feel the desire to tell an athlete that 'if you don't know how to push yourselves, then you should not be here'. But I live in the real world and I know that athletes have to develop their mental capacity and they need some form of encouragement along the way. So, I have learned to frame these types of comments in a more helpful way, such as 'I can't make you do it, you can only do it yourselves'. In turn, of course, athletes also have to learn the signals from the coach that indicate when more effort is needed.

We are now encouraging athletes in New Zealand to be more confident in their communication by asking questions and to challenge all of the coaching and support staff more in terms of what are we doing, why are we doing it – it is part of their education. I also tell them, 'I don't mind you asking questions but if you are "questioning" without some understanding or a solution in mind, then you may well be on the wrong track'. We try to help educate our athletes about how best to ask a question. Occasionally, athletes get annoyed (athletes are prone to being rather intense) and resort to yelling and shouting. If this is a regular occurrence with a particular athlete, then there are certain ways of dealing with it. In the heat of the moment, we could always fight fire with fire and tell them that their behaviour is inappropriate, but in my experience this is more likely best resolved in a more structured conversation after training. If a display of frustration comes from someone who rarely shows impatience, then that may need more care and consideration. However, a coach should deal with incidents like this on a case-by-case basis. In my earlier coaching days, I am sure that I could have been more patient with athletes and, had I done so, I suspect I would have enjoyed even better results and made the training atmosphere better for everyone. I now try to be more measured in response to conflict and disharmony. Athletes still have to learn professionalism and how to get their point across without creating tension or allowing frustration to control them – this is the way it has to be in racing and so it must be learned in practice. Coaches need not shy away from confrontation, but will more than likely benefit from creating an environment where athletes are not afraid of asking questions.

TECHNICAL APPROACH

When I started in the sport we had wooden boats and wooden oars. We had little technical equipment and to move a boat well and gain advantage over your opponent you had to be a fluid, well-coordinated and skilled practitioner. Many younger coaches and rowers now have only worked with modern materials and sometimes they may not quite understand the 'feel' of the boat. They have a lot of clinical knowledge of rowing but some of the art has been lost in the drive to modernise our sport.

As a former cox I'm always thinking about the process of rowing as a whole. In terms of achieving an outcome through coaching drills, this can be contextual. For example, Murray and Bond have been through a range of different styles in their rowing journey including the influence of people such as Drew Ginn, a former Australian champion that I coached for many years in Australia. As a result, when I became their coach in 2013, I picked up a fairly set product and knew that it wasn't for me to try and change much about how they row. My role has been to work with them on how to refine their style; to discuss other ways of thinking about it, to consider other race strategies and so on. I have taken a much more applied holistic, race performance viewpoint related to their skill processes. So I do not necessarily try to change a specific skill but instead try and develop an idea or a concept that we have shared and agreed to explore together. This could be about how to maximise the run of the boat or how we synchronise. Murray and Bond spend very little time performing drills and when they do, it is for a very specific purpose. At the moment, they have their own starting drill of wide grip with feet out which helps them to establish a coordinated movement pattern early in the session. For a crew that has established excellent stroke mechanics and boat feel, there are few purposeful uses for drills.

When coaching my younger athletes who are still learning to put the pieces together, in terms of hands body slide, hang, push, pull, I coach the individual a lot more. I also coach the crew a lot more, in terms of style and technique and what we

Men's pair in training. *Credit: Steve McArthur*

are looking for. Over the years there have been many changes in rowing style, but essentially the technique of moving the boat efficiently remains the same. It's a question of polishing it, drilling it and improving it.

In my present work with the New Zealand men's eight, there is a much more evolution in terms of technique and drills play an important role here. I should first point out that I think it is often unhelpful to simply copy drills that other coaches and athletes use. I certainly would not recommend making technique changes without first gaining a solid understanding of what the likely effects of the change will be. This is a policy that I have maintained throughout my coaching career. There are too many unique factors that are specific to individual athletes and each crew to expect that what appears to work for another boat, can work equally well for the one in front of me. For example, if a crew rows in a particular way, then you need to train a particular way and rig the boat a particular way. If a crew is more even-paced, then they may need to train with a nice steady rhythm all the time and undergo more endurance training. If a crew has the capacity to produce an explosive finish, this places different technical demands on them and this needs to be thought about in terms of practice. The important thing about the technical aspects of developing high-performance rowing is that these must accommodate the specific capabilities of each athlete and crew.

I usually include some sort of technical drill during the warm-up for each water session. The specific drills are matched to the technical objectives for the week and adjusted to suit the needs of each crew. I do, however, have a few favourite drills that

I often find helpful including pause drills and roll-ups. The pause drills are used across different parts of the stroke to match the technical objectives. For example, we might take a brief pause just after the release on every third stroke to try and encourage smooth finishes and promote better feel for the balance. It is important to remind the athletes that the goal is to use the drill to improve their overall rowing. The continuous strokes between each pause are a good time to reinforce this message. I also find roll-up drills helpful. So we might have part of the crew holding the balance, while the remaining athletes roll forward on the seat from finish to catch placement. This is very helpful to encourage athletes to set their body position well in advance of arriving at the catch. Again, I make sure to watch the athletes closely once we finish a drill to help ensure that improvements from isolated movements are successfully transferred to normal rowing.

There are occasions in a training session when an athlete is not able to respond to my coaching on a technical point and I have exhausted my own repertoire of ways of tackling this. I might then ask another coach to take a look. I'm always happy for another coach to give my athletes advice – as long as they keep me in the loop about what has been done or said. I would never ignore another coach's input and views on the problem. The other key decision about a technical 'fault' is to weigh up the detriment to performance. There are a lot of ugly rowing styles out there that are moving boats extremely fast. Too often as coaches we get caught up with the aesthetics of the stroke pattern – and we need to make a really conscious decision about how the aesthetics appears in terms of the performance of the boat and the individual. If it doesn't affect

Men's eight in training. *Credit: Steve McArthur*

boat speed, then don't worry about it. I can give you an example from when I was working with Professor Theo Khorner, formerly of the German Democratic Republic, and one the greatest coaches in the world. We were both coaching James Tomkins, one of the greatest athletes in the world. I had coached James at school and he was not good at squaring and placing the blades in the water. Theo asked me to give him the megaphone and he kept on saying 'now, now, now' when he wanted James to square the blade and get it ready. One result of this was that James's heart rate was much higher than normal because, as he said, he had so much more to think about when this world famous coach whom we all respected was shouting at him. I had to weigh up the relative importance of this advice, especially when I realised the small amount of water that was being missed – and James was still getting hold of the water quicker than any other rower in the world. As I did not consider it relevant, and because the 'cure' was unlikely to make James go faster, I ignored Theo's advice. At that time, James was already a world champion and he went on to win three Olympic gold medals. As a coach you need to judge what's important and what's not.

Another example I would give is that one of my fellow coaches, who was coaching an eight, became obsessed with the rower in the three seat who was 'skying' his blade, shooting his slide and always out of sequence. This coach was spending almost three-quarters of the coaching session working on this rower's faults, often stopping and talking to him about the problem. I had to point out that he was ignoring the rest of the crew – the guys who are going to win you the race. The coaching and training time that these crew members were missing was amounting to as much as one week in seven. Sometimes you have to stop worrying about individuals; if they are reasonably competent rowers they will fit in better once the crew begins to move the boat at race speed. Trying to fix the problem can result in slowing the boat down. Sometimes you have to stop looking at the aesthetics and keep the key people training and concentrate on improving their fitness.

SUPPORT SERVICES AND TECHNOLOGY

It would be easy to think that with the modern technology available, we can quantify the 'feel factor' in terms of forces and angles, but I'm not totally convinced we can. Coaching rowing is still, in my view, both an art *and* a science. Along that continuum I place myself somewhere in the middle. Around 2000 I began to lecture at a university on sports coaching. My aim was to teach the students the difference between the art and science of coaching – a subject very dear to my heart. My experience with wooden boats and oars gave me the 'art' side, and my brain gave me the 'science' side and also the willingness to embrace the use of technology and the sciences of physiology and biomechanics. I use aspects of science and technology every single day but I try to synthesise the importance of these to any given crew on any given day – and that is the art side of the process.

Currently, rowing is the top funded Olympic sport in New Zealand. This has improved the access that we have to support staff on-site as well as enabling us to hire several sports scientists from overseas. All 15 support staff with the rowing programme are contracted to us by High Performance Sport New Zealand. Approximately, half of them work with rowing on a part-time basis while some are also contracted to other sports such as track cycling. There are sufficient offices and working areas for the support staff within our training facility at Karapiro. These individuals have brought a wide range of expertise with them, including massage therapy, physiotherapy, sports medicine, psychology as well as the strength and conditioning training, physiology and biomechanics that I mentioned earlier.

We also have several dieticians who work part time with the rowing team. At present, the athletes provide their own nutrition supplements, so our dieticians have an important role in advising each team member to make well-informed choices about safe, effective and most importantly, legal nutrition supplements. The nutrition support staff also advise athletes about helpful dietary changes, which may include suggestions on what to choose from a sample food menu or they may even offer cooking lessons to athletes in order to help enhance their self-catering abilities. The dieticians also take regular skinfold measurements from each athlete and this provides helpful insight about their body composition. The information and knowledge shared between support staff is used to help athletes make dietary adjustments to enhance physique. For example, the dieticians can collaborate with our team doctor to help interpret and respond to blood profile data, especially with respect to any nutritional deficiencies. Personally, I also think it is important that the coach is kept informed about what the support staff are thinking. So, in the case of the dieticians, I put time aside at regular intervals to speak with the nutrition support staff in order to find out what I can do to reinforce their messages. Often, this is simply reminding the athletes about their nutritional goals at the end of a training session.

Overall, I think that our team of support staff make important contributions to our daily progress. They also have an important role in innovating our training practice and competition strategies. This might be in terms of trialling out new ways to polarise our training or suggesting rig changes that help optimise our sustainable race pace. In a collective sense, perhaps the most important outcome that I have noticed in the New Zealand approach to the way we use support staff is an apparent reduction in the amount of injury and illness, at least compared to my past experiences in Australia. Indeed, it is very rare that our athletes get injured or lose more than an occasional session to illness. Possibly, I think that the athletes in New Zealand have been more willing to embrace the work of our support staff, due partly to the excellent education support provided by our sport science and sport medicine teams.

FINE TUNING FOR RACING

At the very high levels of competition, integration is about understanding race strategies. For example, in the 2015 World Championships I had done a lot of work with our men's pair of Murray and Bond about what speed we needed early on in the race; we were trying to be quicker in the first 500m. I have had a lot of feedback from people around the world noting that we had changed the race strategy, which was not really the case. We might explain what we really did but some things have to remain a secret for the time being! I also received a lot of feedback about the eight, with people noting the changes in rating and rhythm, something that was achieved through a great deal of hard work. We did hours and hours of practice and drilling the rhythm so that we could repeat it under pressure, and practising the movement stroke after stroke so that it provides the important mid-race pace. To me it is all linked together in an integrated way. If athletes do not understand that then it is the coach's responsibility to explain it until they do understand. In my opinion that is what will achieve a better result.

FINAL THOUGHTS

In terms of training sessions, we have a standard routine based on the daily programme, and the athletes will know the warm-up routine for each boat class, though I might still give a reminder about what the expectations are related to the point they have reached in the overall programme before the start of a session. With the more senior athletes the briefing is likely to be minimal, apart from some short reminders. With the eight there is likely to be more of a varied structure, for example rowing in pairs, and I might have a brief discussion with them to clarify the aims.

During a session on the water I often do not say much at all, especially when I'm coaching Murray and Bond in the pair. I could easily say almost nothing for three-quarters of the session because they know what to do, and I'm simply keeping a watchful eye on them or starting and ending timed pieces. Over the years, I have become better at following the maxim 'less is more'. As a former cox, I was used to talking a great deal, but even then all I did was make key points and try to encourage the crew to think for themselves.

It is important to remember that there is plenty of potential for misunderstanding, especially during long tiring sessions. Just recently, I had an athlete who approached me after training and asked why I was trying to get him to make a specific technical change. In fact, I had been addressing another person in the crew. This was a useful reminder that I need to keep checking that I am sending messages across the water clearly and these are being received as I intended. The problems of communication can be even more subtle than this. For example, I recall talking to a crew about 'flowing around the finish'; it later transpired that they thought I was talking about 'slowing around the finish'. These episodes can create frustrations for coach and crew, so it is useful to review session objectives in ways that enable coach and crew to demonstrate that everyone is thinking in the same way and working towards the same goals.

I use a range of methods for debriefing crews depending on the type of session and the focus in that particular week. The men's pair generally have a short debriefing where we re-affirm key points from the day's session, then I give them a quick snapshot of what we're going to do the next day. This could last for as little as 30 seconds. However, a debriefing with the men's eight is usually longer and has a different structure, partly because there are many more people involved as well as the greater number of factors involved with a developing crew. Sometimes I encourage the athletes to debrief themselves. For example, we have a score chart for our pairs and we encourage them to rate themselves. But if people are cold, then we do not encourage them to hang around; getting some rest is just as important as all the other aspects of training. Generally, I would ask them how it went, rather than me immediately offering my opinion, but occasionally I need to be more direct, particularly if I am not happy with how the session has gone. There is always myriad things to deal with, especially when considering matters of technique. However, it is not necessary to try and do everything at once and the training year is long. I am usually with these athletes twice a day, six days a week for most of the year, so there is no need to make pre-training and post-training debriefs lengthy. After all, most of the improvements achieved by high-performance rowers happen during on-water training and competition.

I regularly have guests in the coaching launch with me. Sometimes it is other coaches who might believe that doing so will help them discover the 'magic formula' of creating successful crews. I am generally pleased for others so see how we operate. It is important that we share knowledge for the good of the sport. I also invite family and friends of the athletes to join me on occasion and this helps them to gain some understanding of what it means to be a full-time athlete. Because athletes are living away from home, it is also an opportunity for members of their wider support team to meet up and see them in action. Moreover, when the men's eight are in coxless boats the coxswain is almost always present in the coaching launch. I encourage all of our team coaches to be open to having guests in the coaching launch, but some of them find it inhibiting or distracting.

We might have 'secret' sessions from time to time, but generally we do not hide what we do. In truth, it is very hard to protect the intellectual property of our athlete preparation. For one thing, we do our boat-based training in a very public place. Also, our athletes use social media extensively and do many interviews for newspapers, magazines or university student projects, so most of the information about our coaching methods is readily available anyway. I can understand why readers might be interested to learn about what we in New Zealand believe are the secret ingredients to success in international rowing. It is tempting to provide simple 'answers' to complex processes in order to provide a sense of understanding. Yet in truth, I don't think there are many so-called secrets in international rowing. Many of the world's best rowing coaches find employment with various national teams during their careers. If there really were any great secret to international rowing performance, then these ideas and approaches would surely transfer along with the coach. Also, we all make many friends across the world and are happy to chat about ideas with like-minded individuals at regattas and other FISA events. Indeed, there are various coaching conferences where we share our approaches and details of our training systems with anyone who wishes to attend. For athletes and coaches who have never attended international events such as these, I can appreciate why they may think there are secrets to discover. In a sense, I suppose that all of this information does remain secret until an aspiring coach or athlete realises that they need only look for it. There is much that can be learned from books, conferences and conversations, but perhaps more than anything else, the willingness to keep learning from the experiences of daily training and competition is the greatest secret to success in rowing.

Another aspect of our preparation that I would like to improve is the access we have to top quality competition. For example, I would like to be able to offer our men's eight better chances to test their athleticism against well-matched opposition. Ideally, it would be great to be able to fly in a top crew from overseas to do some match racing with us. Of course, we travel to race at World Cup regattas, but these events have obvious constraints that limit opportunities to try out new combinations or race strategies. We do occasionally send our crews over to Australia or North America for competitions, but this is expensive and lengthy travel periods are disruptive to athletes' personal lives and training regimes. For the moment at least, we try to make best use of the competitiveness that exists in our wider squad set-up to provide competitive challenge. This can include breaking the larger boats down to smaller ones for training pieces, as well as operating time trials across multiple boat classes by staggering the start or ranking boat performance against prognostic benchmarks.

Lastly, and perhaps this is a reflection of the length of time that I have been involved in rowing, I think it is important that coaches and athletes never stop learning. There is a tendency for people who accumulate success to become more closed minded. This happens most often when people narrowly attribute their successes to the things that they did. There are some coaches that perform well, particularly with school age athletes – and they become self-satisfied because they believe it is their talent rather than the talent of the athletes that has brought success. I think one of the best ways to help keep an open mind to progress and improvement, especially self-improvement, is to keep learning from other people. I certainly think that it is good for coaches and athletes to develop their understanding of scientific approaches. Ultimately, an entire training season is really just one big experiment about what training features might contribute to improving 2000m performance. We just cannot easily isolate improved rowing performance to single causal factors in the way that many traditional scientific studies are constructed to do. For this reason, I think aspiring coaches and developing athletes will gain a better appreciation of their own training approaches if they have a willingness to learn about anatomy, biology, physiology, biomechanics and psychology, as well as gaining insight from experienced rowers and coaches. This willingness to learn is increasingly important now that we have lots of new technology to help document features of rowing technique and training. Ultimately, it is the effective and evolved combination of art and science that will advance rowing performance in future generations of rowers.

Johan Flodin Head Coach, Norway

Johan was World Rowing Coach of the Year in 2013 and the coach behind Norway's remarkable 2016 Olymypic regatta results that saw bronze medals for the men's double sculls and lightweight men's double sculls. As a rower, he won two World Championship medals in the lightweight men's quadruple sculls before moving to the open weight quad, finishing sixth at the Atlanta Olympic Games in 1996. Always interested in the movement of rowing, Johan completed a Master's in Physiology during his rowing career. After rowing he went on to become a school head teacher. Although he spent many years working with 2010 World Champion in the women's single sculls, Frida Svensson, he did not become a full-time coach until he took up the position of Head Coach in Norway after London 2012.

During my career as a rower, I was always interested in physiology and training methodology, so it was natural for me to become involved in the coaching process and to participate in discussions with my coaches. What I learned during this time was the importance of understanding the process, which gave me a sense of 'ownership' and involvement in it – a factor that has had a strong influence on the way in which I now work with the athletes I coach.

While I was still competing, I completed a Master's degree in Physiology, Pedagogics and Psychology, so a move into coaching at the end of my rowing career was a natural progression. Initially I worked as a volunteer part-time club coach, gaining a lot of experience which led to me working for several years with Frida Svensson who became World Champion in the women's single sculls in 2010. My main employment was in education and I became the head teacher of a school. It was not until after the London 2012 Olympics that I became the head coach of Norway – my first appointment as a full-time coach.

TRAINING ENVIRONMENT

In terms of facilities, we have two main training centres in Norway. Our water-based training takes place on a 3km lake at Årungen, which is about 30km south of Oslo. This lake was used for the 1993 World Junior Rowing Championships. We have a small centre there which has a kitchen, so it is possible to stay there for a night or two. The boathouse contains our boat fleet and there is a very small gym with two ergometers. We share the facilities with two other clubs. We can usually row there from mid-April through until Christmas – then it is frozen for a few months. It is a simple place, but it works well for us. The lake is lined with eight lanes during the warmer months and is

Årungen Lake – where most of the Norwegian team's training is performed. *Credit: Tine Bjonge*

The boathouse training facility that the Norwegian team share with other rowing clubs. *Credit: Tine Bjonge*

essentially only used by rowers and a small number of canoeists. Most of the national team athletes live in Oslo and travel to the lake by car.

We also have use of the Olympic centre in Oslo, called Olympiatoppen (http://www.olympiatoppen.no), which is shared with all the Olympic sports in Norway. This has a gym, a few ergometers and accommodation where we can stay overnight. It also has test facilities, a small clinic with doctors and physiotherapists – and we can get advice on sports psychology, training and nutrition. The National Olympic Committee is based there and they ensure a good exchange of information between the various sports, so I have regular discussions with coaches from other disciplines – such as cross-country skiing, for example. It is a great environment in which to train and to learn.

I am one of the two full-time national team rowing coaches. Our annual budget is about half a million Euros and this has to cover all our activities including transport, regatta costs and training camps. I know our budget is very small compared to our main competitors, but this does ensure that we spend money carefully. I actually like working with limited resources because I think that it keeps me focused on what is important and I certainly don't feel under resourced. We just have to be careful in how we plan each trip, what tickets we buy and even make sure we drive the trailer economically. With practice, it gets easier to find good value for money and I enjoy the challenge of finding a good deal.

Although rowing is Norway's most successful summer sport, it is still difficult to find commercial sponsors and we do have to argue our case with the government each year to maintain our funding through the National Lottery. In fact, we receive a large proportion of what our Olympic Committee receives; they are very supportive of rowing.

TRAINING AND CONDITIONING

Of course, the winters in Norway can be very severe. Nearly all of our accessible water is frozen from January to March. During this period, we maintain our training volume with cross-country skiing, cycling, running and CrossFit workouts. We also have boat-based training camps in warmer countries such as Portugal, so we can still do a basic amount of rowing in the coldest months. But only about 60 per cent of our total training volume each year is on the water or the ergometer.

Because we have a lot of bad weather, and especially the high winds, we need to make a lot of use of the ergometer as a training tool. However, it is important that we use this time as preparation for rowing in a boat – so there is always an emphasis on technique. We do not put athletes on the ergometer and then leave them to it; we have the same approach to providing technical feedback on the ergometer as in the boat. We know that ergometer rowing can be really tough on the body, but if we focus on the right things it seems to work well for us. We make occasional use of the dynamic ergometer in cases where a rower has a back problem, for example, or we need to work a specific aspect of technique training.

Our strength training is mainly organised around free weights (see Table 1 on the next page for an example week) – and here the programmes are always individualised.

Table 1: Gym based training (session structure)

1) 15 min of steady state warm-up (e.g. rowing, cycle, run)
2) Stretching for 10 min
3) Weight training session (see below)
4) Power training on Concept 2 ergometer - 5 x 10 sec max effort with 110 sec rest (5 min rest after completion, then repeat again for a second set)
5) Cool down and stretching for 10 min

Exercise	Sets	Reps	Rest	Total lifts
Squats	3	6	150 sec	18
Dead lift (straight legs)	4	6	150 sec	24
Dead lift (straight legs)	3	6	150 sec	18
One leg squats	2	6 on each foot	120 sec	12
Bench Press	4	4	150 sec	12
Bench Pull	5	5	120 sec	11
Chin-ups	4	6	120 sec	11
Excentric sit ups	5	8	120 sec	40
Total	30			146

There is a general programme for the different groups but, for example, our lightweight rowers have different needs to the heavyweight rowers, so the programmes are quite different. We work very closely with the strength and conditioning professionals from the Norwegian Olympic Committee and they help inform the specific exercises and approaches needed for each athlete.

We also work closely with the Norwegian Olympic Committee to plan our annual training volume. They have a great deal of knowledge and research based on cross-country skiing – and they are encouraging us to think about 'training design' rather than simply 'training volume'. Our experience is that there is little to be gained if the aerobic training volume is increased from 800 hours to 1200 hours. Currently, we do around 1000 hours per year of aerobic training (including approximately 600 hours of on-water and ergometer rowing), but this is under constant review in terms of how effective it is. In terms of rowed distance, we cover between 6000 and 7000km each year (including on-water and land-based rowing; see Figure 1, depending on boat type. Therefore, the average volume of rowing is around 125km per week, but there is a lot of variation between weeks. During the competition period, when the weather is more favourable for on-water rowing, our weekly volume is usually somewhere between 150 and 200km.

We take care in planning and monitoring the intensity of each training session. Each athlete uses their heart-rate monitor to make sure to adhere to the prescribed training zones. Figure 2 displays the distribution of relative exercise intensity during rowing. Overall, between 10 and 15 per cent of the annual training volume is performed at moderate intensities (i.e. blood lactate 2.5 to 4.0mmol/L) and between 5 and 10 per cent at high intensities (i.e. blood lactate >4.0mmol/L). Accordingly, between

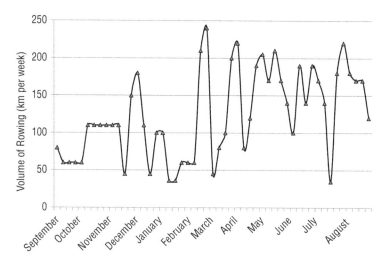

Figure 1: Weekly volume of rowing (ergometer and on-water) for Norwegian national rowing team

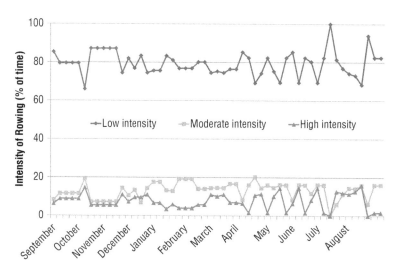

Figure 2: Weekly distribution of intensity during rowing (ergometer and on-water) for Norwegian national rowing team (Note: low intensity = <2.5 mmol/L blood lactate; moderate intensity = 2.5 to 4.0 mmol/L blood lactate; high intensity = >4.0 mmol/L blood lactate)]

75 and 85 per cent of our annual rowing is performed at low intensities (i.e. blood lactate<2.5mmol/L).

In recent years, we have shifted slightly more towards a greater proportion of low intensity training at the expense of higher intensity training. This change is partly due to the conversations that we have had with our colleagues in the Olympic cross-country ski programme. We think that the rowers experience slightly less soreness between training sessions thanks to the greater emphasis

Table 2: Sample Race Training Week: June (Senior Men's Double scull)

Day	Training	Rest	Stroke rate (strokes/min)	Intensity	Distance (km)
Monday	Aerobic cross training: 75 min (no rowing)				
	Rowing: 3 x 20 min	3 min	20 to 24	I2	20
Tuesday	Rowing: 5 or 6 x 2000 m	3 min	24 to 26	I3	20
	Weights and power training on Concept 2 (5 km)				5
	Rowing: steady state paddle	n/a	16 to 20	I1	15
Wednesday	Aerobic cross training: 90 min (no rowing)				
Thursday	Rowing: intervals 5 x 3 min (change rate every 1 min)	4 min	32 - 34 - 2000-m race rate	I5	18
	Rowing: steady state paddle	n/a	16 to 20	I1	18
Friday	Rowing: intervals 5 to 7 x 10 min	3	24 to 26	I2	20
	Individual training choice (e.g. rest, cross-train, row, weight training)	n/a	n/a	n/a	n/a
Saturday	Rowing: intervals 2 sets of 8 x 500 m	1 min for intervals and 10 min for set	26 to 28	I4	20
	Rowing: steady state paddle	n/a	16 to 20	I1	12
Sunday	Rowing: steady state paddle	n/a	16 to 20	I1	18
	Weights: short session for 60 min				
				Total	166

Table 3: Training Intensity Zone Outlines

Training Zones	Duration	% heart rate max	% VO2max	Lactate (mMol)
1	1-6 hours	45-65	55-72	0.8-1.5
2	1-3 hours	66-79	56-81	1.5-2.5
3	50-90 min	80-86	82-86	2.5-4.0
4	30-50 min	87-93	87-93	4.0-6.0
5	15-30 min	94-100	94-100	>6.0

on low intensity training. Tables 2 and 3 present an example training week and training zone categories, respectively.

ATHLETE SELECTION AND TALENT DEVELOPMENT

Perhaps the biggest challenge in Norway is finding talent. We have a population of only five million and few Norwegians ever get to try rowing, though the number of athletes involved has been growing in recent years. There are approximately 30 competitive rowing clubs in Norway and the top clubs often have crews competing at Henley Royal Regatta in England. These are the athletes that form the majority of the selection pool.

Our national selection process is organised through the National Olympic Committee. Essentially, club coaches send in ergometer test results for their best athletes from which we identify the athletes that have the greatest potential. The hardest decision is *when* to remove a talented athlete from their club environment to come and train with the national team group. Before this happens, we are careful to talk to each athlete and make sure that they have a good understanding of what is involved in rowing with the national team. However, all rowers up to the age of 19 stay with their clubs. Of course, these youngsters will go to international competitions, but it is my policy, supported by the National Olympic Committee, that they should stay in regional teams until the age of 20. If we take away the best juniors to join the national squad, then we risk damaging the long-term health of the club system. Finding talent in a country with a small population is not easy, but we do have good oversight of all the athletes and we value the relationship with the club coaches and their athletes. In a system that has limited resources, both in terms of people and finances, the national team results are highly dependent on the success of club level rowing.

We also try to identify potential talent from other sports. We look for 17- and 18-year-olds from other disciplines who have become accustomed to serious training. In Norway, this is nearly always from cross-country skiing. We give them the opportunity to join a rowing club and train twice a week or more to get them up to a reasonable technical standard where we can judge their potential. This needs a well organised system and it is costly. We know that there is a big drop out of really good swimmers, cyclists and cross-country skiers who could be great rowers. Presently, we are working towards a stronger talent identification system along with the National Olympic Committee. We hope that by working with Olympiatoppen, we will be able to identify a valid and robust set of test procedures to help identify rowing talent from the wider pool of athletic youngsters. If they have not quite made it in their first choice of sport, then it would really good to give them another opportunity to do a sport to which they may be better suited.

COACH AND ATHLETE RELATIONSHIP

I would describe my philosophy of coaching as 'sensitive and democratic'. I work hard to develop a close connection with a small group of very good athletes. We have a planned training programme which provides overall guidance, but for me it is important to have regular discussions with the athletes about how to individualise the training on the basis of their needs and feelings. I think that this is particularly beneficial in the small system that we have. It means that we can take care of every individual in a positive way. So it is this close connection with the athletes that enables me to discuss how they feel about what we are going to do over the next few days. My aim is to give them a big part in the process of their own development.

If you were with me on a coaching session, you might be surprised by how positive I am. I might point out a few problems or a few things to work with, but I also point out things that have worked well. I have the feeling that if you point out the things that are going well, problems usually disappear. I am also very consistent. I follow the plan for the session even if we run out of time and lose something at the end. So, in summary, I am positive, consistent and maybe I will say less than other coaches because I believe that 'less is more'. I am not a 'morning person' so becoming a rowing coach has been a challenge. Fortunately, even if I go to an early morning training session a little bit fatigued, I quickly feel energised by seeing our athletes striving to improve. So it is the job itself that energises me. I also receive great motivation from working with a good Olympic Committee that supports our development and has confidence in me – that is so important.

Of course, there are also times when I have to put my foot down – and to say, 'this isn't good enough'. I think that working with strong athletes and individuals can produce tensions, and that the training environment can be affected because somebody is behaving badly. In such cases, I need to be tough but I have learned to be careful in these moments. I recall some interesting feedback from one of my rowers. He said, 'you don't need to raise your voice, it's very obvious when you are happy or not'. I hope that these experiences have helped my interactions with athletes. However, there are still tough moments and perhaps the toughest is when we have to make final athlete selections. To compose the best teams, objective measurements and a little bit of 'handcrafting' are needed. Ultimately, these decisions cannot be democratic. Especially in these moments, I have to be a bit tougher than my personality would normally allow – and that has been a learning process. I'm in my 50s, and I'm still learning how to manage rowers.

Thor Nilsen is one of the coaches who has been very influential on the development of my coaching philosophy. I have learned a great deal from his keen interest in the coaching process. One of the main pieces of advice he gave to me – and which I have tried to follow – is to 'keep it simple' because rowing is a simple sport and we, as coaches, have a tendency to complicate it. This is an important lesson for two reasons. First, I think that a coach can spoil the overall competence of an athlete by trying to correct lots of small things. Second, if I am trying to explain something, in the stroke sequence for example, that I think is complicated, then for sure the athletes will think it is too. Keeping it simple means there is clarity on both sides.

It is my belief that 'performance is the sum of all behaviours'. Of course, it is important to develop technically and physically, but in the end what makes a difference is good behaviour by the coach and athletes on a daily basis. One of the key things that we do at the start of each training year is to discuss as a team how we are going to be the best group in terms of our training environment. As a result of this discussion, we agree on a list of behaviours that will help to create the best environment possible to make progress towards our goals.

Team behaviour goals

Our list might look something like this:
- always keep training as a priority
- help each team member to get better
- solve problems at the simplest level without need to involve more people
- be in the right place at the right time with the right equipment
- seek solutions rather than problems
- be communicative with team members
- support the team goals as a team player

I spend plenty of time with the other full-time coach and we often go running together in the middle of the day to discuss current training issues. We might also review video clips on our smartphones. It is also important that we both invite club coaches to come and see what we are doing. This hopefully helps develop the standard of club coaching and the relationship with the national group, but we also pick up useful ideas from club coaches, many of whom are very experienced and insightful. On other occasions, we may be joined by experts from the Olympic Committee staff who come and observe how we communicate with the athletes during on-water training. They make helpful suggestions about how to improve the interactions. However, I find it harder to focus on the rowers when there is someone else in the launch, so I don't like such visits to happen all that often. I really like to feel close to the athletes and I do that best when they have my complete attention.

At least once a week, members of the national squad train by themselves. This allows me to have time to do the necessary team administration and allows athletes to take more responsibility for their own training. I also hope that by giving the athletes a regular reminder about what training without a coach is like, that they are reminded of its value. I want our time together to be the finest thing that we do. If we were always together, then the training could become like tap water; I always want our training to be like champagne.

Although I might not be at every training session, I do believe in enhancing the coaching at certain times of the year, especially as we approach a major regatta. The training will then become really intense, and I might be coaching two or three times a day on the water – and also between workouts. However, even in these more intense periods, our crews do not really compete against each other on-water since that would mean having 'winners' and 'losers'. I want all of the crews to end a training session feeling that they are 'winners'. I want them to feel that they were in the right zone, with the same stroke rate and making best use of the training plan. I certainly do not want to let competitiveness change the goal of the session. Therefore, we work together rather than compete against each other. I believe that it is important to define 'winning' more carefully so that training does not become confused with competition.

I think that rowers appreciate that I am a person who is stable, consistent over time and someone that they can trust. I don't want them to look at me and think 'what kind of person will Johan be today'. But if I am feeling a little frustrated with their lack of progress, then I tend to become more quiet and analytic as I try to discover and understand the problem. It doesn't mean that I'm working hard not to look frustrated, I'm quiet because I'm trying to work out the problem. Frustration for me rarely turns to aggression.

In terms of maintaining my own motivation, I try to stay connected with some good memories from the past and also with the plans that we are creating for the future. I enjoy working with highly motivated athletes, and I find it easy to share the experience with them. I believe that motivation is established before we go on the water. The athletes know what they have to do and the kinds of feelings they are going to experience. For example, it might be hard physical work followed by technical rowing. It might be that on one day the results are not good because the athletes are tired. In this situation I need to motivate them by explaining the purpose of the workout. I believe that if athletes do not know the purpose of a workout and how they need to respond, it can really hurt and is de-motivating. I take a lot of pride in looking into everybody's eyes before every workout to see if there is anything that is bothering them. This for me is very important. Also the concept of 'mindfulness' is an important motivational tool. I try to get the athletes to focus on the fantastic feeling you get when the boat is going well; when you feel 'at one' with the boat and the crew. The aim is to carry this feeling through to the next workout in order to regain motivation for the next challenge. Of course there are a few workouts every year that do not work well.

Sometimes problems with crews persist. For example, I have a double that, after winning the World Championships, lost their form completely. It is important to remember that every problem does not necessarily have a technical solution. You have to accept that there might be physical or emotional disturbances. In such cases when the problem appears to be difficult and the solution is unclear, we will go back and try to find other ways of dealing with it. For example, we might use free weights to find the right biomechanical connections. Also we might go back on the erg. Although I don't believe it's possible to solve every problem in the boat; neither do I believe that there is a problem that cannot be solved. I think it can be done but you have to find the key. We are a small squad so we do not have the luxury of being able to find replacements easily. In order to find solutions to the challenge that athletes pose, we as coaches need to change our approach so that we find a way to make every 'flower bloom'.

I believe that one of the keys to getting 'flowers to bloom' is by using the 'individualisation of training programmes'. For example, one athlete might perform badly because they are tired and in need of a rest; another might have had a poor training session because of a technical fault that can be corrected by giving them a particular exercise to practise. Of course, it is important that they all follow the main training programme but also have the opportunity to take a slightly different path to achieving their own individual goals. For me, individualisation means that you actually listen to each athlete each day to find out where each individual is in their own mind so that you can plan ahead. It's easy to get lazy around individualisation. It doesn't mean that the athletes can do what they want – and it doesn't mean that my job is any easier. On the contrary, it actually needs more thought and preparation. If you have a training scheme and one person does not fit the scheme, then in a large squad such, as they have in the UK, you can change your athlete. We do not have that choice, instead we have to be more aware of the individual recovery needs of each athlete and allow much more flexibility.

TECHNICAL APPROACH

I know that different coaches place emphasis on different parts of the stroke. For me the important thing is what is happening around the hip, especially at the finish of the stroke. The hip is where I start my analysis of each new rower. I then work outwards to the limbs and to the oar. I look for an early body preparation into the catch position during the recovery. I want to see rowers sitting up tall in an aggressive position at the catch. It is also critical to get the length of reach at the catch from the position of the pelvic bone rather than extending the shoulders. We do core stability work three or four times a week to help with this.

Our training sessions always start with a briefing for the whole group. This sets the aim for each workout and outlines the details of the training and who is working with whom on that day. Usually we have two coaches available at the same time and we try to organise it so that everyone can get as much as possible from both coaches. The training group I work with at any given session is usually between five and 15 athletes. In smaller groups, we continue our pre-training briefing and this will include talking with each boat about the specific technical points and any other individual refinements (e.g. any special tasks and verbal cues for use during training). All of the squad then spend 30 minutes warming up on the water together. After the session, we tend to debrief at the whole group level, unless something has not worked well when we might deal with the boats separately.

SUPPORT SERVICES AND TECHNOLOGY

It has been beneficial to make use of the technology that is now available to measure forces and angles in the boat – but we only use it a few times a year. We don't have much biomechanical support available in Norway and instead we hire Valery Kleshnev, an international expert in biomechanics, to visit our training centre two or three times a year. The data produced can be very specific, for example, when Olaf Tufte returned to training in 2014, the biomechanical data indicated that his stroke length was about 10 per cent too short and that the peak oar force was occurring too late in the drive phase. Olaf won the Olympic single sculls in 2004 and 2008 and a bronze medal in the double scull at the 2016 Olympics. We used the biomechanical data to increase his flexibility as well as reducing the span between the oarlocks to get his effective stroke length back. We also encouraged him to drive his legs harder earlier in the stroke, which shifted the peak force towards the catch.

One challenge that comes with this new technology is the sheer volume of data produced. I find it challenging just thinking about how much is available and how best to use it. There are some coaches who think that if you are not using this

Norwegian openweight men's double of Borch and Tufte who won bronze at the 2016 Olympic Regatta. *Credit: Steve McArthur*

technology then you are not really serious. We are getting better at managing these data collection systems, but our aim is make its use more efficient and effective. At the moment it is a work in progress for us.

One alternative to using sophisticated biomechanical data collection systems is to simply take video recordings. There is a Norwegian company that manufactures one of the best drone video systems in the world. They have a GPS device that you put on the boat and you programme the drone to film exactly what you want to see throughout the session. This system gives wonderful overhead shots and also allows us to make manual estimates of stroke length, including how much of the stroke is distributed in front of the oarlock. I like the automated nature of this system since I can get great video and still put all my focus into my coaching. I think that this type of advanced drone system will be our next step. Perhaps we could offer more real time video feed to the athletes in the boat, including some on-screen display of stroke length or crew timing.

We have various support personnel that contribute to our team on a day-to-day basis. Sport medicine, for example, accounts for about 10 per cent of our annual budget. Some staff, such as our physiotherapist, travel with us to international regattas. We also explored the possible benefits of acupuncture with the support of a trained nurse who worked with our athletes at least twice a week all through the year. This proved so beneficial that our acutherapist now travels to regattas with us to help the athletes stay calm and relaxed before races. I appreciate that many people, including some of our own Olympic team support staff, do not think this is the best use of our limited

Norwegian lightweight men's double of Brun and Strandli, who won bronze at the 2016 Olympic Regatta. *Credit: Steve McArthur*

funds. Nevertheless, we continue to use this complementary therapy because it is popular with the athletes.

We also have the support of nutritionists and dieticians through Olympiatoppen, an organisation that supports the training of all Olympic sports in Norway. These experts are very important to help manage our lightweight athletes and they have encouraged our lightweights to reduce body weight much earlier in the season. Some lightweight rowers in other countries leave their weight loss until the main regatta season, but we take an active interest in body-weight management earlier in the training year and the nutritionists take skinfold measurements at regular intervals to help estimate body composition changes. All of our lightweights must be able to make their race weight within 48 hours from April until the World Championships in August. It is normal for our lightweights to have to lose 1 or 2kg in the final 12 hours before a weigh-in and they do so by eating less and then using strategies that promote acute dehydration in the last few hours.

The nutritionists also advise us about the use of legal performance enhancing supplements and we have explored the use of sodium bicarbonate and beetroot juice with some success. We have also considered the possible benefits of caffeine, but with less success. Rowing regattas are already stressful enough and too much caffeine can make athletes over-aroused. Of course, many of our athletes enjoy drinking caffeinated coffee as part of their own routines and that is left to each individual to decide for themselves. Our lightweight rowers, for example, often consume coffee after a successful weigh-in.

We do not have quite as much sport science support in some areas. For example, I personally take responsibility for ensuring that the athletes are logging their workouts using our Polar watches. I ask the athletes to record all their training routines and to upload their heart rate and GPS logs to the software provided by Olympiatoppen. This lets me monitor each individual's progress and make effective estimates about how well the team is adhering to the training plan. Generally, this approach works well, as long as everyone takes responsibility for themselves. It helps that most of our athletes receive funding from Olympiatoppen and one requirement of this support is that they upload their own information to a central data capture system. Most of our team are very good at doing so, but sometimes they need a little encouragement. I do find this a worthwhile approach to monitoring and controlling training, although it can be a little time consuming.

FINE TUNING FOR RACING

There are several things I do to help prepare our athletes in the final weeks of the season. Perhaps one surprising thing that I like to do is to give the athletes a week off. On our return we will maintain the same number of training sessions while increasing the intensity of our workouts. For the last two weeks, ahead of the World or Olympic championships, we decrease the volume of training by between 30 and 40 per cent. With an important event approaching the coaching naturally gets more intense, both on and off the water, and this is partly why I think it is helpful to start final preparations by letting the athletes have a short break. I also find this helps to keep my motivation high when I am with the athletes and tends to promote better discussions across the group. I have also learned to avoid saying things to athletes when I don't feel that I have anything to add. I think it is good for athletes and coaches to have quiet periods, which may last from a few minutes to an entire week.

FINAL THOUGHTS

Almost all of current rowing team are part-time students and most will do some sort of part-time employment during the year to supplement their income. Most do get a small living cost grant from the Norwegian Olympic Association depending on their performance level. The top rowers may get around 12,000 Euros per year, while the typical grant for most of our rowers is closer to 6000 Euros per year. This money does not go very far in Norway, where the cost of living is very high. Our athletes really do have to work at living cheaply. It would be nice if we could increase their funding and turn them into full-time athletes, but I think it is good for our athletes' personal development to have interests outside rowing. If an athlete received a good salary for rowing, so much so that they excluded all other career development, then there is a risk that the athlete may feel like they must keep rowing simply because there is no alternative. Of course there are advantages for full-time athletes, particularly in terms of energy levels and recovery time. But I don't think much else would change in our collective approach to the sport.

I would, however, like to invest in better logistical support in order to free the coaching team from spending many hours doing things that have no or limited benefit to performance. For example, it would be great if we had more staff to do boat maintenance and to drive the boat trailer across Europe to regattas and training camps. At the moment we have to do a lot of this work ourselves. I would much rather be able to spend more of my time improving my knowledge of rowing and coaching, as well as reading some of the latest sport performance research. Right now, for example, I am very interested in finding better ways to reduce the risk of illness and injury in rowers. I think athletes are the best judges of when they are getting ill or injured, and am convinced that there is a role for good questionnaires or biomarkers (e.g. white blood cell activity) to help athletes learn to read their bodies. I think the science of immune function in athletes is still relatively unclear and this is where more money can direct time and research to improve the individualisation of advice that we give to athletes, which might improve our performance outcomes.

I believe that it is very important to talk with other coaches about high-performance rowing and to exchange ideas so that we learn something from each other. Also I read books about the psychology and philosophy of sport – and also about language. I believe more and more in the importance of language in how you manage yourself and your athletes, and how you work together towards achieving goals. You can look for other things but if you can develop yourself to become a decent human being, that for me is the most important attribute that a coach needs. Just being older seems to work if you continue to be curious. Coaching is about making yourself understandable – and less is more.

If you are planning on a career in coaching, then you will need really big ears! Try to sneak in and listen to other coaches; watch what they do and hear what they say. What can you learn from their approaches that could be applied to your own situation? It is also very important to develop a good understanding about technique and physiology so that your philosophy of rowing stands on a good base, that way you will not be too easily influenced by different coaches and their different approaches. Your own philosophy will develop over time. You should regularly ask yourself 'what is important for me?; what is it that I am aiming for?'. You might have an ideal model in mind, but it is important to be willing to adapt and adjust to what is actually possible.

I worked with Frida Svensson in Sweden who became the world champion in women's single sculls in 2010. She was not the most technically or physiologically gifted athlete, but she succeeded anyway. What was important for me was that she could achieve an economy of movement and make the most of the attributes she did have. I think that these experiences of rowing in Scandinavia, with all its imperfections and resource issues, have made me far better at concentrating on what I have in front of me. Many of our European football teams have developed a business model where they seek to buy the best players from all over the world in order to strengthen their team. They spend eye-watering amounts of money to buy the best players only to have spectacularly disappointing seasons (followed swiftly by a new coach). I think we are fortunate that rowing is not like this, and indeed probably could never be like this. However, some high-performance coaches aspire to have better financial resources in order to secure better athletes in their programmes, though of course this would be through national talent identification rather than overseas recruitment as happens in football. This idea may seem appealing at first, but the coach with plenty of financial resource may undervalue the athletes that he or she already has and spend too much time and energy seeking better raw material. What I do know from my own experiences is that any athlete can surprise a coach. Performance breakthroughs can happen at almost any point in a career and sometimes there are no obvious signs in advance. I think I have learned to be more open minded about what it takes to be a world-class rower, in part, because I have to work within reasonable resource constraints. This has made it easier to focus all of my attention and energy on what I can control, something that is especially important when things are not going so well.

Simon Cox
Performance Director of Rowing for Czech Republic

Head Coach in Switzerland from 2011 to 2014, Simon Cox helped build the lightweight men's four crew that made the London 2012 Olympic final. He then split the boat into a lightweight double and pair for 2013, with both boats medalling at the 2013 World Rowing Championships.

Simon gained his formative rowing experiences at Emmanuel School in Chiswick, on the River Thames in south-west London. Simon remembers that period with affection and admits it has proved influential on his own style. In 2014 Rowing Australia asked Simon to coach its Men's Eight, a role he undertook until 2016. He is currently the Performance Director for the Czech Rowing Association.

In 2008, I was hired by Swiss rowing to coach their junior national team. Soon after arriving I was given the additional role of working with the lightweight group in support of Tim Foster, who was the head coach at that time. Tim was part of the British coxless four that won gold at the Sydney Olympics and had moved over from London about a year before I arrived. In many ways, I think this made the transition to coaching in another country much easier. We had both been part of the University of London rowing team some years earlier, so we shared many similar ideas about developing high performance rowing and we both had a similar British mentality about many things. Tim was already making good changes with the senior group when I arrived and we worked closely over the next few years. We had many discussions about the differences between rowing in the UK and Switzerland and these helped us build new strategies for developing high performance pathways for Swiss rowers as well as achieving a more cohesive and targeted approach to athlete development. We often rotated coaching duties, especially since we were the only full-time coaches with the national teams, so I gained a lot of experience working with the full range of Swiss rowers. When Tim left in 2011, I became coach of the senior team and another full-time coach was employed to support the junior programme. There was subsequently another part-time positon created for the under-23 group, but the coaching team was small, and worked closely to ensure that all aspects of the programme ran smoothly. My previous 12-plus years of coaching at various clubs, universities and schools in the UK stood me in good stead for the many and varied challenges involved in making a small nation successful on the international stage.

I worked as head coach of the Swiss team until the end of 2014, and this chapter describes many of the improvements that helped raise the standard of international rowing in Switzerland, especially in preparation for the 2012 Olympic regatta and beyond. I am proud of all the improvements in Swiss rowing to which I contributed, not only in terms of the headline medal-winning performances, but also the raised level of expectation, professionalism and openness to 'what can be done' if there is real desire. The biggest gains occurred in the men's lightweight and open weight events. For example, at the 2007 Munich World Championships, the Swiss Rowing Federation entered 13 lightweight and heavyweight men across four boat classes (lightweight 2X, and heavyweight 1X, 2- and 8+) with a highest placing of third in the B final. Seven years later at the 2014 Amsterdam World Championships, which was to be my final competition as head coach, we had 12 lightweight and heavyweight competitors in five boat classes (lightweight 1X, 2-, 2X and heavyweight 1X and 4X). This time, we had three boats in the A final, including gold (and a world record) in the lightweight pair and bronze in the lightweight single. Underpinning these improvements was a higher level of performance from all the athletes that participated in the national selection process. Even after my move to Australia in 2015 to coach with the national team, I still enjoyed watching Swiss rowers continue to progress their international results and I look back on my experiences there with great fondness. I hope that the ideas and descriptions of what was changed in Switzerland during my tenure will be helpful to other rowers and coaches who are keen to advance the standard of rowing in their own club, university or national team.

TRAINING ENVIRONMENT

Switzerland has 78 rowing clubs, but many are very small and exclusively for social rowing. There are approximately 40 competitive clubs and 1500 registered rowers, ranging from juniors to masters, though many of these too are social rowers. High performance rowing in Switzerland is currently organised as a centralised system based in Sarnen, a small town in the central German-speaking part of the country and home to a beautiful lake on which we did all our training. Sarnen is only 20 minutes from Lucerne, and its central location means it is no more than a maximum of three hours' travel from anywhere in Switzerland.

The centralised rowing system is now well developed and works extremely well. This has only been possible because of the tremendous amount of work done in developing relationships between the national team coaches and the club coaches, club management and athletes. In my initial months and years, I travelled extensively throughout the country doing club visits and presentations explaining, discussing and arguing about what the essentials were to create a successful national team. This building of relationships cannot be underestimated, and the support and understanding developed at this time was one of the bedrocks that led to our future success. Our sport is no different to other walks of life in that it involves relationships and developing trust between people on many levels. By meeting so many of the 'on the ground' club coaches, I opened up lines of communication with individuals who then felt able to call me to discuss an athlete or a problem.

I also issued a nationwide training programme that explained the focus, both technical and physiological, for the national team at each point in the season and how our goals could be adapted to different levels of athlete. This was an excellent means of opening up and engaging in dialogue. I feel very strongly that once a system becomes centralised if the 'ladder' is then pulled up the system will quickly wither and die. It is only by maintaining contact with the grass roots that a continual flow of, not only athletes, but information and ideas can be maintained.

My experiences leading some of the most successful clubs and university programmes in the UK, and my understanding of the pressures for success that the holders of these positions are under, meant I built up a strong rapport with the club coaches whose jobs were dependent on results. It takes trust for a successful club coach to 'give up' their best talents for weekends and longer when they are trying to build club crews. This needs to be recognised, particularly in a small system with limited national team coaching resources and a reliance on the help and 'buy in' of the club coaches. The club coach must be kept involved and their efforts appreciated in order for the system to continue to function.

Lake Sarnen is almost 6000m in length and has few other users, apart from slow moving fishing boats and a few club rowers. The scenery here is nothing less than you would expect to see on a Swiss postcard. The lake is surrounded by steep-sided mountains that rise from an altitude of 400m at the lake to over 2000m at the peak. We could do competitive pieces with as many 20 scullers all starting together and nobody would feel squeezed for water. The conditions on the lake are normally excellent for training, though it can suffer from strong and sudden thermic thunderstorms in the summer and, of course, the winters are very cold. Occasionally, the metal runners beneath the boat seats iced up, which quite literally 'stopped us

Lake Sarnen. *Credit: Felix Dieu*

in our tracks!' So, we typically restricted on-water training between December and March, but apart from these months, we rarely had to cancel sessions on the lake because of bad weather.

Training camps were a major feature of our training year and provided alternatives to training on our home lake. These camps developed over time, as the athletes became not only better able to cope with an increase in volume but also organised their lives around training as a priority. The camps were expanded until each season could begin with a combined cycling and swimming camp in southern France followed by two five-day 'ergometer camps' in December at an army base about an hour from Sarnen. There were great facilities available and we had the capacity to invite the best club athletes to come and train with the national team group. This was an excellent way to develop talent and give aspiring rowers a chance to experience the level of training and discipline expected of national team athletes. It was also an opportunity to develop the athletic skills of the rowers with a particular focus on good weight-training techniques.

After the ergometer camps and at the start of the New Year we would go to St Moritz for a two-week cross-country ski camp. The camp had various purposes: to make the rowers more athletic and robust, to improve their aerobic base as well as improving strength and power through regular weight training, and benefit a little from the altitude. This block of land-based and alternative training ended with the national ergometer championships, which served as an excellent test of physiological development from the winter work and the transition to a greater emphasis on specific on-water training. It was also an opportunity for the national team to be challenged by rowers who were not yet on the team. This was followed the day after by a long distance (6km) water test.

With the change of focus to boat-based sessions, we then had two camps in Portugal, each lasting about 14 days. I have always found 14 days a manageable duration for athletes to cope with the training load, minimise injury risk and to benefit from the change of environment and the removal of any other distractions. These were essential opportunities for extensive boat-based training and building up a large volume of quality water work. The first camp tended to be small boats, while the second camp emphasised crew boats.

The final team selections for summer racing were completed during trials in April. Thereafter, we would often go to a 'non World Cup' regatta of the sort that used to proliferate around Europe. This was important to develop racing experience in a lower-pressure environment where mistakes were not punished so heavily, and the more relaxed atmosphere was better for testing different combinations and boat types. It was also important to expose the athletes to international racing again after the long period of training in isolation. In the spring (May), we had another training block, which included a trip to Varese in northern Italy. Varese is only 3 hours from Sarnen and was a popular place for training as it was the closest 2km buoyed course available. (The Rotsee in Lucerne, affectionately known in the rowing world as 'God's own rowing lake', is only buoyed for a short summer period around the World Cup regatta.) During the competition phase we sometimes took the senior squad on another trip to a canal just over the border from Basel into France, especially if our home water was getting busy with junior and under-23 crews. Finally, we would make a trip to Bordeaux for an on-water speed and finishing camp shortly before the World Championships.

I realise it must sound as if we did a lot of travelling, but most of the training venues are within a few hours of our home base. Even when we went on camps, athletes could still return home if needed for family, university or work commitments (Portugal being the only exception). The costs were largely paid by the Swiss Rowing Federation, who in turn received their income from Swiss rowing clubs and from the government through general taxation. Many athletes still had to make significant financial contributions to cover their camp costs, but again, the athlete's home rowing club often contributed part or all of these costs. I should also point out that almost all of the Swiss rowing team are students, usually doing part-time courses and we were fortunate that many of these courses offered online lectures and opportunities for students to study at their own convenience. Universities across the world are increasingly turning to online, student-centred learning and I'm sure the Swiss are not the only national team to have benefited from this change.

Most of our national rowers did receive a modest level of funding, but it was usually little more than enough to cover their living and training expenses. Once they started to become successful, some rowers did better and either managed to gain commercial funding from sponsors, such as Red Bull, EFG Bank and Schurter (a Swiss Electronics company) or through the Swiss military system. Basically, Switzerland operates a conscription system whereby all adult men are expected to complete a 20-week basic army training course at age 20. For about 10 years thereafter, they are obliged to fulfil annual service requirements which would usually mean performing more training or skill development during a three-week break from their normal employment. However, we were very fortunate that the Swiss military, after a rigorous application process, were willing to support training for international rowing in place of the standard annual service requirement. In this way, the Swiss conscription system was actually a help rather than the hindrance that it could so easily have been. The success of the Swiss rowers on this scheme showed how important it was for the athletes to have a period of learning how to train consistently and at a higher level.

In terms of the facilities at our home training base in Sarnen, there is a modest boathouse alongside the shed of the local rowing club and a sports centre that includes offices rented by the Swiss Rowing Federation for the team coaches, performance director and a secretary. There is also overnight self-catering accommodation for 50 people that is available to athletes, musicians and school groups, and we had many rowers who made good use of the facilities for short camps as well as extended stays.

Initially, as the training quality and volume was being developed, athletes would only come for weekends, but over time, the senior group began to extend their stays until many of the national team members essentially lived in or around the centre full-time. This development and acceptance of Sarnen as the best place to train took some time and work. Initially, the clubs had better facilities and provided a more convenient training environment. It was only by offering something 'better', firstly in terms of the quality of training and coaching and then also in terms of support, equipment and environment that athletes accepted it was the only option if they wanted international success. This change was one of the most important breakthroughs that contributed to better international performances. It meant that a crew could spend more time in a set format and I could spend more time with each rower. It also created more and more opportunities for the athletes to see the collective improvements of the group and to support one another through tougher moments.

Sarnen also has a gym, which contains weight-training equipment and rowing machines sufficient for a group of about 12 athletes at a time. Although it is probably best described as a no-frills land training facility, it was all we needed.

The local facilities and area surrounding Sarnen is fantastic for cross-training. In winter, we included cross-country skiing and then moved to mountain and road bike training in the summer. We had a running track next to the boathouse and endless mountain trails for longer runs. Rowers are understandably inclined towards the outdoors and with so much diverse terrain and training opportunities nearby, I expect most rowers and coaches would find Sarnen especially appealing. It is a great place for a training camp.

TRAINING AND CONDITIONING

When I first arrived in Switzerland, I found that the level of athleticism and physicality of the rowers was too low to support the levels needed for international success. At the time, I perceived a general unwillingness from many in the sport to target improvements in the wider aspects of fitness development of rowers because of a belief that good technique was more important. There is actually an impressive level of general fitness in the wider Swiss population thanks to a national culture that encourages people to spend a lot of time outside, walking, skiing, cycling, jogging and swimming. Compared to most Western countries levels of obesity and inactivity, for example, are far lower in Switzerland. For example, the World Health Organisation data suggest that just approximately 15 per cent of Swiss men aged 35 to 74 are obese, while similar data for England and the United States suggest an obesity prevalence of about 25 per cent and 35 per cent, respectively. Despite this, the relative fitness of rowers who wanted to compete at the elite level was far lower than equivalent international comparisons.

One of my first tasks was to convince the rowers and coaches throughout the Swiss club system of the benefits of developing greater athleticism and physical confidence. Despite initial resistance from many coaches, we made good progress, especially once we had developed a base of robust and athletic rowers, who were less injury prone and able to withstand a higher training load alongside seeing an improvement in results. One of the first changes was to improve the athletes' understanding and skill in using weight training. Many Swiss rowers would avoid the weight room and were completely against the idea of spending three or more sessions a week training there, yet this was the change that happened. Soon after, the training gains in strength and power, along with growing confidence and belief in the conditioning approach, helped to change the general mindset. Formerly, the Swiss rowers were training to be rowers, but with the introduction of a new conditioning approach they also recognised that they were training to become athletes too.

Athleticism is very important to me. Many rowers are prone to listing off all the sporting activities they are unable to do. Yet, I strongly argue that to be a top rower, you have to see yourself as a top athlete who rows. With this in mind, I encouraged the team to embrace many more training alternatives such as cross-country skiing (they were all good skiers). We held cycling and swimming camps, despite initial resistance, especially to swimming. The rowers were often surprised by how similar the terminology used for coaching swimming was to that of rowing, such as the way they had to create an effective 'catch' with the hand while swimming, along with a clean extraction at the 'finish'. Oftentimes, we think of just the direct benefits of a training approach, yet so much about what worked with the addition of swimming to our training regime came from developing a greater understanding of how to create efficient fluid motion, where the hands are directly connected to the water rather than through the oar.

'CrossFit' was another form of training that, although rough and ready, greatly improved the physical robustness of the athletes. We combined this with Sypoba®, a Swiss-developed type of core stability balancing activity. It requires the athletes to balance on a small tilting plate balanced on a central cylinder/wheel while simultaneously performing additional activities. It was excellent for developing core strength, body control and spatial awareness. These activities helped us to develop a good volume and intensity of training while keeping the number of injuries low.

In this instance the specific training for rowing that I developed is best characterised as high volume/low intensity. It has to be recognised that this requires a 'lifestyle' that

Example of a Sypoba based activity that can help develop core stability for rowing. *Credit: photo courtesy of SYPOBA ®; www.sypoba.com*

includes time to train *and* recover. The balance of intensity and volume needs to be made with a view to other life pressures and commitments. Obviously the less time available, in particular for good recovery, the higher the intensity. When I first arrived in Switzerland, many of the rowers struggled to cope with just two sessions each day. Over time and with the careful progression of training loads, the top athletes learned to cope with up to three sessions each day and this allowed us to move our weekly rowing volume (including ergometer) from approximately 140km per week to over 200km per week. Most successful rowers understand the need to achieve high volumes of specific rowing training, but this is not something that can be rushed and the cross-training and general conditioning work that I described above were important to allow us to both build up to and then sustain these high volumes. Almost any reasonably fit trained rower can do a single week of high-volume training, but the rowers that make the A finals at World and Olympic regattas all have to learn to sustain these volumes for months at a time. To illustrate this more fully, it took the Swiss lightweight men's coxless four eight years to develop into World Champions in 2015.

We used GPS and heart-rate monitors to help monitor our training intensity, but these were not something we used all the time. I certainly prefer to encourage rowers who are in the earlier stages of international development to be much more focused on working to a given stroke rate and boat speed during on-water training even if it means the volume has to be reduced.

Once an athlete has a good understanding of the speed of the boat required for good training then I think there is more value to using heart rate to help guide intensity. It takes time for athletes to learn how to equate heart-rate zones with their lactate levels and perceived exertion. My preference is to encourage younger, developing athletes to use their heart-rate monitors during ergometer training rather than on-water training. The ergometer sessions provide much better opportunity for the coach to selectively encourage each athlete to work at an appropriate effort and power output.

With time, the athletes gained a strong sense of training intensity/boat speed control which helped to evolve the intensity of the on-water sessions. However, in the early years of my work in Switzerland, boat speed was what I wanted the athletes to focus on. I am aware that many national rowing teams go to considerable efforts to monitor every stroke for rate, speed, power and the athlete's heart rate, and have extensive records of these outputs which, in turn, can be used to force athlete compliance to a given number. I can understand why this technology-based approach is popular. Certainly, smartwatches and other even more sophisticated feedback systems offer plenty of information that have the potential to improve training sessions. However, it is still the case that all athletes must learn to make internal judgements and decisions about how they are performing and responding to training. Ultimately, athletes need to be able to control their output and when they race they must feel free to perform. Technology should not create a limit or barrier to their performance. The world of sport is full of champions who have managed to go beyond what they thought possible by producing something extraordinary when they had to. Training should prepare athletes to have the confidence to 'back themselves' to do this when it is needed.

One of the key points that I must emphasise in providing the training samples in this chapter is that the prescribed training plan was used a guide to what we were likely to do with a specific group of athletes in these circumstances. All the athletes had a copy of the training in advance. However, I would often change or drop a session entirely depending on how the athletes appeared when they arrived. If they were overly tired and obviously not sufficiently recovered, then we made changes to the plan. Each session had broader aims, such as developing muscular endurance or improving aerobic condition, but there are various ways to achieve

Table 1: Sample Training Week/Preparation Phase: Lightweight Men's coxelss four (November)

Day	Time	Training	Rest	Stroke rate (strokes/min)	Distance (km)*
Monday	Session 1	Rowing: 90 to 120 min	n/a	18 to 20	20 to 26
	Session 2	Rowing: Technical focus with bursts (10 to 20 strokes full pressure to reinforce exercise)	n/a	20 to 30	12
	Session 3	Cross train: 120 min as combination of bike, run, swim	n/a		
Tuesday	Session 1	Rowing: 90 min with power strokes (bungee) 4 x 9 min (as 1 + 2 + 3 + 2 + 1 min; rest 1:1)	5 min between sets	18 to 22	20
	Session 2	Rowing: Technical focus	n/a	20	12
	Session 3	Weights: Standard session of heavy weights			
Wednesday	Session 1	Rowing: 90 to 120 min with bursts	n/a	18 to 30	20 to 26
	Session 2	Rowing ergometer: Intervals 4 x 15 min (rate steps in 5 min blocks)	10 min	(set 1: 18 + 20 + 22) + (set 2: 20 + 22 + 24)	20
		Rest			
Thursday	Session 1	Rowing: 90 to 120 min	n/a	18 to 20	20 to 26
	Session 2	Rowing: Technical focus with bursts (10 to 20 strokes full pressure to reinforce exercise)	n/a	20 to 30	12
	Session 3	Weights: Standard session, heavy weights			
Friday	Session 1	Rowing: 90 to 120 min	n/a	18 to 20	20 to 26
	Session 2	Rowing: Technical focus	n/a	20	12
	Session 3	Weights: Circuit-style session			
Saturday	Session 1	Rowing ergometer: Intervals 3 x 19 min pyramids (4 + 3 + 2 + 1 + 2 + 3 + 4 min)	9 min between sets	(18 + 20 + 22 + 24 + 22 + 20 + 18)	26
	Session 2	Rowing: Technical focus	n/a	18 to 22	12
			n/a		
Sunday	Session 1	Cross train: 120 min as combination of bike, run, swim or Rest day	n/a		
*Distances have been estimated based on the time available for each session and may overestimate actual distance covered				Total	218

these. I definitely did not want athletes to view training as mindlessly 'filling in the diary'. This was especially important in the development of each athlete's weight training strategy. Every athlete had to demonstrate well-developed core lifting technique and performance before moving to the more technical exercises, such as the snatch. The athletes first needed to develop a confident movement with strong acceleration. This flexibility was important in all areas of the development of the national team success story. Although I came with extensive experience of the British approach to high-performance rowing, it was clear to me it had to be a solution to the particular and unique circumstances that the Swiss team were facing at the time.

Table 2: Sample Training Week/Competition Phase: Men's Eight (July)

Day	Time	Training	Rest	Stroke rate (strokes/min)	Distance (km)
Monday	Session 1	Rowing: Long row	n/a	16 to 20	30
	Session 2	Rowing: Technical focus (with short bursts of speed)	n/a	16 to 20 (30 to 40)	13
	Session 3	Cross train: 120 min as combination of bike, run, swim	n/a		
Tuesday	Session 1	Rowing: Intervals 5 x 2000m (rate steps)	10 min	(set 1: 20; set 2: 22 + 24; set 3: 24 + 26; set 4: 26 + 28; set 5: 30)	22
	Session 2	Rowing: Technical focus	n/a	16 to 20	12
	Session 3	Weights: Standard session			
Wednesday	Session 1	Rowing: Long row	n/a	16 to 20	30
	Session 2	Rowing: Technical focus	n/a	16	12
Thursday	Session 1	Off			
	Session 2		n/a		
	Session 3	Weights: Standard session			
Friday	Session 1	Rowing: 90 min with power strokes (bungee) - 17 strokes hard race starts; 30 sec off x 10 (x 3 sets)	8 min (bungee free)	40+	26
	Session 2	Rowing: Technical focus	n/a	20 to 30	12
	Session 3	Weights: Circuit-style session			
Saturday	Session 1	Rowing: Intervals 4 x 15 min (rate step sequence by mins 3, 2, 1, 3, 2, 1, 1, 1, 1)	5 min	(20, 22, 24, 22, 24, 26, 24, 26, 28)	30
	Session 2	Rowing: Technical focus	n/a	20 to 30	12
	Session 3	Cross train: 120 min as combination of bike, run, swim	n/a		
Sunday		Off			
*Distances have been estimated based on the time available for each session and may overestimate actual distance covered				Total	199

ATHLETE SELECTION AND TALENT DEVELOPMENT

Testing was part of a clearly defined selection procedure. Tim Foster, my predecessor, had done a lot of work setting up a selection process similar to what we had in the UK and this was something that I continued to develop to suit the Swiss requirements. Essentially, we held three assessments during the preparation phase (autumn to spring). The first assessment required athletes to submit a 5km ergometer result and then a 6km small boat assessment, the second followed the national indoor rowing championships and the third required another 2km test to be completed. However, we did not restrict entry to the senior assessment process to ergometer scores, something that contrasts with the British system in which athletes have to achieve a minimum ergometer target in a public assessment the day before an on-water trial. We believed it was important to allow as many trialists to participate in the preparation phase as possible due to our considerably smaller talent pool. The athletes that displayed good results during the long-distance trials were then invited to train with the national team group and we formed crews from internal assessments and on-water racing along with my own judgements. These were informed by various pieces of information, including the usual individual monitoring approaches such as 2000m ergometer tests and laboratory tests. From these sessions and tests we invited certain athletes to final trials where decisions would be made about the formation of the summer crews. All the different age groups followed the same testing procedure. This not only made it simpler for the clubs to organise, but also exposed the junior and under-23 rowers to the experience of what was to be expected further down the line. It also made any senior selections very visible to the rest of the rowing community.

I tried to make sure that we always had a purpose for any testing we undertook. Testing was always relevant and I felt it was important that there was a time and a date when the athletes were able to feel that they had 'made it'; they were on the team and had a right to be there. This was a key point in their journey as international athletes. With the small number of rowers I had in Switzerland, options were limited and I was often sure of the selection before we went into final trials, but I still considered it important to make it official.

We would normally do a maximum of three dedicated laboratory-based test sessions each season using a fairly standard format for step testing (i.e. seven stages of four minutes per stage, with lactate samples taken during a one-minute rest between stages). The results were often interesting and certainly the rowers were happy to see the physical evidence of the progress that they could already sense. These tests were a small part of the selection decisions and were helpful in providing a picture of how training was progressing.

For me, selection is always going to be a balance between art and science – and a conversation topic that will go on for a long time. Personally, I have a real problem if I push a crew out to race and do not believe in my heart that this will be the fastest crew, whatever the numbers say. I think in the end you have to trust your own judgement and this is where it is so important to have built up a rapport and trust with the club coaches, so open and often difficult conversations can be had that do not leave a festering background of mistrust once the crew is picked. It is a mix of art and science, but I think one of the beauties of the sport is that, for some reason, certain combinations work when maybe they should not. This is what experience and a willingness to take chances can show. So tying yourself in knots with science can be counterproductive. Sometimes, one individual, who might not make selection based on test results, somehow has the ability to make the boat quicker when put in a certain combination. The size of the team I was dealing with meant that I was able to examine these options before a final trial. It is certainly one reason why I am cautious of only using seat racing. Some athletes are just very good at seat racing, which can mean that immediate results do not predict later results as well as might be anticipated. As a coach, it is important to spot the combinations that 'work' and build on them as a starting point for selection, but to also remain critically minded about the potential for single events as well as an athlete's abilities to confound the selection process.

COACH AND ATHLETE RELATIONSHIP

I think that there is a strong commonality in the winning attributes between successful sports people: they need to be suitably single minded, 'bloody minded' even, to get through the bad times as well as the good. Everyone has tough times in international sport – it's not a smooth progression – and what is needed is a strong self-belief to cope with the training volume, the intensities, the injuries, the setbacks and whatever else is happening. Winners are the ones that cope best with these things. It is a bit clichéd but it is the passion, single-mindedness and determination to succeed that are the key factors. You can't just do it because someone says you should – you have to really believe it yourself. To be able to put yourself through that degree of sacrifice – personal, emotional, physical – takes a lot and if you start to ask if it's the right thing to do, it's gone wrong already. Once you start to question, of course, the level of dedication is mad. In my experience, the mental attributes are fixed and I'm not sure that much can be done to change them. A coach or psychologist can help athletes through a short-term crisis, perhaps by clarifying things, but, deep down, athletes have to believe in themselves. If they have lost that 'fire' then I'm not sure that someone else can get it back for them. Success also takes time, something that is often in short supply, particularly with the pressure on funding now being more and more results based. For lightweights in particular, their best rowing years are often in their late 20s and for them to commit and be supported for this time before they are able to show their best takes a big commitment from all the parties involved.

In terms of my coaching style, I guess my athletes see me as somewhat unforgiving and unemotional. I keep a definite professional distance – I find it easier to work that way – other coaches get in a lot closer to their athletes. I'm very straightforward. I like to set out and agree what our aims are, to agree what we need to do to achieve them and to be clear that this will not be easy. When I have strayed away or not held to this my coaching has suffered. Inevitably, there will be difficulties or disagreements and to deal with these I go back to the common goals. My position is that we are all trying to help each other and that the goals we have in common will help us to work through the problems.

Swiss rowers enjoying a technical paddle before the race season begins. *Credit: Felix Dieu*

Financial support, or the lack of it, is an increasingly common cause of difficulty among rowers, particularly those early in their international careers or who have recently joined a crew of more experienced athletes. I work hard to remind them about how little they actually need to succeed and that while money is an important part of the support structure that makes demanding training possible, success in rowing does not come from being financially driven.

There are also memorable lighter moments that helped strengthen the bond between athletes and coach. I remember an occasion where our lightweight men's four had a breakthrough performance in a World Cup regatta at Lake Bled in Slovenia. They had qualified for their first A final and competed really well. When they came off the water their delight was clear and to celebrate, we thought it only right to go for a drink. At the bar, I offered to buy everyone a beer but embarrassingly found myself ordering four pints of Coca Cola. These were still young athletes who were learning to navigate the intensely competitive world of international rowing. Over time, they matured in their understanding of how elite athletes can behave and even developed a (mostly) healthy interest in celebrating their achievements. Watching young athletes mature both on and off the water is possibly the most enjoyable part of my job.

TECHNICAL APPROACH

In terms of technique there are two key points that I always emphasise, and when I have become distracted away from them or become overly focused on other issues, the quality of rowing has always suffered. The first point is how far a rower can push the boat with each stroke. This is a function of effective length of connection via the pressure on the foot stretcher through the body and on to the spoon, so creating a bend in the shaft to produce the force that sends the boat forward. The second is how well a rower can get the boat to run between each push.

Rowers spend a lot of time on the recovery. Ensuring that each athlete gets the feeling of the boat moving through the water is essential, both for allowing good speed to be maintained and for avoiding wasting the energy that helped create the speed in the first place. The success of the Swiss team was built around getting the basics and fundamentals right. We worked very hard, not allowing ourselves to be distracted by any easy fixes. We had to get a physiology that was competitive and to row a technical model that worked well. We did not chase the additional 1 per cent until we had developed the other 99 per cent as well as we could. That was a big part of the philosophy, working the simple stuff as well as we could. It is very easy to chase the tiny percentage gains and the glamour without actually addressing the fundamentals.

Rowers can achieve a great deal by concentrating on the basics. That was something that the Swiss athletes bought into. It became harder to hold to these principles as they become more successful, but at the level we were starting from we didn't need the fancy gear to get a long way. When it comes to finding that last half a per cent then yes – you have to look at everything – but if you listen to the best coaches, you will find that they don't have magic bullets or secret techniques. They are facing the same problems and issues that we all do, all the way through the pathway of bringing someone from novice to international level. How effectively can you apply your physiology to moving the boat? How little or how much of what you have to offer is wasted in extra or inefficient movements and how much do those movements detract from the boat speed? How do you manage your life outside of training and racing and how much does that affect what you can do in terms of quality and quantity with both on and off the water training?

Technical drills were a regular feature of our training sessions. In particular, I made extensive use of drills that encouraged bodyweight suspension. For example, I especially like a drill where pairs of rowers sit at front stops with their bottoms directly on the deck and slides. The sliding seat is pushed firmly into the backstops so that it cannot move. Next, the rowers have to drive hard against the stretcher and suspend their bottoms in the air until they drop – lightly and unaided – back onto the seat. I also used a good number of hand placement drills (e.g. inside/outside hand off) to try and encourage a good awareness of handle movement without tension or excess movement. One drill that I tend not to use is 'catch slaps'. This is where rowers smack the feathered oar hard on to the water at the catch and then turn it quickly onto the square. Though this may encourage a very positive lifting of the hands, I find it loses any sense of skill, touch, quickness or lightness to the catch and works at a much more gross motor skill level.

I learned a great deal in Switzerland about creating an effective technical approach for high performance rowing. Certainly, I developed a heightened awareness for communication. The Swiss have three main national languages: German, French and Italian, and though I don't speak much German or Italian, my French is OK. However,

Swiss scullers during a long distance paddle. *Credit: Felix Dieu*

I quickly learned that speaking in French created more problems than it solved. So, my coaching was done in English as most of the rowers could either speak English to a reasonable level or someone else in the team translated to whichever other European language was needed. Consequently, I quickly learned to be much more economical and concise in my phrase choice as well as more direct in all communication. It would not work to speak in very broad metaphorical terms to a group of rowers who both have to understand what is being conveyed as well as to accurately relay the message to teammates. This lesson in communication is something that I have retained since returning to coach native English speakers. There is nothing productive in a coach having a 'one-way conversation' about rowing technique development.

SUPPORT SERVICES AND TECHNOLOGY

Using modern technology, it is now possible to measure many aspects of the rowing stroke. However, we made limited use of technology, partly because it was not readily available and partly because I did not want it to become a distraction. We employed Valery Kleshnev of Biorow (a company that specialises in the provision of rowing biomechanical services). He would bring his equipment and work with our crews for three days, twice a year. It was a good way to concentrate on very specific, objective issues and overall it was certainly a valuable approach. It also gave me the opportunity to discuss any technical problems that I had been addressing. The practice of bringing in other people was something that I repeated and this occasionally included bringing in other coaches that I respected and trusted as a way to support the programme both on and off the water. I have no way of estimating how much this activity helped our overall progress, but I think we got the best out of this selective and occasional use of biomechanics measurements. I suspect that had I been offered the opportunity to use biomechanics more often, I probably would have refused. It is clearly a very powerful resource and one that has grown immensely in popularity across all levels of rowing. Yet, the potential benefits to rowing performance that, in theory, the collection of masses of raw biomechanical data make possible, can only happen once there are efficient and effective ways to analyse and interpret everything. For some rowers, it can be an enlightening and excellent way to build confidence in their changes, while for others it can become a source of frustration.

My thoughts on this subject are also based on having now worked in other elite training centres where we could use biomechanics technology at every session if we wanted. There are athletes who would examine the data before deciding whether it was a 'good' session or not, and this can cause a loss of confidence in their own perception and feel. That is when I really learned that it could easily become a distraction. I realise that many readers are likely to be thinking about investing in this technology, or indeed already have all the equipment necessary. What I can say is that when used sensibly and proportionately, biomechanical assessments are a useful tool as long as athletes and coaches do not expect them to provide all the answers. Instead, it is important to have a clear focus for their use. Only in those circumstances do the athletes and coach really get the best value out of the data.

Usually, a pre-requisite for having plenty of support services and outside experts is money. It can cost a lot to access modern sport science and sport medicine facilities. We were reasonably well funded through Swiss rowing, but we didn't have much in the support area. We used a sport science lab to provide blood lactate profiles (using the step test procedure outlined earlier) and to help with fitness monitoring and training intensity control. The test results were used to provide each athlete with individualised training zones, especially for use with ergometer splits. Our athletes would wear heart-rate monitors much of the time, and this helped develop a better understanding of the transfer of the intensity zones to on-water speed and cross-training intensities, but I did not insist on athletes wearing their monitors all the time. Also, I did not routinely download heart rate or GPS data from on-water sessions. Instead, we concentrated on following the training programme and, as athletes became more experienced, I started allowing each rower to make some of the subjective judgements about the intensity zone that they perceived they were using. Of course, we still had stroke rate and other feedback about boat speed and pace to guide our training intensity; something that I think is important for an athlete to learn with or without expensive gadgets.

We did not have access to sport nutritionists, at least not at the team level. I encouraged the lightweights to avoid trying to lose weight too early in the season as I believe that they need some 'protection' against the winter weather and to support the high training volumes. No one would be above 78kg at any point. They would lose weight gradually through the spring until each person was 1kg above the agreed target racing weight for the April trials, but then allow their weight to go back up a little before arriving at regattas with between 1 and 2kg to lose in pre-race sweating. By allowing the rowers to sit comfortably above racing weight until the competition, I think it is probably easier to avoid illness and injury during the many preceding months. We did do individual testing to give the athletes confidence in both how much and how they could lose the weight at the regatta (running, Wattbike or ergometer were the practical options) and yet have no performance impairment.

ALTERNATIVE REALITIES

I am sure that even if I had been offered a large sum of money by a rich Swiss benefactor to improve the international rowing team, I wouldn't actually have changed much. I have already made the point that too many rowers think that their performance would improve by simply gaining more funding. I believe there is likely to be a point where more funding has little to no additional benefit in pure rowing terms. Nevertheless, I would have welcomed an increase in the resource directed at hiring other staff. I spent a great deal of my coaching time working on strategy documents for Swiss rowing to help support club and coach development. I also spent countless hours driving boat trailers across Europe to training camps and regattas and this takes a toll on family life as well as meaning that I started the camp tired. I suspect many readers are surprised to hear that a head rowing coach for a national team spends a great deal of time off the water providing support services. Yet, this is the reality for all but a very small group of well-funded international rowing teams. It would be preferable to have been able to hire a boatman who could do many of these logistical and equipment repair duties, as well as hiring other coaches and strategists to create and deliver national rowing strategies.

FINAL THOUGHTS

I believe there were three main factors underpinning the success of Swiss rowing during my time in charge:

1. We built trust via good communication with the underpinning support structures, especially the rowing clubs.
2. We created an environment where there was continuity of good training. Success is built on minimising the influences that interrupt good training and by the steady development of training volume and quality.
3. We were patient and took our time – it takes years to develop the above two points.

Although the Swiss Federation was small, and had the attendant issues of scale, to my mind these are the golden rules of any international rowing success.

Thomas Poulson Former Head Coach, Denmark

Thomas Poulson was a rower on the Danish national team from 1992 until 2001. In 1994 he joined the LM4- that won gold at the 1996 Olympic Games and in 1999 set a new world record of 5:45.6, held until 2014 when it was broken by another Danish crew. He was head coach of the Danish national team from 2001 to 2014 which, in the 2012 Olympics, won gold in the LM2x, silver in the W1x and bronze in the LM4-. He is currently a freelance coach working as a consultant to US Rowing and the Chinese Province of Liaoning.

I began my coaching while I was still competing for Denmark in lightweight coxless fours. My coach Bent Jensen and I talked a lot about technique after training sessions. He and I could easily spend several hours discussing our progress and thinking about ways to increase our speed. Later, I would help communicate our conclusions to the other crew members. The crew knew that I had a good sense of boat feel and they were willing to listen and respond to the suggestions that Bent and I had made. Towards the end of my international rowing career, Bent would occasionally suggest that I should consider a career in coaching. Initially, the idea did not appeal to me, but Bent had planted a seed in my head. Over time, I started to think about what I could contribute to the team as a coach. I enjoyed thinking about new ideas that we could try in order to improve our chances of success. When I stopped rowing in 2001, Bent invited me to be his assistant, so my progression as a coach was very rapid. I became head coach for the national team in 2006 when Bent was appointed as a national team coach in Canada. I stayed in this position until the completion of the 2013 rowing season.

TRAINING ENVIRONMENT

The facilities and training environment that were available to our athletes while I was working with the national team were pretty basic. There was nothing particularly special about it and I've been to plenty of rowing clubs around the world that have far better facilities. Essentially, all of our training was based at a 2000m lake situated about 15km north of the centre of Copenhagen in an area called Bagsværd. Anyone who wanted to be part of the national team had to be willing to move to Copenhagen and be able to train at the lake. There are very few rowing clubs in Denmark and most are located near the capital, which is home to about one third of the country's five million people. At least this is one advantage of being a small sport in a small country. Most of the team lived within a 30-minute bike ride of the boathouse and could easily get from work or university to training. In many ways, our training environment was pretty similar to what can be found at rowing clubs all over the world.

Lake Bagsværd. *Credit: Thomas Poulson*

The lake was used by all sorts of rowers: beginners, masters and university teams. We also shared the water with the kayak teams, so it would get extremely busy. Every April, a six-lane 2000m course was set-up so that the rowers could share four lanes, while the kayakers shared the remaining two. We never had exclusive use of the lake in the way teams like Great Britain have at Caversham Lake, for example, and we frequently had to get past beginner crews that were using the same lanes as we were. We also had to deal with frequent wash from the other launches and the kayaks. However, we liked training on this lake and found creative ways to make the best use of it.

Coaches often wonder if it's better to train on a 2000m lake or on a much longer body of 10 to 20km or more. In my opinion a 2000m lake is ideal because it means athletes get a mental break at least once every 10 minutes. It's easy to let your focus drift when training on long stretches of water. I think 10 minutes is long enough to do quality, thoughtful rowing, but not so long that rowers are likely to get distracted. I don't really know what the best distance for a training venue would be, but we adapted well to training on a 2000m lake. When I was part of the Danish lightweight four that won gold at 1996 Olympics, we were able to complete an 180-degree turn at the ends of the lake in 16 to 18 seconds. We would often perform 6000m intervals where we never stopped our timers at the end of each 2000m section. In order to improve our performance, we learned how to spin the boat very quickly. We also gained a huge amount of practice in accelerating a stationary boat to full speed. Lots of rowing teams wait for the competition season to begin working on race starts, but the nature of our training environment in Copenhagen made it possible for us to complete hundreds of 'little' racing starts long before summer racing began. Training efficiency has always been a major part of our success and since we don't have the luxuries of plentiful

The Boathouse. *Credit: Thomas Poulson*

training time or multi-million-dollar custom-built training facilities, we found various ways to adapt our training environment to suit our needs.

We shared a boathouse with various local teams. Our national team training group had access to a rented room where we could base our activities. There was a small weight-training room which could accommodate two people at a time and a room that housed 10 rowing machines that we could book in advance. We spent a lot of time training in the rowing machine room, but it wasn't a great space and the cold walls would quickly become layered in condensation during sessions. The boat bays had reasonable space to store our shells and there was no expectation that athletes would own single sculls. Everyone had access to singles, but most of our training time was spent in the boats in which we planned to race. We never trained in eights. Sometimes, people would turn up to our sessions and ask us where they could find the Danish rowing team. As I said, to untrained eyes, our training environment was no different to a typical rowing club.

TRAINING AND CONDITIONING

Before I outline the training approach that I prescribed for our international rowers, I should first mention that I did not expect athletes to do everything that I prescribed on the training plan. At any point in time, I was working with as many as 20 to 25 lightweight oarsmen. Most of the rowers were very experienced and several were Olympic and World Champions so there was a lot of training knowledge in the group. We took a very democratic approach to the training system. I know it is common in other countries that the head coach sets the training and expects everyone to follow it as planned. However, in Denmark, we took a different, more inclusive approach.

Briefly, I would send a five-week training proposal to the athletes and then we would sit together and negotiate each week. Our athletes were not paid to row, but some did get a small government grant that helped pay for food and accommodation. Everyone had to make their own choices about daily training depending on what else they had to schedule in terms of paid work, study, family and indeed how they felt their training was progressing. If an athlete was feeling excessively fatigued or that illness was approaching, then they would make the decision to rest. Our open and shared approach to training management relied on a high level of trust within the team and helped make clear to the athletes that they were ultimately responsible for their training progress.

It's also important to note that we had a very high degree of competition built into the training. The selection pool for the lightweight men's four was large – it reached 40 athletes at one point – so training sessions were competitive. Much of our on-water training consisted of high intensity interval work, so the natural competitiveness that emerged from within the athlete pool was great for helping everyone to develop a strong body and mind. As I will outline next, our athletes had very limited time to train together and when we did, I think many of the rowers were ready to fight for their seat in the top boat. We really didn't use any formal seat racing when selecting crews, just lots of informal swaps during training which kept the athletes guessing and probably heightened the competitive ethos within the group. Sometimes, I had to encourage the athletes to train alone as a way to control the training load. I realise that competitiveness is a key ingredient in rowing success, but, our Danish rowers probably got more than most because of the unique set of circumstances, which included limited time available to train and a bottleneck of top lightweight rowers who were all trying to get selected into either the double scull or the lightweight four. These features probably made it easier for us to develop an aggressive focus on training by racing and not just training for racing.

During our winter training phase (October to April; see Table 1 on the following page), we couldn't do much on-water training. Our lake would become frozen and unrowable. We also have very short hours of daylight in winter and the athletes all have jobs and university classes so there is further compression of training opportunity. The vast majority of our winter training is performed on Concept2 ergometers. However, the athletes would get tired from so much ergometer rowing and would ask to do some on-water training. We found two solutions that helped. First, we would take our boats down to Copenhagen harbour on occasional weekends. We had to pay local clubs to use their facilities and access the saltwater harbour, but at least we could get some time in boats. Also, we usually did two winter training camps in Portugal, with each lasting about 10 days. Predictably, a major consequence of our predominantly land-based approach to winter training was that our annual volume of water work was typically far lower than most other elite rowing programmes who have full-time athletes and kinder weather.

Towards the end of winter training, we would switch from standard Concept2 machines to Rowperfect ergometers. I think this is a good way to help transition athletes from the many months of indoor rowing to the more dynamic technique needed for the competitive season. We also did some supplementary land-based activities as

Table 1: Sample Training Week/Winter: January

Day	Training	Rest	Stroke rate (strokes/min)	Intensity*
Monday	Rowing ergometer - long intervals: 3 x 23 mins (12 mins + 8 mins + 3 mins)	5 min	22 + 24 + 26	D
	Circuit weight training			
Tuesday	Rowing ergometer - 30 mins	n/a	28	B
Wednesday	Rowing ergometer - 50 mins of pyramid training (rate changes every 5 mins)	n/a	20 +22 + 24 + 22 + 20 etc...	D
	Cross training - 60 mins of either swimming, running or mountain biking	n/a	n/a	All
Thursday	Rowing ergometer - long intervals: 3 x 24 mins (8 mins + 8 mins + 8 mins)	5 mins	22 + 24 + 26	C
Friday	Rowing ergometer - long intervals: 3 x 12 mins	4 mins	24	C
	Circuit weight training			
Saturday	Rowing (erg or water if possible) - 60 mins (30 mins + 15 mins +10 mins + 5 mins)	n/a	22 + 24 +26 + 28	C
	Rowing (erg or water if possible) - 12 km of stroke technique training		20	E
Sunday	Rowing (erg or water if possible) - 6 x 1000m low rate maximum effort	as needed	22	C (maybe B)
	Cross training - 60 mins of either swimming, running or mountain biking	n/a	n/a	All

Notes:

2 to 6 km warm-up before each session

2 to 4 km cool down after each session

*Please see Table 2 on the following page for an explanation of the intensity.

well. For example, we included core stability sessions to help reduce injury risk. These sessions were led by a physiotherapist and lasted up to one hour. We would do two or three of these sessions each week in the winter months and then drop back to just one maintenance session when the main regatta season began in May.

We did relatively little weight training. This was partly to do with our facilities and a lot to do with our limited training time. My personal view is that weight training can help rowing performance, but most rowers get greater benefit from ergometers and even cross-training to help develop aerobic capacity. When I was rowing for Denmark in 1999, we set a world record of 5:45.6 for the lightweight coxless four. None of us had done any weight training for years when we achieved that time, and I think maybe we could have gone as much as one second faster if we had been able to find time to do some weightlifting. However, as a coach, in Denmark weightlifting was not something that I prioritised. I usually included one or two sessions per week of circuit style weight training instead, especially in winter (light loads and high repetitions with short rest intervals). However, all weight training was removed from the training plans once we went back on to the lake in spring. Occasionally, a Danish national team rower would decide that he wanted to do weight training and might do as much as three heavy lift sessions per week, but that was pretty unusual.

In terms of training volume, we typically achieved our target of 600 hours per year. This is a relatively low training volume in comparison to other successful elite rowing teams who say they complete approximately 1000 hours of annual training. However, none of the rowers in the Danish national squad were full-time professional athletes during the years that I was the team coach. Most of the athletes were employed or studied on a full-time basis. So we could only plan to do one session per day on Mondays to Fridays and then two sessions per day on Saturdays and Sundays. In a typical training week, we would complete around 10 hours of training in total. In addition, we had to allow time for athletes to travel to training, get changed and meet as a team to discuss the preparation. Only in an Olympic year would we ask them to take extended leave or reduce their working hours or studies, and even then we did not ask this until about six months before the Olympic regatta. So in order to achieve the high training loads needed to be successful in international rowing, we took the approach that we had to be very efficient in our use of training time. Essentially, we trained with a higher average intensity profile than would be normal in elite rowing teams.

A typical week of winter training would include 8 to 10 hours of training, including seven to eight hours of rowing (usually performed on the ergometer). The quality of training time is related to exercise intensity and Table 2 (below) gives an overview of the training intensity zones that we used (I will explain these later). We avoided the highest intensity domain (i.e. Zone A) in winter, but included approximately one to

Table 2: Training Intensity Zones

Intensity	Zone	Heart rate reserve (%)	Target range for a rower with a maximum heart rate of 200 beats/min and a resting rate of 50 beats/min			% of maximum heart rate (to illustrate relationship to heart rate reserve % only)		
A	Zone 5	94 to 100%	191	to	200	96	to	100
B	Zone 4	86 to 93%	179	to	190	90	to	95
C	Zone 3	78 to 85%	167	to	178	84	to	89
D	Zone 2	60 to 77%	140	to	166	70	to	83
E	Zone 1	44 to 59%	116	to	139	58	to	69

Notes:

1) Heart-rate reserve = maximum heart rate - resting heart rate

2) Exercise heart rate = % of target intensity x heart-rate reserve + resting

Example

The lower end of Zone 5 training heart rate for a rower with maximum heart rate = 200 beats/min and resting heart rate = 50 beats/min is calculated as:

Step 1) Heart rate reserve = 200 - 50 = 150 beats/min

Step 2) Exercise heart rate for 94% of heart rate reserve = 0.94 x 150 + 50 = 191 beats/min two hours in Zone B and about five hours in Zone C and D. The balance of our weekly training time was spent in Zone E doing technical or recovery training.

As we approached the summer racing period, we typically increased the training load by including more high intensity sessions with stroke rates progressing towards 32 strokes per minute during longer interval sessions. During the summer regatta season, we reduced the training volume to make it possible to do high quality short bursts of rowing such as 15 x 20 second sprints at maximum effort.

During the on-water training phase of the year, from April onwards, we usually performed 10 to 14 sessions of on-water rowing each week. Once we could train on the lake, we wanted to make our training as specific as possible and we really only used rowing machines on occasions when the weather caused problems for water rowing. In such cases, we would just do the same workout as had been planned for the lake.

Each water session usually consisted of between 16 and 18km of rowing and rarely anything more than that. We sometimes did sessions of only 12 to 14km, but these were usually the very high intensity workouts. I don't actually think it is that useful to talk about our training volumes in kilometres. I prefer to describe training in terms of hours of rowing within the different intensity zones. In one hour of training, a men's coxless four can easily row 16km whereas a lightweight woman in a single scull might only complete 12km. Since I was setting plans for a range of boats, the training load was planned using total time in different intensity zones based on 'training impulse' (as displayed in Table 2 (above)).

Many books and articles are available that describe the ideas that support the use of training impulse. The most popular version takes training time in minutes and multiplies this by a number that corresponds to a training zone. The heart-rate monitor company Polar use this approach when quantifying 'training load' in their software applications. In their scheme, if an athlete is training at 90 to 100 per cent of maximum heart rate (HRmax), this time gets an intensity rating of 5, whereas training at 70 to 79 per cent of HRmax gets an intensity rating of 3. So training impulse for an athlete who spends 15 minutes at 90 to 100 per cent HRmax and 10 minutes at 70 to 79 per cent HRmax is calculated as 105 'trimps' (15 x 5 + 10 x 3 = 105). We used a slightly modified approach that used the concept of 'heart-rate reserve' to set our training loads, but the basis of the calculation was the same. For the purposes of this chapter, the specific details of our calculations and our preference for using heart-rate reserve rather than percentage HRmax are not important, but I do want to highlight the value of using the concept of training impulse.

Combining intensity and volume into a single quantifiable score was very useful for planning training loads and it helped make sure that our athletes were making small but important gains in training overload throughout the season. Of course, each athlete needed to wear heart-rate monitors during their training to make this approach work well. Our athletes quickly learned how to keep their effort within the prescribed range and they would also download their workout data at regular intervals to check for suitable progress. When new athletes joined our group, I would sit down with them and review their heart-rate data after each session to help them learn about managing their training effort and make sure they understood how the training plan worked.

Table 3: Sample Training Week/Pre-Competition: Summer (2 weeks before World Rowing Championships)

Day	Training	Rest	Stroke rate (strokes/min)	Intensity
Monday	Travel to Austria			
	Rowing - long intervals: 3 x 12 mins	4 mins	30	B
Tuesday	Rowing - medium intervals: 3 x 5 mins	4 mins	32	B
	Rowing - short intervals: 3 x 50 secs then 7 x 40 secs	430 secs + 320 secs	≥40	A
Wednesday	Rowing - long interval: 2 x 25 mins (as 15 min + 7 min + 3 min)	5 mins between the two sets	22 + 24 + 26	C
	Rowing - medium interval: 4 x 6 mins	5 mins	32	B
Thursday	Rowing - medium intervals: 3 x 15 mins (as 7 min + 5 min + 3 min)	5 mins between the three sets	22 + 24 + 26	C
	Rowing - 60 mins (as 6 min + 1 min)	Continuous	22 + 28	D
Friday	Rowing - 12 km of technique training	n/a	20	E
	Free time			
Saturday	Rowing 30 mins (as 20 min + 7 min + 3 min)	n/a	24 + 26 + 28	C
	Rowing - 12 km of technique training	n/a	20	E
Sunday	Rowing - medium intervals: 3 x 1500m on race course	1500-m recovery paddle	race rate	A
	Rowing - medium intervals: 3 x 11 mins (as 6 min + 4 min + 1 min)	4 mins	24 + 26 + 28	C

Notes:

2 to 6 km warm-up before each session

2 to 4 km cool down after each session

Morten Lidegaard (assisted by translation of Danish to English)

The summer on-water rowing sessions typically lasted about 90 minutes. Everyone followed the same set training programme regardless of boat type and this made it easy work to encourage and coach all squad members in an efficient way. Again, the relatively short session durations made it somewhat easier for athletes to concentrate on holding their technique and form. However, if I sensed that the concentration was dropping or that an athlete was struggling to listen and respond to feedback, then I would simply move on to another crew. Table 3 (below) shows a one-week sample of training that was used by our lightweight men's four won that won the 2013 World Championships.

Each rowing session started with a warm-up paddle of approximately 4km, which gave me a chance to work with each crew. We would then gather all the boats together to do the main workout for the day. We could set individual training prescriptions when using ergometers, but it would have been impractical to have attempted this during boat-based training. We normally had different boats training together, as well as men and women. So we would set up the intervals with staggered starts to make the work as competitive as possible. The sessions usually ended with a 2 to 4km cool-down paddle. We really didn't do much paddling at rates of less than 20 strokes per minute.

ATHLETE SELECTION AND TALENT DEVELOPMENT

While I was head coach in Denmark, the progression to the national squad was through two stages. First there were talent centres which were essentially targeted clubs who had good coaches and structures that supported athlete development. The coaches would identify talented rowers and keep me informed about their progress and I often visited the clubs to meet and observe the rowers directly. The next level up was the power centre and above that the national squad group. The rowers in the power centre and the national squad train together so that rowers could move up and down between the groups quite quickly. In fact, it is like a national squad at two levels. The aim of having the two groups train together is so that members of the power centre appreciate the level required to make the national squad.

It is not difficult to identify talented rowers in terms of their athleticism and ability to feel when the boat is moving well, but for me the most important part is their ability to believe that they can achieve at the highest level. Within the national squad we are prepared to work with rowers who are not fast in terms of international standards, but if they have belief and are willing to train hard, then we know from experience that they have the potential to win medals. In fact, most of the Danish medal winners were not that fast in the early stages of their development – but what they did have was belief in their own abilities. So we are prepared to develop the talent of those who believe in themselves, because after around 5000 hours of training, they often start winning.

Up to 2013 we did not use erg scores as part of our selection process. For example, in the 2004 Olympics, one of our gold medal winners in the lightweight men's quad had a best erg score of 6:30. With that score he would probably never have been selected for the USA, Australia or Great Britain. However, most of our medal winners do have good erg scores, but because we do not have a lot of rowers to choose from, we need to be even more careful in identifying those who can make the boat go fast.

In my experience, when you put a crew together, you can see very quickly if the boat is going to go fast. When I put Rasmussen and Quist together (2012 Olympic champions in lightweight men's doubles), I could tell after one week that they had the potential to go very fast. Often selection is about finding a blend of technique, personality and ability to move the boat. Just before the 2012 Olympics we did try seat racing on the basis that we might be losing out to other countries. Interestingly, we found that seat racing improved erg scores, possibly because of the additional competitive element. But seat racing was not telling us which combination would make the boat go faster. For example, one of the rowers selected to represent Denmark in lightweight doubles at the 2012 Olympics was ranked 10th in the seat racing

Olympic 2012 lightweight double scull champions Mads Rasmussen and Rasmus Quist racing for Denmark at a Rowing World Cup event. *Credit: Tine Bjonge*

process. Seat racing can be a useful process, but it should not substitute for coaching intuition and judgement about the fastest crew on race day.

COACH AND ATHLETE RELATIONSHIP

I use a lot of energy listening to what the rowers are saying about how the boat is going, and in particular to their reactions to any changes that we have made. Of course, some rowers find it difficult to talk and just want to listen to what the coach tells them. To these rowers I say, 'If you do not give me information about how things are going, then I cannot coach you.' So, for example, if I am trying to correct a problem with the catch, then I need the rower to tell me how the changes feel. A coach can analyse technique by watching a rower (a skill that takes many years to develop), however, in my opinion, the analysis can only ever be effective if it includes a lot of listening. I find that both the listening and watching require huge amounts of concentration. After a coaching session and especially at training camps, I find myself very tired and I need as much sleep as the rowers. I might be sitting still on the coaching launch but my mind is always working at full speed.

When rowers join my squad and we meet for the first time, I spend a lot of time getting to know them because I want them to feel comfortable and to understand the way I work as a coach – I'm very nice to them. I also need them to have the confidence to be honest with me. For example, if a race goes badly, perhaps because they did not push themselves sufficiently hard, of course they know it, and I want them to be able to tell me. They need to know that if they are honest with me, I can help them; if they are not honest with me then I cannot help them. In the first year of training with a new squad member, my main objective is to establish a good relationship with them. I need to invest time in my rowers to be able to make them go fast; I'm not a coach that tries to get quick results then discards rowers if the results do not come.

It can be very difficult when you have a rower or rowers who think that they know better than you. With small groups such as the Danish national squad, this can be more of a problem especially when individuals think that they can succeed without you. Although I am always prepared to listen and to discuss issues, there comes a time when I say something like: 'It's time to stop this discussion. It's me who makes the decisions. It's me who says what we are going to do and how we are going to do it. If you want to be a world-class rower, you have to listen to me. If you do not listen to me, you will not win – and you have to do what I say. I have won my medals and I can help you. If you want to go your own way that is fine with me – but you will not win that gold medal.' Sometimes the coach has to have the last word.

TECHNICAL APPROACH

I think it is very important to teach rowers about incorrect technique. It's easy to think that the goal of improving stroke technique is to eliminate the bad and focus only on the good. One effect of this is that rowers start to dread making 'mistakes', which can make rowers tense and hinder real learning. One reason why children are such good learners is that they are not afraid of making mistakes. For example, if a child attempts to kick a ball, misses and falls over, she often laughs. Then she gets up and tries again and very quickly the misses become miss-directed kicks and before long, the kicks are accurate. The process of making and then correcting movement errors is a really important step in efficient skill development and it is best achieved when the errors are celebrated and not treated as failures. What the child is doing between failed and successful attempts is learning to feel 'difference' – the difference between a goal that is achieved or not. I believe it is 'difference' that is the key to teaching effective and efficient rowing technique. We can help athletes learn from 'difference' if we are willing to teach them what incorrect rowing technique feels like. The brain does the learning, the coach just needs to provide a suitable opportunity for the rower to feel the difference between correct and incorrect rowing technique.

We rarely used specific drills in practice and when we did, they were usually part of dynamic rowing rather than static drills, such as placing catches. Drills never lasted more than about two minutes before we continued with another six to eight minutes of normal rowing. There can be a tendency after practicing drills to go back to normal rowing with the same fault, so we concentrated more on teaching good technique while the athletes were engaged in normal rowing. However, there are drills that I think are very useful when used sparingly. For example, I found it useful to have half of a coxless four row while the non-rowing pair had to hold their blades off the water. This is a hard drill that can frustrate athletes, but it was also excellent to let athletes understand how their oar movement and pressure can throw the boat around. It provided a great opportunity for each rower to experiment with blade force and handle movements in order to show the different effects on the boat, such as balance. We would take this one step further by repeating the drill with each of the rowers on the opposite side and this provides a very good contrast for athletes to learn about boat handling and effective rowing.

I also used drills such as rowing with one arm or square blades, but only very rarely. I think that much of the time spent getting a drill action performed correctly is wasted time. Crews learn how to do the drill well, but then don't transfer that learning to rowing at race pace. I don't think that learning how to row square blades at rate 18 is very helpful for racing at 38 strokes per minute. If you can teach a crew to row fast at 38 strokes per minute, then they can probably row reasonably well with square blades at rate 18, but it's not so obvious that the reverse will work just as well. Typically, I would teach technique while the athletes were just rowing as normal. I would get my motor launch as close to the boat as possible, and then ask a particular rower to make a change that would encourage that sense of difference. If I wanted an athlete to speed up their catch, I would ask him to do this in the extreme, just smash the oar in as fast as possible for 10 strokes. Then, I would ask him to row with a very soft catch for another 10 or 20 strokes.

After that, I would stop the boat and ask the rower to describe his experiences of the fast catches against the very soft catches. Then I would say that I want you to find the balance of making a fast catch, but doing so smoothly and effectively – not to overuse their power to place the blade. Now the rower can blend their experiences towards making a really efficient and skilful catch. Many people think drills are best done when the specific movement is isolated from the rest of the stroke, such as when a rower drops the oar in and out of the water with the boat stationary, however, I doubt this is much help. Yes, she will feel difference, but it is an artificial difference and not the kind that helps develop a sense of what good oar placement feels like at competition pace.

SUPPORT SERVICES AND TECHNOLOGY

The use of biomechanical measurements in rowing is increasingly popular. We started to make considerable use of technology to measure the angles and forces that rowers generate in the boat during preparations for the London 2012 Olympic regatta. We would pay for an international expert on biomechanics to bring his equipment to Denmark to put on the boats. We probably did this on three occasions with the lightweight double that won gold in London that year.

One important benefit that we gained from this approach was the ability to better identify the technique we wanted to achieve. Previously, this was done by eye and intuition but the technology enhanced our ability to be objective in defining what we wanted for each rower and for the crew. This is important to us because in Denmark there are many rowing styles, so we wanted to achieve a more consistent technique, and to have more coaches teaching this. When new rowers joined our national training group, I often found myself having to spend time 'rebooting their system' to get them to row in a consistent 'Danish style'. So, technology offered us a new approach to an old problem.

Most rowers have curious minds and look in all sorts of places to find things that might help improve rowing performance. I am not a scientist in the normal sense of the term, but I do like experimenting and trying out new ideas. Essentially, all a coach is trying to do is find a method to help get the best out of a rower and each training session offers a new opportunity to test what helps and what does not. We are fortunate that Copenhagen has some of the best sport scientists in the world and I was able to get some excellent support from our local university. They had many enthusiastic and talented students who also were curious about how to improve elite sport performance. So, we developed a very productive collaboration between the science students and our rowers to help give us many insights into preparing for races. For example, we experimented with the use of nutrition supplements including caffeine, bicarbonate and β-alanine. Some of these studies are published in academic journals and accessible to anyone who is interested[1]. The researchers helped us to find out how to make suitable use of legal performance enhancers. Caffeine, for example, gave excellent results with our lightweight rowers and the study data helped teach us how to make best use caffeine for training and racing. We found less consistent benefit from sodium bicarbonate (baking soda) and β-alanine (an amino acid that helps make carnosine in skeletal muscle), so rarely used these supplements.

We also worked with the science team to identify how best to warm-up for a 2000m race. We used a limited amount of stretching in our warm-up because our scientists found that too much stretching reduced strength and power. We also found that a 30-minute warm-up on the water was sufficient, especially for lightweights who might need extra time to digest any post weigh-in food and drink. We also found that the best warm-up sequence should include a series of progressively higher rating bursts of speed (e.g. 10 strokes at rate 24, 15 strokes at rate 28, 10 strokes at rate 32, 10 strokes at 36, some strokes flat out then 10 strokes at rating 42 – all with relatively brief periods of relaxation between intervals).

FINE TUNING FOR RACING

Many lightweight rowers don't eat very much, but our Danish lightweights usually ate pretty well for much of the training year. We largely let our experienced lightweights manage their own weight. I know that many nutritionists and sport scientists advise that rowers should lose weight gradually over periods of many months. However, in my opinion, it is possible and probably desirable for lightweight rowers to be pretty heavy 24 hours before a major race. It was not uncommon for our international male lightweights to be as much as 3.5kg over their individual weight limit at 24 hours before a race. Again, we would experiment with individual weight loss approaches in the day before a race. Many rowers could be between 2.5 and 3.0kg above the weight cut-off, but they were able to exercise on the morning of a race and make weight successfully. It was common for our crews to dehydrate on the day of the weigh-in. Much of the potential for dehydration to affect rowing performance is due to psychological concerns. If the rower thinks that the sweat loss will be a problem, then it probably

---

[1] For example: Christensen et al. (2014) 'Caffeine, but not bicarbonate, improves 6min maximal performance in elite rowers.' Applied Physiology, Nutrition and Metabolism. 39(9): 1058–63.

will be. So, we used the science to help each rower learn how to make an effective short-term weight loss approach and then how to rapidly restore the lost fluid. In this way, a crew of four lightweights could carry up to between 6 and 10kg of muscle that we would otherwise have had to lose to weigh in 'comfortably' and to avoid sweat runs. Of course, sometimes a rower would get it wrong and miss the weight target but gain useful and individualised experience about what they need to do to control their body weight in the days before competition. In my opinion, it is helpful for rowers to have a little extra muscle as well as higher body fat through much of the season. This seemed to reduce our risk of injury and illness and it was certainly preferred by most of the rowers.

In the final weeks before a major regatta such as the World Championships or the Olympics, we would not use rowing machines for our training sessions because I think this can damage a rower's boat feel, even very experienced rowers. The only exceptions to this were when the weather made on-water rowing unsafe or impossible and we needed to preserve fitness.

FINAL THOUGHTS

Danish rowers get very little funding to help them, which made it hard to balance training with everything else. The very top rowers got a little sponsorship as well as some money from Team Denmark, but they still had to earn money for long periods. I do wonder how well we would have done if we were able to pay our athletes to row on a full-time basis such as they do in Great Britain, Australia and elsewhere. Even in the US, the university rowers are well funded through scholarship systems and other programmes. One thing is for sure, it would allow us to retain more of the talent in Danish rowing. There are likely to be lots of better rowers in Denmark who don't continue to the national team crews because they do not want to struggle financially. Our rowers were not be able to train for more than about 16 hours per week during my time as head coach, but I wonder how much better we could have done with a bit more money. I'm not sure that I would change the main training approach but we might well have done more work on weight training.

Another way we could help improve the international results for Danish rowers would be to develop a coach education programme. During my time we had no formal structure of coach education in Denmark. The national coaches would meet from time to time with club coaches to explore specialist topics such as biomechanics or nutrition, but there was no structure leading to a coaching qualification – unlike football in Denmark where the top coaches need to have a coaching-related degree from a university. What we are interested in is identifying what makes a successful coach. For example, why is it that one coach with 20 rowers might provide one member of the national squad, yet another coach, with the same number of rowers will provide 10. Of course, if a successful coach leaves a club, we see the level of success fall. Success is clearly related to individual coaches. One of the factors of these successful coaches is what we call in Danish 'fire soul', which I think translates loosely in English as something like 'fire in the belly', a combination of burning enthusiasm, inspiration and motivation. Most of these successful coaches are happy to see their rowers move on to the national squad and take pride in their subsequent achievements but some want to hold on to them and keep the success to themselves.

There was also a large gap between the small group of top coaches, who mainly worked for the National Team, and the many club coaches. I think we could have improved the national team performances if we closed this gap. We have examined the coaching structure in other successful rowing countries, but we cannot simply copy those approaches because most would not fit with the Danish culture and our way of doing things. Perhaps, if we were more supportive of providing financial and education support for our developing coaches, we could improve the pool of national talent. Then maybe we would see Danish rowers doing well in other boat classes and in more open weight events.

Part 2

National Rowing (Universities and Clubs)

Ben Lewis
Ben Lewis, Head Coach, Thames Rowing Club, London, UK

Ben has been involved in rowing for over 20 years and is a veteran of 13 Henley Royal Regatta finals. As a rower he won the Ladies' Challenge Plate and contested five other finals; as a coach he has achieved three Thames Cup wins, another win in the Ladies' Plate, the Visitors' Challenge Cup and two other composite victories. He represented Great Britain as a rower and has since developed athletes to gain selection for the senior and under-23 teams as well as coaching the GB under-23 4+ to a bronze medal in 2010 at the World U-23 Championship. He is currently Head Coach at Thames Rowing Club in London.

This chapter describes the development of a men's sweep rowing programme during a one-year preparation for Henley Royal Regatta. Hopefully, it will give interested readers a sense of how we built a successful squad and adjusted to the challenges of club level rowing. I expect that many of the challenges that I describe are common to rowing clubs all over the world. Of course, there are specific aspects to what I will discuss that are unique to rowing in the UK. Nevertheless, many rowers and coaches throughout the world aspire to compete and win at Henley Royal Regatta. There are many opinions and ideas about how to achieve this aim and no simple recipe for success. Yet, there are features that distinguish successful rowing teams and, for obvious reasons, many of the features that distinguish successful club level teams differ from successful features of international rowing programmes. This chapter details the specific approach that I used with Thames Rowing Club, which delivered two crews into the final of the men's club events at Henley in 2015. In sharing my experiences, I hope it will offer direction to others who are equally passionate about developing a high standard of rowing performance in a club setting rather than a university programme or high performance centre.

Henley Royal Regatta is an annual rowing event held in Henley-on-Thames in the English countryside about 30 miles west of London. It is the absolute pinnacle of rowing for clubs, schools and universities around the world, and indeed even among Olympians it is thought of as a very special place to row. In comparison to modern rowing regattas, Henley retains the traditional British regatta format of two boats competing in a straight knockout contest across multiple rounds of a draw. There are no second chances or repechages and the boats usually compete just once per day. The abruptness with which a crew exits the regatta is felt all the more acutely due to the at times perceived 'unfairness' of the course, which is straight on a bendy river, lending advantages and disadvantages at various points of the course. Years with high stream can see this exacerbated.

The course itself is constructed each year with wooden posts and booms that separate the 2112m racecourse from the navigable portion of the River Thames. The water is usually pretty bad as the combination of wind, opposing current and passing motorboats creates a washing machine feel for racing crews that is far from ideal. The best that a Henley competitor can hope for is to draw a station that turns out to be a little less disruptive to rowing than the competitor's station, or with a bit less stream at the start and finish. There is no physical divider between the racing crews. Instead, the umpire in the following launch directs crews to remain on their allocated station, according to an imaginary line along the centre of the course. All these uncontrollable variables can create frustrations

Thames Rowing Club winning the Thames Cup in 2015 at Henley at Henley. *Credit: Tom Wilkinson and www.mentalimagesphotography.com*

and distractions for competitors, especially inexperienced athletes who can easily be overwhelmed by the physical and emotional challenges of the regatta. Yet, perhaps the single most exciting yet daunting aspect of racing for all Henley competitors is the many thousands of spectators and revellers lining the banks from start to finish by the weekend. The sheer size and scale of Henley Regatta is unlike anything else in the world.

I had been employed as a full-time coach at Leander and Molesey boat clubs between 2006 and 2013, with a year in the USA in between changing clubs. Prior to moving to Thames, I had already coached several crews to victories at Henley. Significantly, I coached a Molesey Boat Club men's eight to victory at Henley in 2012, where the losing finalists were from Thames Rowing Club. Six months later Thames invited me to become their head coach with a real focus on the men's squad, and I started my employment in August 2013 with the clearly stipulated aim to develop a Thames Rowing Club crew into a Henley winning crew for the first time in almost a decade.

There are only three events for club-level oarsmen at the regatta, all for sweep rowing only and each is known by the name of the cup that the winning crew receives. There is the Wyfold Challenge Cup for coxless fours, the Britannia Challenge Cup for coxed fours and the coincidentally named Thames Challenge Cup for coxed eights. The eligibility rules for these club level events are determined by the Regatta Stewards and although these do occasionally change, athletes who have competed at a senior world or Olympic event are excluded along with specific groups of individuals such as anyone who has won a medal at a world under-23 rowing championship. Furthermore, schools and university crews are also excluded from the club events and have their own events at the regatta. The idea is that men and women with jobs and careers can compete with other rowers of a similar standard from the UK and around the world.

Although Thames is one of the biggest and best-known clubs in Britain, they had not won a men's club event at Henley since 2006 and had not won the Thames Challenge Cup since 1934. My first season with Thames, in 2013–14, went well and we developed a strong squad of experienced athletes, but Henley 2014 taught us that we still had significant progress to make. I also learned a great deal about adapting to the challenges of a new club with oarsmen who had far less time available for training than I had enjoyed at my past clubs. Leander and Molesey each received significant public funds as designated high performance rowing centres in order to produce a pathway for developing Olympic athletes. As a result many of the athletes had put their careers and personal lives on hold to focus their efforts on rowing. However, most of the athletes at Thames had demanding full-time occupations and all their rowing-related activities had to be fitted around work.

TRAINING ENVIRONMENT

Thames Rowing Club is situated on the Putney Embankment in London, near to the start of the Oxford and Cambridge Boat Race course. We train on the tidal stretch of the River Thames where the water can become extremely rough, especially when tide and wind are in opposition. We share the river with thousands of other rowers and canoeists, as well as London river traffic and pleasure boaters. The river narrows significantly at low tide, but at high tide we have approximately 200 metres of water between banks so there is at least reasonable space. Although the distance that we can row is essentially unlimited, we do most of our training on an 8000m stretch upstream from our boathouse in Putney.

The Thames Rowing Club boathouse is surely one of the best in the country. It overlooks the river and has been refurbished to a sufficiently high standard that it is rented out for weddings and social functions. There is a large gym with 30 rowing machines and a weightlifting room that is also home to an indoor rowing tank (non-pumped). When I first arrived the rowing machines that we used were pretty old and battered and the weight-training equipment was older and even more battered. However, our boat fleet was very good and we had access to almost everything that we wanted for training and racing. We also had large changing areas, showering facilities and warm sitting rooms where we could meet and discuss our preparations as well as eat meals together. The top-quality facilities at Putney gave us a number of advantages. All of our athletes could train simultaneously and feel that they were part of a very large team. Many club programmes struggle to boat a single eight oared crew of competitive athletes, but at Thames, we were able to cope with as many as 70 athletes at a time. Thus, our facilities enabled us to develop and support a large pool of talent, which in turn encouraged more and better athletes to join.

The Thames at Putney at low tide. *Credit: Don Somner*

The Thames at Fulham. *Credit: Don Somner*

The Rowing Tank inside Thames Rowing Club. *Credit: Don Somner*

The Gym. *Credit: Don Somner*

Thames Rowing Club Boathouse. *Credit: Don Somner*

Rowers have to deal with the challenges of training and competing for an outdoor sport. In most cases, rowers have at least 2000m of water to train on, which is helpful given that large volumes of distance must be covered to acquire the skills and conditioning needed for competitive success. However, there are plenty of examples of clubs, universities and schools that have relatively poor training facilities but still produce extremely competitive crews. We are fortunate at Thames to have comparatively good facilities, but I studied and rowed at Oxford Brookes University where the facilities were certainly primitive, at least when I was a student. At that time, Brookes had one facility for land training near our campus and then we would travel 20 miles to a boathouse that was really a cow shed with boat racks made from scaffolding. The equipment was not well maintained as there was no professional boatman and the coach also ran his own business and did his coaching as a sideline. Our weights bars consisted of home-made concrete filled cans with a weight written on the side in permanent marker. However, these basic facilities helped create a sort of 'Rocky' environment, especially when ice coated the windows in deepest winter. We developed an attitude that it was what we did with the blocks of concrete and dented rowing machines that mattered and we did have good capacity to cope with the basic needs of a large squad of rowers.

As with many rowing coaches, much of what I believe matters to rowing performance came from my own experiences as an athlete. Oxford Brookes is arguably the most successful student rowing team in the UK and has won countless events at Henley Regatta as well as supporting the development of many senior international rowers including multiple Olympic champions and medallists since 2000. The approach at Oxford Brookes taught me a great deal about the importance of creating a team atmosphere conducive to high performance rowing. The quality of training facilities was far less important than creating the right training atmosphere. Our head rowing coach at Brookes was Richard Spratley, a brilliant motivator and architect of rowing success. Richard knew how to create an effective environment for rowing, both in physical terms but even more so in the way that he created an atmosphere that was inspirational. It is not easy to identify all the things that he did which gave rise to the right atmosphere, but certainly competitiveness was at the heart of everything that we did. Richard created a training environment that motivated large numbers of students to get out of bed at weekends and perform the most physically demanding of training sessions through the dark and wet winter months.

At Thames, I was far less concerned about the equipment available or water restrictions than I was about creating a training atmosphere that pushes all team members to challenge their physical and mental limits. Above all else, I believe the training environment must be a vibrant, energetic and exciting place to be. We make sure that we reduce crew cliques early on, have as much fun as we can and keep everyone thinking they are part of one team. Of course, tempers sometimes fray between athletes and coaches, or other athletes. I think tension is hard to avoid in a highly competitive training environment, especially when the training groups focused on beating each other to get into the best crew they can. However, the training location and associated environment needs to be welcoming and somewhere the athletes look forward to going. It must have a challenging atmosphere and provide opportunity for athletes to feel rewarded for all the hard work they do. The environment should allow athletes to create a toughness, both on and off the water, that is independent of the coach. Athletes need to learn to nurture their competitiveness in a way that helps each team member to push their limits, and that ultimately does not rely on the physical presence of the coach.

Obviously it is much easier to state the qualities that I wanted from our rowers at Thames than it is to explain how we created it. However, I certainly think that establishing clear and objective performance standards (e.g. 2000m ergometer targets) as well as celebrating personal best performances with each athlete is really helpful. I also think that our determination to keep training even when the weather and training conditions were unpleasant really helped develop the type of training environment that I envisaged when I was first appointed to the job.

TRAINING AND CONDITIONING

In order to win the Thames Cup, I believe a men's eight must be capable of breaking 5:40 for a 2000m effort (assuming flat and warm water with a helpful breeze). This is a real challenge for oarsmen who are unable to train more than once a day on weekdays. Many club level eights are capable of breaking 5:50, but finding a further 10-second improvement for our crew was a major objective of our training approach.

My previous experience of coaching winning Thames Cup eights at Henley was with crews that had an average body weight of approximately 87kg and an average 2000m ergometer score of 6:10. Those crews never actually achieved the sub-5:40 on-water target during their seasons, but they came close and it would likely have happened had we raced even better opposition with improved water conditions and in both cases training times suggested this was doable. Both crews won their events by a comfortable margin. Hopefully, this helps give a more objective sense of the performance targets that the training and conditioning process should target for success in the club events for men at Henley Royal Regatta.

The reality of coaching club athletes who work 40-hour weeks is that training has to be efficient. In our programme, we decided to limit the weight training to just one session per week and concentrate a greater proportion of our time to aerobic training, especially on-water and ergometer rowing. There is only so much that can be achieved with one weight training session per week and we certainly did not expect this session to produce lean muscle gains. Instead, the main purpose was to enhance the strength of each athlete's ligaments and tendons to help reduce our injury risk.

Essentially the problem boiled down to this – could I get guys in their late 20s well into their rowing careers with weddings, kids and the other trappings of life to go the same speed as athletes that trained 15 to 20 per cent more and very little work to worry about or tire them out?

The essence of my conditioning approach at Thames was to encourage our athletes to cover as much rowing distance as possible within the time constraints of daily life. Critically, training intensity had to be relatively low in order to maximise the volume of rowing. Many ambitious club crews start their training year with great enthusiasm, which can quickly lead to training sessions that are performed with excessive intensity. These sessions can feel like the right thing to do at the time, but the reality is that such crews significantly compromise their training volume if the intensity is too high too soon. Also, adding too much intensity to a club level training programme makes recovery difficult, especially over sequential days of training and even more so when multiple sessions per day are included. It can also make athletes miserable, sick and injured, which is quite depressing for everyone. With these considerations in mind, our training approach at Thames emphasised performing as many strokes as possible within the UT2 and UT1 (see Table 1 on the following page) training zones as far as time would permit. We also included no more than two 'very hard' sessions each week, one on the ergometer and the other in a sweep boat (not always the eight).

I have always been a believer in 'working all the systems'. Even early on in the season, it is beneficial to challenge the body with intensity at least once a week. As the season developed, we gradually increased the relative amount of time spent in the highest intensity zones. Our typical week (see Table 1) started with a Monday session where the goal was always about distance. Monday's session was usually on the rowing machine in winter (November to March), but we occasionally switched to a water session in the weeks immediately preceding important events such as the Fours Head (November) or Eights Head (March). Tuesday's session was typically land based, such as a run or the weight-training session. Wednesday was set as the 'hard' day of the week and utilised the ergometer. This session served as a potent aerobic training stimulus as well as an important opportunity to gain objective performance data on each athlete to help evaluate their training response through the season. Thursday sessions were initially conceived as land training on the rowing ergometer, but often we were able to perform this on-water. Friday was a day off and was important to enhance the recovery in time for the large volume of weekend training, which is typical of the British approach to club rowing. We scheduled two sessions on each weekend day to begin at 7a.m. and end around 12p.m. Most of our weekend training time throughout the entire year was performed on-water in crew boats.

The training programme was prescribed in two-week blocks, but I did not always send a copy to the athletes. Instead, we had a standard weekly structure, which the athletes learned to repeat and to adjust to suit their needs. The target for rowing distance was typically in the range of 120–150km per week, assuming all sessions were completed.

The Wednesday ergometer session consisted of 30–40min at rate 20 with near maximal effort per stroke. The goal was to develop power per stroke while maintaining good technique. This has become a common session in schools, clubs and universities in England and gives useful information about training gains. Once the team performances began to plateau, we introduced long intervals at rate 26 work for about 7000m. Periodically, we replaced this session with a 5000m ergometer test (rate cap of 26 strokes per minute), the results from which showed

Table 1: Winter Training Programme/Standard Weekly Structure: Thames Rowing (January)

Day	Training	Rest	Stroke rate (strokes/min)	Intensity	Distance (km)
Monday	Rowing ergometer - 2 x 10 km	2 min	19	UT2	20
Tuesday	Rowing ergometer - 40 min steady state	n/a	19-21-19	UT2/UT1	10
	Rowing - training in coxed or coxless fours	n/a		UT2 / UT1	18
Wednesday	Rowing ergometer - 3 x 2500 m (rate capped)	3.5 min rest	24	UT1/TR/AT	12
Thursday	Rowing - technique paddle in pairs*	n/a	18-20	UT2	12
	Rowing - long paddle in eights	n/a	18-20	UT2 / UT1	18
Friday	Rest day				
Saturday	Rowing - Long steady state paddle in pairs	90 min + continuous	18-20	UT2	20
	Rowing - medium intervals in pairs: 3 x 6 min (rate capped)	2.5 min	24 to 28	UT1/AT	12
Sunday	Rowing - medium intervals in pairs: 2 x 8 min (rate capped)	20 min (row back to the start)	24		14
	Rowing - power strokes in eight: 20 x 10 strokes	Equal work to rest	20 + 30 + 20 +30 (repeat to end)	TR / POWER	14
Notes:	* a weight training session can replace this session			Weekly total distance	150
	Intensity classification				
	UT2 (55 to 70% max heart rate)				
	UT1 (70 to 80% max heart rate)				
	AT (80 to 85% max heart rate)				
	TR (85 to 95% max heart rate)				
	Power (>95% max heart rate)				

that approximately 70 per cent of the team achieved personal bests in December and March testing.

ATHLETE SELECTION AND TALENT DEVELOPMENT

Each September at Thames, we were presented with a selection of quality rowers who were mostly between 19 and 30 years of age. At the start of the 2014–15 season we had about 60 of them. We divided everyone into more manageable training groupings based on the results of an initial 5000m ergometer and an assessment of each rower's on-water technique. We also considered each person's competitive rowing background as well as their general availability for training. It took about six weeks to develop a basic rank order of squad ability. Thereafter, we formed the 'senior squad' of rowers. These were the 16 individuals who the coaches believed had the right material and potential to win at Henley during the 2014–15 season. The next task was to identify a careful rank order of senior squad rowers through further training and testing.

We emphasised selection based on performance in the coxless pair. We were able to buy six new and used Filippi pairs thanks to income generated through the hire of our function room for weddings and parties. We quickly reduced the senior squad of 16 athletes to 10 based on pair handling and other training data. We had planned to do a comprehensive pairs matrix, but instead we reduced the amount of testing to a series of race pieces performed over two days with selected swapping of rowers to find the selection order. There were still some aspects of selection where we had to rely on judgements rather than point to the more transparent test data we collected, especially on matters such as seat order. The final confirmation of our selection process was completed through early season regatta results and a training camp.

In the UK, the transition between winter training and spring race preparation is marked by the 4¼ mile Head of the River Race in London. The event is exclusively for men's eights and is contested by over 400 crews in a time trial format. The course is the Oxford-Cambridge Boat Race course but in the opposite direction so the finish line is about 100m beyond our boathouse in Putney. The majority of competitors are club oarsmen from the British Isles, but there are also a variety of elite rowers from the British team and several European countries. Our first eight finished 9th in 2015, ahead of what we believed would be our main rivals in the Thames Cup. Our second eight finished 17th, also beating almost all our main rivals. These early results gave us confidence about our strength and depth for the summer season and began to push us towards racing in the club eight events at Henley rather than the club four events.

In April, we refined our crew selections during a training camp in Seville in Spain. We often do this trip in the spring. It is a huge logistical effort as we have to drive our boats on two trailers along 1600 miles of French and Spanish roads. The athletes have to take time off work and make a significant financial contribution to cover their flights, accommodation and other costs. Overseas camps are now very popular among rowing clubs in Britain during the Easter period. Many clubs use the camps for an extensive period of testing and seat racing, but on this occasion we were able to use our camp almost exclusively for conditioning. The senior squad athletes spent the first part of the eight-day camp performing long, low intensity paddling in coxless pairs before moving into fours in preparation for a 2000m time trial on the final day. Ultimately, we decided to prioritise the senior squad athletes into a top eight (Thames Cup), then the next four best athletes went into the coxless four (Wyfold Cup) and finally the athletes ranked 13 through 16 went into a coxed four (Britannia Cup).

Table 2: Spring Training Camp: 8-Day Programme: Thames Rowing (April training camp)

Day	General	Detail	Stroke rate (strokes/min)	Intensity	Distance (km)
Saturday	Remove boats from trailer and rig				
	Rowing - steady state paddle	Tech & Drills	18-20	UT2	12
	Rowing - steady state paddle	UT2 & Pause Drills	18-20	UT2	12
Sunday	Rowing - steady state paddle	20km UT2	18-20	UT2	20
	Rowing - steady state paddle (UT2) and intensified section	18km with 2 x 3km r21	18-21	UT2 + UT1	18
	Rowing - short session with technique focus	8km Tech - backing down drill. Roll ups		UT2 + UT1	8
Monday	Rowing - Long steady state paddle	20km UT2	18-20	UT2	20
	Rowing - Long steady state paddle	20km UT2	18-20	UT2	20
Tuesday	Rowing - Long steady state paddle	20km UT2	18-20	UT2	20
	Rowing - medium intervals 3 x 2000m (rate capped)	3 x 2km r24-28	24-28	UT1 / AT	10
	Rowing - short session with technique focus	40 min of static drills	N/A		4
Wednesday	Rowing - steady state paddle	20km UT2	18-20	UT2	20
	Rowing - medium intervals 3 x 2000m (rate capped)	3 x 2km r24-28 (switch combos')	24-28	UT1 / AT	10
	Rowing - short session with technique focus	40 min of static drills	N/A		4
Thursday	Rowing - Long steady state paddle	20km UT2	18-20	UT2	20
	Rowing - medium intervals 3 x 2000m (rate capped)	3 x 2km r24-28 (switch combos')	24 to 26	UT1 /AT	12
	Rest				
Friday	Rowing - steady state paddle in set crews for tomorrow	20km UT2	18-20	UT2	20
	Rowing - technique session in set crews for tomorrow	12km Tech + Drills. Starts	18-20 / 40+	UT2	12
	Rowing - paddling to include 3 x 250m in set crews for tomorrow	Shortened race warm up. 3 x 250m	(free rate)		1
Saturday	Rowing: race warm-up and 2000m all out effort #1 (unconstrained)	Internal race v. either similar speed boat	(free rate)	FLAT OUT!	7
	Rowing: race warm-up and 2000m all out effort #2 (unconstrained)	or use a stagger	(free rate)	FLAT OUT!	7
Notes:	Recovery is key!			Total distance (8 days)	257

COACH AND ATHLETE RELATIONSHIP

I have mostly coached athletes aged between 19 and 30 years. My basic rule is to, 'treat them as adults unless they give cause to do otherwise'. Occasionally, this has been difficult because some of these athletes were older than me and several were friends. I also think that it is important to include experienced athletes in the decision-making process. The coach makes the final decision, but it is valuable to offer all athletes the opportunity to give their opinions about what selection processes and training sessions we should use.

Athletes make a choice about the amount of commitment they want to offer and can drop out at any point in the season. So, it is important that the experience of club rowing is enjoyable and challenging at the same time and a coach must not allow their personal enthusiasm and passion for success drive athletes away from the sport. One way to gauge the mood and desires of athletes is to chat informally with them and show interest in how they are handling the various demands placed upon them, on and off the water.

During the 2014–15 season, there were two moments when I had to show some very strong leadership. The first moment was in October when we had gathered as a team to discuss a nagging feeling I had that we were not training hard enough. I had noticed that some of the athletes were cutting corners and I highlighted the need to refocus our efforts to ensure we continued making progress. The second key moment was the day before Henley Royal Regatta. By this point, my top crew was the eight and they had just completed a warm-up row without purpose or obvious discipline. I was worried that the crew had become over-confident in their capabilities and were losing focus, so I made my thoughts loud and clear through the megaphone. The crew looked stunned after what they seemed to think was 'a decent row'. However, I wanted them to set their standard higher for the final days of preparation. The next water session was much improved and we moved forward as a team, but the episode served as an important reminder to us all about the need maintain a strong focus on our daily progress. As the crews developed and enhanced their trust among one another and with the coaching team, we gained further successes in early season racing which helped build self-belief and excitement.

TECHNICAL APPROACH

There are three fundamental elements that I believe are essential in successful rowing: stroke length, power and rate. In theory, the higher the stroke rate, the faster the boat but there is an obvious trade-off between the two at a certain point. Power can be improved through gym work as well as a solid base of on-water endurance and is the main reason why we emphasised lots of distance in boats. Stroke length is probably the most controllable of the three fundamental elements. Importantly, it is effective stroke length that matters to boat movement – not simply moving the oar through a 90-degree arc. I spend many hours emphasising and developing effective strong length.

The rowing stroke is really quite simple but we can easily make it complicated. I think the legendary Australian coach Steve Fairbairn got it right over a hundred years ago when he said '[rowing] is as simple as bending down and picking up a piece of paper'. The problem is that many rowers with an oar in their hand want to start working the handle rather than hanging from it and working the foot stretcher. Of course, for every 'technician' in the sport there is an equally successful 'hammer'. However, the best rowing crews perform the fundamental things well – they row long strokes, they use their large muscles in a logical sequence and they do very little to interrupt the boat run. Rowing 'styles' can vary and international teams often have their own distinguishable style, but successful international rowers make long effective strokes, have great power and above all else, they make rowing look easy.

My thoughts about technique development have two guiding principles. The first is that athletes stop listening after about a minute or two of a coach speaking, so explanations must be brief and concise. The second is that 'feel' cannot be taught – rowers either have it or they don't. I believe in the need to drill, drill and drill again in order to ingrain technique. The boat feel, as with physiology, improves by completing many miles of rowing. But given that most programmes are under an element of time pressure, sitting around and describing the perfect stroke is less preferable to having rowers practice their stroke technique. I make regular use of video analysis and this is one activity that most rowers enjoy and are consequently better placed to see what I see and have asked them to focus on. We typically used video sessions on most weekends of the season, but even more so on training camp and in the weeks immediately before a major event.

Helpful hints for technique development

- Introduce several exercises at the start of the season to develop the technique 'framework' for the stroke. Repeat these daily in the warm-up.
- Video regularly but don't let rowers obsess over the results.
- Be patient. Each rower has their own technical 'thumbprint' and it can take time to change.
- Practice makes permanent. Every poorly executed stroke that they row will ingrain faults.
- Limit early season water sessions to a focus on technique development. Use land-based training such as ergometers, weights and cross-training to develop fitness.

I believe that the foundation of good rowing technique is built by establishing a strong ability to maintain the sequence of hands–body–slide. If it is not well developed in training, the pressure of intense racing will soon reveal the failure and there is likely to be a subsequent loss of quality in the overall rowing stroke. I learned the importance of this point from the great coaches that I had as a rower. I think that the best way to develop a strong sequence of movements in rowing is to have athletes perform a variety of pause drills at different segments, and our Thames athletes spent many hours doing these. I found these especially useful at the end of long, steady state on-water sessions when athletes are most at risk of losing their sequencing.

Overall, our technical approach was essentially quite basic and encouraged everyone to row long off the finish, place the oar at the extent of the reach, build pressure through the pin and sit tall throughout the drive to avoid a loss of body weight control and hold an optimum body position to apply power. Once our rowers could demonstrate this in coxless pairs, we found our success in the fours and eights.

SUPPORT SERVICES AND TECHNOLOGY

I'm sure physiotherapists, psychologists, physiologists and boatmen are on the wish list of every rowing coach, but none of these was formally available to us at Thames. We were fortunate to have a small army of generous volunteers who assisted with boat maintenance and rigging and we had a small amount of money to pay for an occasional sports massage therapist to help. I expect that few clubs have much in the way of resource directed to support services, despite their potential benefits. As a consequence, I have tried to develop my own education to incorporate a wider knowledge of sport science and other support.

Many high-performance clubs still expect the head coach to take care of everything. However, it is increasingly important that the coach is able to focus his or her time on key aspects of performance, such as one-to-one technique coaching, while allowing specialists to assist with other vital areas. Good coaches should certainly have a working knowledge of these other areas, but I think it is now more important than ever that coaches are able to consult with sport scientists, physiotherapists and strength and conditioning experts. A cost effective way to do this is to read relevant literature and attend conferences and seminars. In particular, I am a great fan of the writings of the legendary Steve Fairbairn who was head coach of Thames and started the Head of the River Race in 1926 to provide an incentive for rowers to increase their training volumes. While Fairbairn probably wrote more about preparation for rowing competitions than any other coach in history, he died long before the era of telemetry and hypoxic tents. There were no definitive answers about what I should prioritise in terms of support services, technology and outside experts in order to enhance our crew performances. All I can offer is a brief description of my opinions and experiences of some of the more popular approaches currently in use.

I think that club rowers probably do not do enough training volume to warrant the use of blood lactate profiling to establish training zones. I also had too many rowers to do this level of detailed work, which would have been expensive and time consuming. I also think that most coaches are reasonably proficient in sport psychology, rigging and other areas where national teams may employ dedicated specialists. I think it is actually very hard to achieve much as a coach without a diverse skill set. One area where coaches can be particularly sensible is in terms of developing training programmes, which minimise injury risk. This reduces the need for physiotherapy and I think some sports massage and flexibility training does help reduce injury. So, even in our situation where support service provision was minimal, we were able to reduce our need for professional support by taking more care over our training approach and making good use of our limited discretionary funds.

During the 2014–15 competition season, we engaged the services of a strength and conditioning coach who also doubled as a masseuse. She helped improve our athletes' posture and enhanced their flexibility and range of motion. I found her services really valuable and she understood the need to work closely with the goals of the coaching team and to identify the needs of individual athletes such as improving shoulder stability or hip movement.

Thames had also invested in a biomechanical telemetry system in 2010 to monitor oar force and boat movement. We used this regularly during the 2013–14 season, but much less so during the 2014–15 season, in part because I was much happier with our on-water performance in 2015 and also because we were making good use of video analysis. I do think biomechanical analysis has its place, but it is probably best to use when rowing on calm water. The Tideway stretch of the Thames where we train is usually turbulent and unstable so far from ideal conditions for biomechanical telemetry assessments. We still found uses for this equipment and it does give very interesting data and observations, but it is only a small piece of a very large and often complex puzzle.

The most important support that I had was a team of volunteer coaches who helped manage the progress of all our athletes, especially those further down the selection rank order. I had regular updates from each coach about how their group was developing and the coaching team also met frequently to have broader conversations about the effectiveness of the overall programme. These meetings were also used to help plan and review decisions about athlete selection. I especially valued these conversations because they offered an important rehearsal opportunity to articulate why specific seat orders or crew line-ups were chosen before having to do so face-to-face with disappointed athletes.

Dave O'Neill Head Coach, University of Texas, Austin, USA

Dave O'Neill was a founding member of the Boston College men's club rowing program during his freshman year at the school. He won medals at the US Rowing Nationals, the US Olympic Festival, the CRASH-B Sprints and the Canadian Henley. O'Neill earned a Bachelor's in History in 1991. He then led the college's women's rowing program for seven years before taking over as head coach of women's rowing at the University of California at Berkeley. In 16 seasons at Berkeley he won two NCAA team titles and led the Golden Bears to 12 NCAA top-four finishes.

His influence has been felt at the US national and international levels as well. O'Neill is currently in his second stint as the lead coach for the US Women's under-23 national team after serving in the same capacity in 2006–07, winning gold in the women's eight at the 2006 World Rowing Under-23 Championships and gold in the women's quadruple sculls the following year. He graduated to the senior team in 2009–10 and coached the US women's team to four silver medals at the 2009 World Championships.

He was appointed Head Coach at the University of Texas in 2014.

Like many rowers in the United States, I became hooked on the sport during my first year of university studies at Boston College. Although the program was a small, upstart club team, the experience changed my life and I am truly grateful that nearly 30 years later I have a career in the sport.

I have always been interested in outdoor education and the skills that we learn by working as a team in pursuit of a common goal. Much of my coaching has been built around developing the mindset, culture and environment that produces the best results for individuals and teams. I think this holistic approach is more suited for coaching in a university and team setting, where education and personal development are essential. The sport science aspect of sport is used to support this process, but it's not an overriding theme of our program.

The growth in popularity of women's rowing in the USA has been incredible over the last 20 years, and as a consequence has provided many opportunities for both rowers and coaches. The level of competition at the NCAA Championships has increased significantly as the crews have gone faster and faster. The top eights at the Division I level are comparable to under-23 national team eights in terms of talent and sheer speed.

Most NCAA women's rowing teams at the Division I level have between 50 and 75 women on their roster during the spring racing season. Team members can range from novice walk-ons (i.e. athletes who joined the team with no rowing experience) to Olympic medalists. Bringing all these athletes together into one team is one of the biggest challenges facing a college coach in the States.

The team aspect is an integral part of the NCAA Championship Regatta that completes the rowing season each May. The winner of the championship is determined by a points system based on three events, I Eight, II Eight, and Four. So, the squad that ultimately competes at the NCAA regatta is 20 rowers and three coxswains. I personally love it that the NCAA champion is the team, as I feel this adds a special dynamic to our sport.

TRAINING ENVIRONMENT

In many ways our program at the University of Texas at Austin has everything a coach could *want*. We certainly have everything a coach might *need*. The program is very well supported in terms of funding for staff, athletic scholarships, equipment, travel, and support for the student-athletes to succeed academically. Nearly everything the team members need for performance is provided, including nutrition, gear, laundry service and sports medicine. In fact, our program may very easily be better supported than many national teams.

The weather in Austin allows for year-round training on the water. I have not had to program around a 'winter season' for a number of years. While there are NCAA restrictions on practice days and hours of training per week, our team does row on the water throughout the year. However, about half of our workouts during the winter are land based.

Ergometer Room *Credit: Courtesy of University of Texas Athletics Department*

Our lake is just three miles from campus and nearly perfect for training. Motorboats are not allowed to create a wake on the lake, and this is welcome news to all rowers. There is a straight 2000m stretch with one bridge, and it is possible to row 8000m without stopping. However, I rarely go more than ten or twelve minutes without a break. This is important to help the athletes stay focused.

Austin is a vibrant and active city where it is easy to have an athletic, outdoor lifestyle. There is a great running trail that surrounds the lake and our team make use of it on a regular basis. The biggest negative we encounter in training is the number of stand-up paddleboards (SUPs), kayaks and canoes, which seem to take over the water on a sunny Saturday or Sunday afternoon.

The University of Texas athletic department, which many believe to be the most powerful in the country, is fully committed to a high-level rowing program. This support places an added responsibility on our team and has been a positive influence for us. Our team recognizes we are part of a big athletic department that has historically been among the best in the country and rich with tradition. 'Texas Pride' is palpable and empowering.

Coaches at collegiate programs like Texas typically see themselves not just as coaches but also leaders and educators. I certainly do. The purpose of our team is for the overall education of the student-athletes. The lessons learned through the pursuit of athletic excellence are incredibly valuable, and what the student-athletes learn through rowing is just as valuable as what they learn in the classroom.

Lake view *Credit: Courtesy of University of Texas Athletics Department*

The mantra that guides me through each day is 'the main thing is to keep the main thing the main thing'. Since the *main thing* is success at the NCAA Championships, continuous progress towards that goal is the priority every day. This singular pursuit guides my thinking and decisions on a daily basis and helps eliminate distractions. Never jeopardize the ultimate goal for short-term success. For example, I never train the team or put together a priority crew for the fall head races. I find this to be a distraction from the ultimate goal of going fast at the NCAA championship in May.

Establishing a strong team culture is essential to the team's success, and the role of the head coach is critical. I am keenly aware of the mood of the team, especially during the high stress periods of crew selection and racing. Every time our team is together, whether it is on the water, on the erg or in the weight room, is an opportunity to cultivate a culture of hard work and winning attitudes. The culture of the team is developed from the outset and remains a constant theme throughout the year. This cannot be stressed enough.

The team's culture is developed and strengthened at every workout but particularly through times of struggle. Overcoming adversity and challenges happens on a regular basis. Invariably, this culture is called upon later in the year, particularly at the season-ending championship where some unforeseen circumstance could derail us from our goals. A strong team culture prepares us to overcome any obstacle that might stand in our way.

TRAINING AND CONDITIONING

Our team starts training together in late August when classes begin. Some of the athletes will have trained at a high level over the summer, and others will have done very little. Since our team is in training throughout the academic year, the summers are a good time for the student-athletes to go away for summer school, have internships and make use of time without training demands.

Because the group will be varied in terms of levels of fitness and the championship is nine months away, the approach for the first three to four weeks is rather slow. Training in the fall is entirely geared towards developing an aerobic base.

During the fall semester, approximately 74 per cent of the workouts on the water are focused on skill development with rates around 18 to 24 strokes per minute. New concepts and individual skill instruction are typically taught in the eights, and supplemented with small boat training to give the athletes a chance to continue to work on their skills on their own.

The top athletes on the team spend about half of their workouts in singles, pairs and doubles during the early preparation phase of the year. While the eights are clearly the priority crews during the racing season, the level of competency in the small boats, especially the pairs, is quite high, and many of the top NCAA programs, including ours, now use singles and pairs as an important part of their training and selection throughout the year.

The volume of our training increases during the fall as the team develops strength and fitness. Two to three workouts per week are higher intensity (anaerobic threshold) with one of those always being on the ergometer. I rarely use total kilometers for the

Working on skills *Credit: Courtesy of University of Texas Athletics Department*

weeks as a gauge for training loads since we do so much training off the water. Rather, I track the number of hard efforts we do over a three-week cycle and monitor the progress of the top 20 athletes on the team. Understanding that any individual can have a bad day is important, but if the majority of the group is failing, I know that something is wrong with the training.

My thinking on weightlifting has developed over the years. The approach that I have taken in the last few years is to use the weight room workouts to focus on 'becoming a stronger athlete' and injury prevention. The goal is to get the athletes stronger, so they can handle a greater training load in our specific sport. Developing peak power in the weight room is not a focus.

I understand the value of Olympic lifting, especially cleans. However, I have not seen a correlation between athletes at our level being good at this lift and being strong on the water. The movement is so specialized and technical that it is an Olympic sport in itself. My feeling is the student-athletes should focus on being good at one Olympic sport, rowing, while they are at our university.

A fair amount of cross-training is integrated into our training, especially running. The team runs two to three times a week and will cover at most 20km total for the week. While this is not a lot of a running, it can be a fair amount for rowers, especially given the amount of other training that we are doing. One of the main reasons for the

Table 1: Sample Training Week/Preparation Phase: Preparation phase (February)

Day		Training	Rest	Stroke rate (strokes/min)	Intensity*	Distance (km)
Monday	AM	Rowing: Intervals 4 x 3 km	5 to 7 min	24 increasing to 32	4	18
	PM	Rest				
Tuesday	AM	Rowing: Technique development session	n/a	18 to 22	3	20
	PM1	Cross training: 30 to 60 min easy run (or cycle)				
	PM2	Weight training (metabolic circuit)				
Wednesday	AM	Rowing: Intervals 4 x 2 km	6 to 8 min	28 to 32	4	16
	PM	Cycling: 2 x 25 min (steady state)	5 min			
Thursday	AM	Rowing: Intervals 4 x 12 min with focus on power per stroke	5 min	20 to 24	3	18
	PM1	Cross training: 30 to 60 min easy run (or cycle)				
	PM2	Weight training (metabolic circuit)				
Friday	AM	Rowing: Technique development session	n/a	18 to 22	2	12
	PM	Rowing ergometer: 30 min	n/a	22 - 24 - 26 (by 10 min section)	3	10
Saturday	AM1	Rowing: Intervals 2 x 5 km pairs fours, eights)	row back (15 to 20 min)	28 to 34	4	20
	AM2	Running: 8 km followed by abdominal/core circuit session				
	PM	Rest				
Sunday		Rest				
					Total	114

*Intensity is subjectively estimated based on the expected challenge/effort of the session (where 1 is very light, 2 is light, 3 is somewhat hard, 4 is hard and 5 is very hard)

running is to put in extra minutes of aerobic conditioning without putting additional stress on the body where rowing injuries typically occur (e.g. lower back and ribs).

Running is also beneficial to help our rowers maintain an optimal body weight for peak performance. Obviously, body weight can be a sensitive topic among collegiate athletes and I have found running to be the most effective and least stressful way of achieving this goal since running requires the athletes to move their weight efficiently. Of course, it is important to build the running gradually and not overdo the mileage. Foot, knee and hip injuries can occur if too much running is done too soon.

Of course, the ergometer is an important part of our training, and the team continues to do erg workouts through the racing season. This has been particularly helpful in reminding the athletes what it means to 'pull hard' and in holding them

Table 2: Sample Training Week/Competition Phase: Competition phase (May)

Day		Training	Rest	Stroke rate (strokes/min)	Intensity	Distance (km)
Monday	AM	Rowing: 1' on/1' easy x 7 (3 sets)	8 min	34 to 44	5	16
	PM	Rest				
Tuesday	AM	Rowing: Technique development session	n/a	18 to 22	3	18
	PM1	Cross training: 30 to 60 min easy run (or cycle)			2	
	PM2	Weight training (aerobic circuit training)				
Wednesday	AM	Rowing: Intervals 4 x 1500m (selection)	6 to 8 min	32 to 36	4	15
	PM	Cycling: 30 min easy pedal				
Thursday	AM	Rowing: Intervals 3 x 12 min with focus on power per stroke	6 min	20 to 24	3	15
	PM1	Cross training: 30 to 60 min easy run (or cycle)			2	
	PM2	Weight training (aerobic circuit training)				
Friday	AM	Rowing: 4 x 250m race starts (race simulation)	8 min	36 to 44	3	12
	PM	Rowing: 12 km	n/a	22	2	12
Saturday	AM	8k, race course x 2	n/a	22	1	8
	PM	4k, race course x 1	n/a	22	1	4
Sunday		Race (Race line-ups or selection pieces)				10
					Total	110

accountable. It also builds trust and confidence among teammates during this critical time.

Most of my coaching career has been spent in parts of the USA where we can row year-round. This is certainly a good situation, but too much time on the water can be tough to manage since rowing is such a monotonous sport. Too much rowing can become problematic in terms of motivation and remaining injury free. Keeping the athletes enthused and fresh is important, so there are plenty of days where we train on land even though on-the-water rowing is an option.

ATHLETE SELECTION AND TALENT DEVELOPMENT

A critical component of coaching at the NCAA Division I level is recruiting. Identifying talented, prospective athletes and bringing them to your program has become increasingly important. Recruiting is a never-ending process because bringing the right athletes on to our team is the lifeblood of our program.

Aside from coaching the current rowers on the team, recruiting easily consumes the most amount of time for our staff. This process has been criticized, but it is a necessity for coaches at our level. In fact, rowing programs at all levels from junior clubs to elite national teams do some form of talent identification and recruiting. However, the recruiting we do is much more visible and obvious, and I believe this is from where much of the criticism stems.

Much of our recruiting success has come from developing a good reputation. This might be called 'building a brand' in the business world. Prospective rowers and coaches recognize that being on our team is a worthwhile experience, and being proactive in letting others know about the opportunities on our team is important.

Crew selection is more often associated with actual coaching than recruiting, and it is also a critical piece of what we do. Coaching is all about making decisions, and I have said for years that, 'if I make good decisions, I'm a good coach'. Some of the most important decisions we make as coaches are during selection of crews.

The selection process on our team is ongoing throughout the season, and changes within the crews can happen at any time. The power and flexibility rests in the hands of the coach, and this is a big difference from many national teams where committees and procedures might dictate crew selection. Being clear and totally transparent about the process and how decisions are being made is of utmost importance. Results from all erg workouts and timed pieces on the water are always shared with the team, and athletes are free to keep track of that information on their own.

The stress for both athletes and coaches surrounding crew selection is always high. When athletes feel the process is secretive or unfair, the team can be ripped apart, and performance ultimately suffers for those who were selected.

Something I make clear to the team each year during the height of the selection process is that I do have opinions on who should comprise the priority boats. Once this is acknowledged, I then make it clear that I also have an open mind, and this openness is really what is most important. The athletes seem to appreciate that honesty.

I take many factors into consideration when selecting athletes for crews. Objective data (erg tests, time trials, races against time standards, etc.) is collected which is then used to make a subjective decision. Athletes are reminded to 'paint a complete picture of their all-round athletic abilities' and that selection is not done on one particular day or week.

Of course, results closest to the NCAA championship are given the most weight, However, it is possible for even the best rowers to have a bad day, and I am keenly aware that one bad day should not discredit weeks and months of good work and success. Keeping this perspective has prevented me from making some very rash decisions over the years. For example, if our one of our most proven athletes loses a seat-race to someone that I believe is slower then I will most likely do the switch again later in the week, and maybe even a third time to confirm. Consistency is valued over a singular outstanding performance that might be hard to repeat.

In fact, I find that seat racing by itself is not a good method of selection. Being good at seat racing can be a skill at which some rowers are better than others, and this does not always produce the fastest crew. It is far more important to select the best crew, not simply the best athletes or those who are skilled at seat racing.

While the decisions of who is in and who is out of a crew are often subjective, favoritism can never play any part in the process. Seniority, scholarships, and performances from past years are not considered when selecting the crews. Coaches and athletes will typically agree that the person who will make the boat the fastest on race day is all that matters.

Steps need to be taken to assure the athletes that performance is the only criteria in how decisions are made. I have found that transparency throughout the entire year is helpful in minimizing confusion. Again, objective data is always used to come to the subjective conclusion, and it is important to always share this information with the entire team. Whenever we do timed pieces on the water, those results are written on a whiteboard after the workout, and typically a few team members take a photo for their own records. This is perfectly acceptable. I have found that the more I share this basic information, the less confusion and uncertainty the athletes have surrounding selection.

COACH AND ATHLETE RELATIONSHIP

More than anyone, the head coach sets the tone and atmosphere of the team and the boathouse, and this is a responsibility I do not take lightly. Over the course of their college careers, the student-athletes will spend more time with the rowing team than anyone else, so the head coach will have the greatest impact on their collegiate experience.

It is important to be honest at all times. As a coach, there are plenty of times throughout the year when bad news needs to be delivered to the team or individuals. During these conversations, I am always straightforward and direct without being curt or rude, making it clear that those receiving the bad news feel respected and valued is paramount. This is particularly true during final selection for the squad that will row at the NCAAs. Tough decisions need to be made and hard conversations need to be had. The athletes are typically exhausted, both physically and mentally, so I am keenly aware how this news is conveyed to the individual and to the team.

There are always issues and situations that arise, and problems are always dealt with immediately. I never shy away from having the difficult conversations, and I never let problems fester. This is particularly true when it comes to team dynamics. For example, conflicts between teammates are always addressed immediately and resolved quickly, even if this means sacrificing the workout for the day. There have been days where the team took a bigger step forward by resolving an issue within the team than we might have achieved on the water. By doing this, a strong message is sent that team culture is a priority, and the workouts that follow are typically very productive.

I do not get overly involved in the lives of the team members away from rowing. By no means should this be construed as me not caring about the women as people, quite the contrary. I care deeply for the general health and well-being of the student-athletes. I have simply learned that keeping some distance allows the coach-athlete relationship to remain focused on rowing and not be clouded in the drama of everyday life. Of course, situations arise where I need to be involved, and I do so without hesitation when I must.

I want to avoid situations where athletes are vying for my attention. The appearance of favoritism can ruin the team culture. Therefore, I choose to remain as professional as possible in our interactions. While it is important to keep the mood light and jovial at times, a clear line needs to be established between coach and athlete.

Rowing makes us better people. A big part of my coaching philosophy is coaching the life lessons that sport has to teach us. The pursuit of excellence in a team environment is what our team is all about. Rowing forces self-improvement. Leadership, resilience, accountability, and dealing with failure and stress are all part of the process.

My goal is to empower the athletes to make decisions for themselves and to act on their own. I am fortunate to coach some very bright women, and they usually know more about the sport and their path to success than they might think. It is my job to lead them to answer their own questions and realize that they can solve their own problems. While it can be difficult in a collegiate setting, I take steps to minimize my involvement. The experience should not about me; it is about them. *I know I'm doing my job well when I don't have to do anything.*

TECHNICAL APPROACH

The technical approach I take is typically very simple and easy to understand. I have often said that I can go through an entire workout and say only three words: harder, longer, and relax. The combination of these three simple concepts is key to moving the boat and flowing with the crew.

First and foremost, the technique I coach is geared towards a long, powerful drive. Being 'drive oriented' is taught immediately. A long connection to the water and the ability to put maximum pressure on the blade face is paramount. Therefore, most strokes we take are with a fair amount of pressure. While the stroke rating and intensity are low, it is important to understand connection, so almost all of our rowing is done at a firm pressure.

I spend a fair amount of time on proper body positioning during the stroke. A particular emphasis is placed on this early in the training cycles. General awareness of where you are sitting on the seat and your side to side movement goes a long way in putting the rower in the strongest and most comfortable position. Being comfortable on the seat with a strong core throughout the rowing stroke is a skill that needs to be learned and re-learned throughout the year.

The concept of being relaxed during the drive is taught from the outset. I find this important for three reasons. First, the efficient use of the muscles in our legs and back requires that the upper body be relaxed. Understanding how to move the boat with legs and body ('hanging on it') becomes easier when the rowers can relax their shoulders and arms. Being able to engage one set of muscles while relaxing another is key to applying power efficiently. Turning one group 'off' is just as important as being able to turn another 'on'.

Second, being relaxed in the drive phase creates a better sense of length in the water. Staying relaxed and delaying the use of the arms while maintaining pressure on the blade puts emphasis on the use of the legs and body. I often say 'stay long across

Developing strong body position at the catch. *Credit: Courtesy of University of Texas Athletics Department*

the knees'. By this I mean feel a long, solid connection to the water as the handle comes past the knees during the drive. This is most easily felt when the rowers are relaxed.

Finally, being relaxed is critical in feeling the flow and rhythm in the crew. Rowing efficiently is more than simple timing. Feel and flow takes the rhythm to a higher level, and the ability to relax, even during the drive, makes it much easier to maximize the efforts of the collective unit.

The main gathering point for the crews is typically at the back end of the stroke, i.e. the release. 'Rhythm at the finish' is a regular call. It is important for the crew to stay connected to the water while the arms are drawing into the body. Being relaxed and releasing the blade cleanly will add to the rhythm and stability of the boat. A smooth transition to the recovery phase is important as the hands move away from the body at the same speed they came in on the drive. The three drills that I use to emphasize proper connection and flow around the finish are pausing at the release, rowing with 'feet out' and rowing with 'eyes closed'.

The crews I coach tend to row with less forward body angle than most. This allows for added compression with the seat. Being in a strong position with the body allows for maximum length and power with the legs, and this also decreases the risk of back injuries. While the finish of the stroke is where we establish the rhythm, we focus on the front end (catch and leg drive) for the speed – 'boat speed at the catch' is another regular call. A lot of time is spent on proper placement of the blade and the initial connection to the water. The legs initiate the drive, and it is important to be sure the leg-drive is connected to the body.

The legs and body working together and the connection through mid-drive is a point of emphasis. I encourage the rowers 'to bend it through mid-drive'. This helps encourage length through the drive and keeps the focus on being connected to the water. I often say, 'use the muscles between armpits and knees to move the boat'. That everything should be relaxed during the drive is too often overlooked in my opinion.

Obviously, the recovery is an important part of the stroke. The rhythm and flow is essential. As stated earlier, the arms should float away from the body at the same speed they moved on the drive. There should be no jarring motions, especially at this point when the system (combined mass of boat and rowers) has the most momentum. Allowing the chest to flow forward once the hands are extended will give plenty of reach with the upper body. Minimizing the upper body movement is important. A gentle break of the knees is encouraged, and the slide generally happens at one constant speed into the catch. I try not to overcomplicate the speed of the slide, but rather encourage relaxation and flow with the rest of the crew.

I rarely find myself telling athletes to 'slow down into the catch'. When individuals have the proper fitness, feeling and comfort level, they rarely 'rush' into the catch, so it is good to stay focused on getting them to those levels. More often than slowing rowers down into the catch, I tend to encourage them to move a little quicker on the slide. When the movement up the slide is done too slowly, feeling and flow are sacrificed, and the catch is typically sacrificed as well. The slide should be an easy, natural movement where nothing is forced.

During the early learning stages of the year, I spend a lot of time coaching proper body-position into the catch. It is critical for the rowers to be in a strong, yet comfortable, position from half-slide to full compression. This is important to allow for maximum run of the boat, and the rowers should be well aware of their weight on the seat rather than the footboards. I coach the athletes to 'bring the stomach forward' and 'sit tall into the catch' rather than saying 'don't lunge into the catch'. The rationale for this is for them to focus on what to do rather than what not to do.

A high priority is placed on core strength and being well supported in the lower back. It is really important for the rowers to be both strong in the core yet relaxed in the upper body at the catch position. Again, 'sitting tall into the catch' is always a focus. I have experimented with having the athletes relax their posture, sit lower in the boat, and focus on a lower center of gravity. However, this led to an increase in injuries, so the costs outweighed any potential benefits.

While there is always a technical focus at every workout on the water, I generally keep the drills pretty simple. The most common drills I use are the pair add-in (i.e. 'add a pair'), rowing with eyes closed, rowing with legs only or legs and body only, and the assortment of pause drills. I have found that keeping the drills simple and consistent allows the rowers to see improvement, and, more importantly, relate the drills to continuous rowing.

SUPPORT SERVICES

One of the advantages of coaching at a large Division I program and at a school like the University of Texas is the resources and staffing available to our team. Sports medicine, logistical support, boatman/rigger, strength coaches and nutritionists are all assigned to our team. These individuals are easily accessible and deeply invested in our success.

Having a good strength coach who knows and respects our sport can have a tremendous impact on the team's performance. My experience with strength coaches has varied over the years. Some coaches have little to no experience with rowing, and they might be set in their ways of doing things. The lifting program might have little or no variance from another sport, and this can certainly be a cause for great frustration.

I have also had the opportunity to work with strength coaches who develop programs with the input of the rowing coaches where there is a free exchange of ideas, experience, and opinions. Obviously, this is a much better situation, and I am fortunate that this is the mindset at Texas. Our team lifts two times a week, and this has proven to be time well spent. The lifting program is designed by our strength coach, but she regularly checks with me on the intensity of the workouts and actual exercises she has the team doing. Most importantly, she is always aware of how the lifting is adding value to what the team is doing on the water, and this is greatly appreciated.

Our program is also fortunate to have the services of a full-time boatman. As we all know, rowing is a very equipment intensive sport, so having one person dedicated to keeping the shells, oars, launches (i.e. coach boats) and electronics in working order makes the daily routine much easier. When we host races, our boatman is called on to put in the racecourse, docks and too many other duties to list. Finally, driving the shell trailer is an important part of the job, especially during the racing season since Austin is often at least 1000 miles (1600km) from many of the courses where we race. Having a dependable, good-natured, and committed boatman as part of the support team makes a big difference in the day-to-day operations of the program.

Developing a good rapport and trust among the doctors, athletics trainers, and physical therapists is also extremely important to the success of the program. I have learned to trust the opinion of the sports medicine staff, and they always have the final say as to whether an athlete can train and/or compete with an existing injury.

We have a certified athletic trainer (ATC) dedicated to our team, and the value of this talented individual cannot be overstated. Injuries are inevitable, especially with the amount of training we do. Having a good relationship with the athletic trainer can make or break the year, and it is important to trust the opinions of the medical staff. Everyone wants to do a good job and do what is best for the athletes, and good communication among all always works best. When everyone has the most and best information, the smartest decisions can be made, so open communication is critical.

It is important that everyone involved be aware of the short-term and long-term goals. Over the years, I have found it best not to sacrifice long-term goals in order to achieve short-term success. This is particularly true when dealing with injuries. I am much more cautious with injuries than I was earlier in my career.

FINAL THOUGHTS

Since women's rowing became an NCAA sport in 1997, the standard of rowing has been raised significantly and the speeds have gotten faster and faster. The effects have been felt at all levels of women's rowing. Of course, the most noticeable change has been at collegiate level, but there has also been a positive impact at both the junior and elite levels in the United States and beyond.

Opportunities for female rowers have increased through athletic scholarships, and there has also been a rise in the number of junior women rowing in the United States as better and better athletes are being attracted to the sport. Twenty years ago most collegiate programs relied on walk-ons to fill their rosters. While those women continue to play an important role on most teams, the talent base for most programs are team members who rowed as juniors.

The juniors are pulling faster and faster erg times, and the skill level keeps getting better. Years ago there may have been one or two junior women pulling under seven minutes for a 2000m erg. We now see scores under 6:50 from juniors. This is certainly impressive and not uncommon. Three junior women from the United States went sub-6:50 at the 2016 CRASH-B Sprints.

The experience and knowledge of the junior coaches has increased as well. Both long-tenured coaches and younger coaches just starting their careers have shown tremendous skill and talent in preparing their athletes for success in our sport. Many women transition from their junior programs into the priority boats of top collegiate crews, and credit must be given to their junior coaches. These women are well prepared as they are skilled, strong, and tough.

The effect of the NCAA has impacted the elite level, as well. The USA women have become a powerhouse at the World Championships and the Olympics. Since the level at collegiate level has been raised, the talent pool for the senior team has increased, and these women are better prepared to take the big step up in training and expectations that are now required on the senior team. The combination of strong, talented women and terrific coaching at the elite level has produced an impressive series of international regatta results for the USA women's teams.

Most of the top Division 1 programs have rowers from around the world, and Texas is no exception. I believe this has been beneficial for all parties involved. The collegiate teams are better, and the rowers typically have a terrific experience. Since the level of racing is so high, the women return to their national teams well prepared for the under-23 World Championships and beyond.

The growth of collegiate women's rowing in the United States over the last 20 years has been remarkable, and I believe the level of racing will continue to get faster and faster. The coaches are becoming more professional, knowledgeable, and experienced. The athletes are simply stronger and faster, and there are more of them. More teams vying for the top spots at NCAAs is also raising the bar, and athletic directors are taking a greater interest in seeing their rowing teams succeed. All of these factors will push us to go faster and faster, and I, for one, welcome that challenge. 'Hook 'em Horns!', as we say in Austin.

Mark Fangen-Hall Senior Coach, Rowing Australia

Mark Fangen-Hall has over 25 years of experience as an athlete and coach at some of the most illustrious boat clubs in world rowing. He was assistant coach to Robin Williams at Cambridge University, Head Coach of Kingston Grammar School, Surrey, and Head Coach of Queen's University Belfast (all in the UK). He moved to Australia in 2011 to become Head Coach of Mercantile Rowing Club in Melbourne, and in 2014 became a senior coach with the Australia national team, also based in Australia's second city. His crews have won gold and silver medals at various World Championships.

I was a club oarsman at best. With some of the other contributors to this book coming from the highest of levels, I am humbled by my inclusion and it goes to show that there are many ways to progress in our sport. However, as a coach there are certain things that you *must* do – do the required learning, gain experience and most importantly, formulate your own style and your own ideas. What follows are some of mine; I hope you find them interesting.

My love of rowing was born out of my father's involvement in rowing during my childhood. My understanding of programming was directly taken from two hugely successful coaches, Jürgen Grobler and Robin Williams. Lucky seems a grossly inadequate way to describe it. However, I believe I am now at a stage where I have a solid understanding of the sport and that has led to a desire to learn even more.

When I was starting out in coaching I looked up to the well-known coaches and wondered what they did to make their crews so good. As I progress I come back to the age-old saying – 'keep it simple'. At its simplest our work should provide an ability to deliver this simple sequence: 'Connect, lever, release and run'. Then repeat it – a lot.

I suspect my athletes think I am never satisfied and to a certain extent I do not mind that. Without being dismissive of present or recent performances, I want them to know that our goal is to develop better performances. There is currently a great deal of emphasis in Australia on the use of 'world best times'. What will the next Olympics bring and what will it take to win there and beyond? What is certain is that those who put a ceiling on performance are soon left behind. I am constantly impressed at what people, let alone athletes, are actually capable of. Someone betters the performance we thought untouchable and so we need to adjust all parameters and benchmarks to keep up. Personally, I am not in the game of 'keeping up' so I want to let go of the notion of accepting limitations. Instead, I think it is essential to consider the road to improvement as continuous and without end. This may sound futile, but the athlete and coach who accept this understanding are then best placed to appreciate the journey. The results along the way are important steps to improvement but they should not become the only focus of the journey. I believe this is a basic principle of development.

Within Mercantile and Rowing Australia the words 'trust' and 'transparency' are some of the cultural foundations that underpin the separate programmes. This is key at all levels. It seems simple and obvious but can be overlooked when club politics interfere. At Mercantile, we have a code of conduct that all athletes and coaches must sign when they join. We revisit it regularly and if we, the leadership, do not uphold it then we expect the members to let us know – and they do.

One of the key phrases of Rowing Australia is 'fair but not equal'. The first time that I heard that it really hit home. Unless you have limitless resources you cannot be equal to all. The best boats invariably go to the best athletes, especially when they have earned that right. High performance club athletes earn the right to have better attention, support and equipment. However, athletes must realise that often their best performances come from within and do not rely on the latest technologies, feeling great or favourable conditions. It frustrates me that some athletes think they cannot row well unless they have the latest gadgets. I think some technologies can hamper learning of the art of rowing and quite often I find personal bests in training are set directly after the biggest and heaviest blocks of training. Fairness though is crucial to ensure athletes stay at the club. If rowers try hard and do what is asked of them, then they will get rewarded and that can mean more support or the chance to row with better athletes. It is up to each athlete to demonstrate their abilities and to do that they only need a consistent intent and determination to complete all set training and competition.

The key principles of coaching rowing

Although these are my principles, I suspect that they are relevant to most coaches at most levels all around the rowing world:

- keep it simple
- keep it safe
- openness and transparency will ensure trust
- connection, leverage, run
- row further more often
- reward effort not results
- fair but not necessarily equal

TRAINING ENVIRONMENT

Melbourne is a world-renowned city with many world-class facilities and an Olympic legacy. Much of Melbourne's rowing takes place just minutes from the Central Business District at the famous Boathouse Drive, where Mercantile is located. Similar to the Embankment in Putney in London, this is home to seven different and quite separate rowing clubs.

Boathouse. *Credit: Sarah Banting*

Once a male-only club for the merchants of Melbourne, Mercantile has been producing and developing many of the finest rowing athletes, male and female, for the Australian Team for decades. In 2001, the club employed their first professional coach, Ian 'Scud' Dryden, previously from Cambridge University. While the club's principle aim is to develop athletes on to the various national teams, we do so in the belief that our long-term success depends very much on Mercantile being a club first and foremost.

Mercantile recently undertook a major refurbishment whereby only the outer walls of the boathouse remained in place. Everything inside it was pulled down and we started again with the aim of building a new home that reflected our outlook on 'performance' and 'inclusion'. The new facilities include men's and women's changing rooms that are of an equal size, a gym that is equipped to meet the very latest thinking in strength and conditioning, a bar and function area that allows the club to meet socially but without absorbing too much of the available floor space and above all a shed that can accommodate a growing boat fleet.

Mercantile is fortunate to be able to sub-lease boat bays to two schools, one male and one female, and this is a very important aspect to the make-up of the club. Like many sporting clubs we see ourselves as a club who support family values, so having juniors in the club is crucial. Our challenge is to remain true to those values while excelling in the elite category.

We train on the River Yarra which meanders through the heart of the city. Originally called Birrarung by the Aboriginals who first settled here, the current name was

Gym. *Credit: Sarah Banting*

mistranslated from another Wurundjeri term 'yarro-yarro', meaning 'ever-flowing'. Many other Australian rivers do not flow all year around. Despite flowing out into Port Phillip Bay a little further downstream, the tide is minimal and the stream mostly flows in one direction. We can row upstream for about 9km, but after 3km there are many bends that require a suitable fin and rudder configuration to get around. Indeed, one of the bends is referred to as the Big Bend and by this you can get a flavour of Australian understatement. It is easily 180 degrees plus, and the full bend is no longer than 150m in length. It takes a skilled cox to steer an eight through it at full speed without stopping. However, this is what they must attempt for the Head of the Yarra every November.

Downstream is even more exciting as this leads to the Docks and the open ocean, so quite literally there is no end if that is your intention. The docks can only be accessed when the port authority gives permission. Rowing through the docks though is an experience that I never tire of. There are tributaries such as the River Maribyrnong that allow us to row a further 15km plus before turning for home and Jennie's legendary breakfasts. Sessions out to Williamstown and back are 30km plus, although you then run the risk of missing Jennie's breakfasts altogether. In general, the river is good water for rowing training, however, the growing popularity of rowing in Melbourne, especially with juniors, has led to overcrowding issues at certain times. The river is also open to water taxis and tourist ferries, all of which jostle for their right of way.

Currently, the boat fleet in Mercantile is extensive and we have six men's eights and three women's eights. This is backed up with 12 fours and 20 pairs. We also have

Yarra River. *Credit: Sarah Banting*

six club single sculls, but most athletes are encouraged to buy their own boats – a golfer has their own clubs and a cyclist has their own bike, so in my view a rower should aim to have their own single. All the boats we buy come from the Australian boat builder Sykes. The boats are used year round and are often shared by different crews. Some high-performance athletes are given exclusive use of a pair, but only after they have proved their potential with good competitive performances.

TRAINING AND CONDITIONING

The coaching team at Mercantile is led by the head coach and supported by an assistant coach, both full-time paid positions. All the other coaches are volunteers. We have long-term coaches and over the years a number of them have been though the club system and moved on to impressive full-time coaching roles.

Within the team I encourage all the coaches to take ownership of their athletes and crews. I believe that once a coach feels supported in what they would like to do then they are able to fully lead their crews. As long as they stay within the club guidelines and the overall strategies set out by myself and the committee then I think they/we are more likely to achieve success. My job as head coach is to support them and sometimes, when necessary to provide a guiding influence. Once the coaches are clear about the messages and goals that I provide, I encourage them to work across a range of our crews so that the athletes benefit from a variety of coaching approaches.

Mercantile works very closely with Rowing Australia and the Victorian Institute of Sport and we all share a common outlook on competitive rowing. For us, it was a natural relationship that resulted from similar thinking about training and competition and I believe that it makes sense to work with the national governing body in this way. The clubs in Australia recruit, develop and nurture athletes from school upwards. Once an athlete achieves success on a national team they can be awarded a scholarship on a tiered system from their home State Sports Institute. They then train and compete for the State Institute, usually on a daily basis, with their parent club acknowledged in all competitions. The athletes can still return to their club crews for important domestic regattas. The clubs therefore are the providers to the State Institute, which in turn develops the athletes to continue on to national under-21, under-23 and senior teams.

The Australian rowing season is, like the actual seasons, out of kilter with the northern hemisphere. Winter training is generally June to November, pre-competition training is November/December through to February and the regatta season is from early February through to the nationals in April. May is what is termed the 'off season'. As such, there can be a dual approach to training which can result in 'conflicting' seasons for club athletes and those on the national teams preparing for World Championships – generally held in the northern hemisphere. On top of this, school academic years are organised around the calendar year so clubs compete to attract new junior/under-23 members directly prior to the regatta season, which is over halfway through their operating season. It's complicated.

The Australian domestic season is based around the nationals, which are held in late March or early April. Consequently, the winter training block and hence the beginning of the training year starts in May and goes through to the end of August, a period of 16 weeks. There is not much racing on the calendar apart from small local competitions. The pre-competition phase then starts with some limited head racing through to Christmas. This then leaves January to March as the all-important competition phase. April is regarded as down time where most will take some four weeks off water work.

The training programme

There are many 'programmes' out there. However, one of the principal qualities of all the programmes I believe in is 'work'. Continuous work. However, work doesn't need to be hard labour. It frustrates me that rowing has the image of a super tough sport, only mastered by the masochistic. I agree it can be made to be super tough but a well thought out biomechanical and technical model should make it less demanding as one develops both technically and physically. That said the work within the programme is progressively high in volume and focuses on easy free movement to move a hull at speed for long durations.

I base the philosophy of my programme on John Wooden's Pyramid of Success[2] and within that constant ideal I add and stress the element of 'fun'. I want the training to

---

[2] Coach Wooden's *Pyramid of Success*, 2005, John R Wooden and Jay Carty, Regal Publishing.

be fun *and* challenging. Challenging can be fun and while some aspects of the training may not be pure fun at that moment, in time the sense of achievement gained is rewarding and that surely is enjoyable and even fun?

From the outset I ask the athletes to feed back into the training programme so they have a sense of ownership. They are far more likely to train consistently well and then push on if they believe they are part owners of 'their' programme.

The programme aims to become 'familiar' within weeks of starting and certainly in presentation I do not alter the outlook. I stick to the same format each cycle so people get into a rhythm on which they can then depend. I publish a general programme with dates and the basic daily information at the beginning of each phase, which are:

- Winter – May to August
- Pre-Competition – September to December
- Competition – January to April

I then post the detailed weekly programme every Friday prior.

Both clubs at which I have been head coach were operating on comparatively lower levels of training volume per season when I arrived. By low I mean less or equal to five water sessions a week and, of those, few if at any went above 16km. Erg work was sporadic and really only done in poor weather. Gym work was mostly voluntary and there was no general strength and conditioning programme. I immediately instituted a progressive programme to build up the athletes' general capacity, which would go something like this:

Table 1: Sample Training Week/General Capacity: November (Level 2 group – medium load)

Day	Time	Training	Rest	Stroke rate (strokes/ min)	Intensity	Distance (km)	Session duration (min)
Monday	06:00	Rowing: Small boat training (aerobic steady state) + 15 min stretching + 10 min run	n/a	16 to 18	T2	20	100
	(own)	Core stability and strength work on own time	n/a			n/a	20
	(own)	Weights + 15 min stretching	n/a				80
Tuesday	06:00	Rowing: Small boat training (2 x 5 km threshold pace) + 15 min stretching + 10 min run	10 min	24 to 26	T4	20	100
	(own)	Core stability and strength work on own time	n/a			n/a	20
	(own)	Rowing ergometer: 16 x 12 power strokes – max effort per stroke	max recovery	all at rate 32	T6	n/a	30
Wednesday	06:00	Rowing: Small boat training (aerobic inc. 4 x 2 km) + 15 min stretching + 10 min run	10 min	18	T2	20	100
	(own)	Core stability and strength work on own time	n/a			n/a	20

Day	Time	Training	Rest	Stroke rate (strokes/ min)	Intensity	Distance (km)	Session duration (min)
	10:00	Weights: Circuit session + 15 min stretching	n/a				80
Thursday		Rest					
	(own)	Rowing ergometer: 3 x 25 min at 2 mmol/L blood lactate + 15 min stretching	2 min	18	T2	20	75
	17:30	Rowing: Big boat steady state incl. 3 x 12 intervals + 15 min stretching	10 min	18 to 24 to 18	T4	26	110
Friday	06:00	Rowing: Small boat training (aerobic) + 15 min stretching + 10 min run	n/a	16 to 18	T2	20	100
	(own)	Core stability and strength work on own time	n/a			n/a	20
	(own)	Weights + 15 min stretching	n/a				80
Saturday	05:30	Rowing: Small boat training (4 x 2 km) + 15 min stretching + 10 min run	10 min	(20, 24, 24 + 26, 24 + 26 + 28 + 32)	T4 to T5	20	120
	10:30	Rowing: Medium/big boats (steady state with drills) + 15 min stretching + 10 min run	n/a	16 to 18	T2	16	80
	13:00	Cycling: 75 km ride + 15 min stretching	n/a		T2	(75 km cycle)	180
Sunday	(own)	Rest day OR top up any missed cardio sessions (stay at <2 mmol/L lactate)	n/a				
					Total	162 (row) + 75 (cycle)	1315 min (~22 hours in week)
		Intensity zone classification system					
	T1	Light aerobic (60 to 75% max heart rate and <2.0 mmol/L blood lactate)					
	T2	Moderate aerobic (75 to 84% max heart rate and <3.0 mmol/L blood lactate)					
	T3	Heavy aerobic (82 to 89% max heart rate and 3.0 to 4.0 mmol/L blood lactate)					
	T4	Threshold (88 to 93% max heart rate and 2.0 to 4.0 mmol/L blood lactate)					
	T5	Maximal aerobic (92 to 100% max heart rate and >4.0 mmol/L blood lactate)					
	T6	Suprmaximal aerobic					

In terms of capacity, volume is still key and doing as much as one can is bound to reap rewards. The first two years of the competitive programme are periodised and then after a solid base is acquired the better or more experienced athletes can move to block periodisation. For both I run on weekly cycles, with Sundays off, as I find training on longer cycles does not suit the average athlete who can also be juggling work, university or family, and sometimes all three.

I use a simple formula for my periodised cycle of four weeks, generally based around each month. Each week is a regarded as a Level of Training and assigned a number from 1 to 4 with 1 being a recovery week and 4 being the hard/high volume week. Water volume is measured in kilometres and I aim for the following:

- Level 1: 100–120km per week
- Level 2: 130km per week
- Level 3: 150km per week
- Level 4: 170km plus per week

The technical model within the programme is very much based around my understanding of the art of rowing. I wanted to experience Australia for a number of reasons but one of them was the presumption that Australians in general rowed like the 'Oarsome Foursome', the men's coxless fours Olympic Champions from 1992 and 1996. Unfortunately, they don't. That said, there is a strong belief in Australia that you can row very fast with a better understanding of how and why rowing boats move on and through water rather than simply relying on raw power. This thinking is based on connection, leverage and run.

Apart from the pure technical sessions, all the water sessions for the competitive squads are based on training speeds calculated from prognostic gold medal times. If we are true to those training speeds, we can accomplish high volume in realistic time frames. A distance of 18–24km is standard though if in a bigger boat 25km plus should not be seen as anything other than normal. Done four times a week, that's half the loading already. I have often used my 100min challenge – how far you can go in that time – as a means to pushing the distance barriers. You can choose the boat you want to do it in and, at first, most favour the big boat but after a few goes the ones you will be interested in will opt for the smaller boat (unofficial selection already at work). My rules are: meet at the club at a prearranged time for a warm-up. We then start a countdown clock and people are free to go where they like, rowing as many kilometres as possible. They must return to the start point on the 100min mark exactly or you lose distance for every second you are late. This way they learn otherwise neglected skills as well as pushing their physical boundaries.

It is important to acknowledge variation of modality within volume. For a while I was anti-running, especially for heavyweights. Few heavyweight rowers can run well enough to ensure volume to be at the correct levels. Lightweights on the other hand are far better at running (and they would say rowing too). What I now encourage is running over shorter distances at pace, this way the heavyweights get the benefit of an additional stimulus but everyone can get great work done in a short period of time. 'Short' distances would be doing repeats up to 1600m. Ideally you should use a track, but any 'course' of about 400m will work.

Cycling is an obvious cross-training modality but I suspect like most other coaches I am always concerned when the athletes go out on the roads. Wattbikes are good but, like the ergs, dull if you go over the hour mark – and for me the hour mark is the minimum when building base levels or training T2 (UT2). The Wattbike though is great for alternative threshold and high-intensity interval training (HIIT) sessions. Cycling up hills is the best and whenever the opportunity arises I will always get the athletes out on the hills. Even if it means driving them from climb to climb, it is worth it.

We ensure athletes know their lactate levels and corresponding heart rates and we use these for all water and cardiovascular work. After sufficient training hours (18–24 hours per week for two full seasons) an athlete can move on to a hybrid periodised/block training programme. It is here that they can train on their threshold levels up to three times a week with one additional session (either on water or on the erg) focusing on tempo work. This will remain true through the season, right up to the key competition weeks where one or two race preparation sessions will replace one or two threshold sessions or one threshold and one steady aerobic session. This can vary from crew to crew depending on their individual requirements.

Gym work, weight training or strength and conditioning could take up a whole chapter in itself. I still find there are many common misconceptions in this area of training, especially for women and lightweights. My view is that when done well it is crucial. The gym work though must have added value to the water capability as well as capacity. This is why I describe gym work as 'resisted movement patterns', realistic to the rowing stroke. We try to replicate the stages of rowing movement and then add resistance. With this in mind the resistance does not need to be huge, indeed more often than not less is more. Without doubt there is a selling job to get the less experienced female athletes on board and to ensure the heavyweight men do not become influenced by the amount others are lifting. Power-to-weight ratios are important and if an elite male competitor is over the 95kg mark then his erg score had better be below 5:55. Female weight is still a sensitive subject but I try and talk about it empathetically to make it less of an issue. Using power-to-weight ratios helps in this.

Does capability override capacity or visa-versa? We can argue both cases but I believe capable athletes who have trained very well for a consistent period of time, and we are all aware of the 10,000-hour theory, will succeed best. I think that if you learn how to row well first and then add capacity, you can row to a very high level. Therefore, I start with the art of rowing, enjoying the sport and then add capacity. That way you can engage the love of the sport first and then build the engine.

Erg Training

I use the erg in two ways. Firstly, for beginners or someone with low training history it can be used for technical learning and introducing volume. For newcomers, I set time challenges and repeat once each week with other erg sessions focusing on technical sequencing. For developing athletes, I still have time-based sessions but would have tested their lactates and set corresponding intensities (watts or splits). My standard 2mmol sessions are 3 x 20min in a Level 1 week, 3 x 25min in a Level 2, 3 x 30min in a Level 3 and 3 x 35min in a Level 4 week. The rest between each set is between two and five minutes depending on ability to hold consistent watts and heart rates.

In addition to the 30min test my threshold sessions are based on a total of 40 minutes' work and repeats. For example, 2 x 20min with intensity set for 4–6mmol blood lactate. Early in the season the challenge is to be consistent so start at the 4mmol level and build as one sees improvement. Variations would be 4 x 10min or 8 x 5min but with the reduced time, increase the intensity up to the 6mmol levels and adjust the rest time accordingly.

High intensity interval sessions are becoming more popular. However, because of the nature of the rowing stroke I tend to prolong the sessions to look something like up to 2min 'on' with 1–2min 'reduced intensity' with from 10–20 repeats depending on drag, rate and, of course, training history. With the longer reps the intensity is reduced so the session is more accurately labelled as 'threshold interval work'.

The use of sliders in the longer sessions is not a bad idea. Sliders were the standard in Australia but now, to stay in line with the other mainstream rowing nations, all erg monitoring is done on the static erg. I like to vary it up though, as so much can be learned while on the slider. As long as the athletes do not become set on any one variation I think they should be able to choose how they complete the long distance erg sessions. This goes for drag factor too. On the water we are open to outside conditions, so why not vary the loading on the erg. For some this can make the difference to training or not training when fatigued.

The second approach is for the athletes with a developed training history; then the erg becomes more of a monitoring tool. Distance work should never be replaced but monitoring capacity is best done on the erg. Here, I use the 30min open rate as often as bi-weekly. However, every other 30min may be completed at 90–95 per cent effort. This way they have done a max 30min and a training threshold every four weeks (one cycle). The threshold effort will be based on 90–95 per cent of their previous best effort depending on their current state. The other monitoring ergs I use are 2 x 6km at 90–95 per cent of the functional threshold watt of the 30min test and then the benchmark tests of 5km and 2km.

The ergs sessions are specific to lactate levels previously taken. This way they are also individual, which I see as important. Erg data is collected either by the coach or better still by the athlete and logged, so self-monitoring is a natural consequence to their training. In all cases it must be reported to a central database.

The HIIT sessions mentioned previously are part of a range of sessions that are good for both beginner and elite alike. The beginners like them as they avoid the long monotonous sessions and the elite athletes like them because they can open up the engine and see how they rank with their teammates.

Core stability

I find I still have to sell the concept of 'core stability' to my athletes but with each passing season it seems to be better understood. I think of it like this: if a skyscraper lost its middle 10 floors, saving only the back wall, it would obviously collapse. Now, I'm no architect but to me that image could replicate a side-on skeleton losing its rib cage and unless we replace the ribcage, or the 'missing floors', with stabilisers and supports, our bodies will collapse too, especially when loaded up.

On water I really like the concept of pushing the feet back under still handles and driving as close as you can to a 'bum shove' without actually fully bum shoving. To my mind this can best be achieved by holding firm through the core prior to the placement and connection. I talk about firming up from spine to belly button. To demonstrate this, I get an athlete to sit on an erg and hold the handle deep in their lap above their pelvic bone and row legs only holding the handle in place. When they do this the relationship between handle and seat is obvious but to do so they all report having to hold firm with the core muscles. When they push on the stretcher the handle returns with the seat as if they are held together, and in effect they are. I then ask the athlete to move the handle out to a normal out-stretched position as if they are at the catch and to repeat but maintain the relationship between handle and seat through a firm core. To do so they must fill in the missing floors and 'grip'. Without actually 'pulling' the handle it will return with the seat due to the connected core grip as well as the leg drive. Indeed, I find the best effect on speed is to allow a slight lag from seat to handle – let the seat lead the handle. This is close to a bum shove and sometimes it will actually be the beginnings of a bum shove. I don't worry about this – just continue to 'grip' prior to placement and fill in the floors. All of this is possible with developed core strength and stability. I want my athletes to do it every day and as part of their daily routine; at home while watching TV, in the classroom, or before each and every session.

ATHLETE SELECTION AND TALENT DEVELOPMENT

Over a season I encourage athletes to select themselves. When they take ownership of their programme they will develop at such a rate that the selection process becomes part of the continued journey. By taking regular monitored data from both water and land – and never forgetting to publish it – the athlete ladder becomes apparent soon enough.

Over the years I have found that the majority of athletes within any one squad I have coached are of a similar standard. A few are either very good or off the pace and selection for them is not really a debatable issue. Most occupy the middle ground so selection 'decisions' usually come about when comparing similar athletes and, to make it really interesting, usually when deciding the final seats. While I have used seat racing to select the final seats I only think it's fair on the athletes to do this if 'seat racing' has played a part in previous regular training. Done with targeted intent it can provide not only ongoing and regular data but also familiarises the athletes with the processes as well as close racing. It can also help iron out the deficiencies of this test, although it can just as easily go the other way if it is not properly thought through.

I do use the erg as part of a selection decision and will weight adjust the scores using the Concept 2 formula. Prior to any test though the athletes will know what their target score is. However, success on the erg only gets the athlete to the next stage, be it seat racing on water or time in a boat to show skill development or compatibility prior to any further water testing.

If selection comes down to a considered coach's call then I think that should be accepted as a necessary part of the job. We see this in other sports and in rowing the flow of a crew is very important and it is the coach's eye that considers the flow. This though is a contentious issue and open discussion at the beginning of each and every season is required to set out the parameters and guidelines the coaching staff will adhere to in coming to a considered opinion. Inclusion of other club officials is crucial as third party knowledge and opinion ensures fairness is adhered to in a consistent manner.

I aim to deliver selection decisions as soon as possible after any selection process and I prefer to start with the decision and then explain the detail. Long drawn out preambles, sometime after the event, always cause resentment and possibly anger. If there is a close call on a seat race, I use the result as the starting point and the thought process is there for all to see. If it's a considered call, I outline the facts then call it straight out.

I like to offer a contingency to a deselected athlete, be it another crew or race but I will avoid repeating selection because it only causes muddled thinking. Besides that, most of our races are one-offs and you cannot go back and try again. Hence, selections based on single races can be used to train for heighted levels of competition. I think most clubs are able to do this. Post selection, showing gratitude for effort given and acknowledging that the team needed everyone's involvement is the very least one can do.

The school athletes we attract are very much used to rowing in the eight. Each state has its own school Head of the River for both girls and boys. Raced over 2-km courses these interstate competitions hold the greatest appeal to junior athletes, coaches and parents alike. There is very little small boat training or competition. I find this remarkable because it has a knock-on effect, as once a pupil leaves school and decides they want to continue rowing they will join a club who will do most of their training in small boats. The first couple of years therefore are limited as the skill base is not where it needs to be. Dropping young school leavers into small boats though can quite easily turn them off the sport altogether and at Mercantile this is a challenge. Our aim for ambitious athletes is to get them on to the state team and then the national under-23 team and to do this they must qualify for trials via the small boat. This sudden change in approach to training and selection could be a reason for the large dropout rates that are now a real concern in our sport.

Our current solution is to use the big boat and the medium boat through the training week as a means to continue familiarity. As they progress the number of small boat sessions will increase over the big boat sessions.

COACH AND ATHLETE RELATIONSHIP

An athlete does not need to like you and personally I would never become a 'friend' to any of my athletes while they are competing. That said I always strive to be friendly, supportive and always 'there' for them, but there is a line that should not be crossed. Some may disagree, and that is fine but I prefer the understanding on both sides that the relationship needs to have a boundary to get through the highs and lows and to have a chance of long-term success. I heard another colleague talk of creating neighbourly relationships with his athletes – so the sort of relationship that most would like with our neighbours, friendly and supportive but not overly familiar. I run the risk of being seen as removed and maybe even distant, but on the whole I think athletes prefer this positioning as much as I do.

I have always adhered to the 'fair but not equal' approach. With careful explanation I have used this same approach at Mercantile. It goes without saying that a club does not have limitless resources and therefore at some stage the best will get more of the better resources than others. You earn the right to have the superior equipment and support services. However, it is important for coaches to remember that everyone should feel supported in their development. It's the careful managing of these various relationships that take up most of coach's non-rowing time.

Specifically, I am interested in watching and developing group cohesion – a topic that has intrigued me since my university days studying this very subject. Many factors have an influence on group cohesion but I see individual mood as a leading factor. How we effect mood is one of the most important factors in coaching. I enjoy situations and surroundings where I am among easy going and relaxed people with a sense of purpose and a shared intent on a common goal. My off-water objective then is to create an environment where athletes feel at ease and part of the club structure so that they can develop in a challenging but not confrontational atmosphere. Their motivation develops from this familiar and supportive daily environment.

It is important therefore not to allow the training culture within the shed to become the domain of any one group or squad. Everyone must feel they have a part to play in the successful development of the club and from this their own development will gather pace. To beginners and newcomers I play the role of a teacher and, as they develop, I become more of a guide rather than a person they need to rely on. I believe we learn best by trial and error rather than by instruction alone. My preferred style then is to set up conditions whereby people can evolve and progressively self-teach without fear of failure. I am there to support and guide but the athletes soon learn to take control. With all the different and differing personalities it can be quite a juggling act.

Allowing athletes to take ownership is a long-term approach and for some can be frustrating, especially in this 'instant' world in which we find ourselves. Mistakes need to be made and sometimes repeated in order to fully learn. This takes time and patience from athletes and coach alike.

I think there is a belief within rowing that rowers are the toughest of all. I doubt that. That said, the school athlete looking to move up to the national level needs to understand that the training is long and can be challenging at times. Initially I like to show them that it is not impossible and anyone can have a go. We stress that the programme takes time so we endeavour to demonstrate early progress to keep the initial enthusiasm high and motivation to continue elevated. Initially a moderated and progressive programme is used and all the time effort is rewarded over results.

TECHNICAL APPROACH

Having now worked with great 'technical' coaches I find this area of my approach to coaching becoming clearer and more certain than ever before. It is also clear to me there are other, just as well-defined understandings out there but what I think is universally agreed on is that rowing is a leverage sport. Therefore, I focus on actual length in the water with an accelerated drive sequence. Fundamentally a combination of length and acceleration create run and thus forms the basis of rhythm. I do think length can be a distraction in terms of more is better. If athletes are over-reaching beyond the desired length, then their ability to drive with acceleration will be compromised.

Biomechanically we know the acceleration curves that are attainable both in the drive and on the recovery so we should have a better understanding of how to construct a complete stroke. The variation comes from the size of boat and crew. However, the basic principles of timing the catch rather than forcing it, a leg dominated drive with a prolonged hang of the body weight off the handle and through the footplate to hold pressure through the finish are all true. Where I think people can really gain more consistent speed and run is on the recovery. The hull will, after a slight dip in speed, continue to accelerate off the finish if there are no inhibitors to that acceleration. The inhibitors can be any number of things but usually start with body weight not being connected through the footplate, body weight 'dumping' into the hull and/or rocking forward against the momentum of the hull prior to the handle/arms extending forward.

On the recovery I like to talk about the body leaving the handle as well as the arms extending. If done literally the handle can stay with the puddle just created. The notion of slow hands or pausing is still debated. Sitting still with no inhibitors to the continued acceleration is, for me, fundamental to maximising speed and efficiency. Once you are able to hold the torso still and free the hands independently then crews can achieve hull acceleration through the finish and release.

In a similar fashion to allowing the body to move with the hull away from a 'stationary' handle we can also minimise momentum rocking forward into the stern against the run of the hull by allowing the hips to move with the hull under the shoulders by 'pressing' the thighs into the bow. This is opposed to rocking forward in a traditional manner. Rocking forward is open to individual interpretation and flexibility. It can also present weight on the foot stretcher too early and with too much negative force. I like the idea of using the single input, the speed of the hull, that everyone should feel at same time and use that speed to get into a set position before half slide. I coach my crews to find it by quarter slide at everything under rate 28 knowing that at a higher tempo it can dilute out to half slide. From here on in though whether at quarter or half slide the bodies and heads need to be still and ready to anticipate the catch so this all-important skill can be timed and not forced. All too often I see people who are not set up, who do not anticipate the front end and then feel the need to reach forward to place the blade. In so doing they lurch forward over their toes and fall off balance. This is slow and damages the speed of the hull when it is at its most vulnerable. Even the best catch will momentarily slow the hull so any extras here will make the hull become heavy, laboured and expensive.

The blade connection to the water is therefore of paramount importance and the recovery as a whole is partly designed to set the posture up correctly so as to allow the best connection for the following catch. During the catch the arms are links to the connectors and the connectors are the latissimus dorsi, glutes and general core muscles supported by the skeleton around.

I like to see how close we can get to a 'bum shove' without actually overtly driving the seat away from the handles. I find that you can squeeze the seat away and allow the handle to follow slightly after and still remain connected. The resulting 'slingshot' is an efficient way to maintain acceleration over a period of time.

The effective stroke, no matter what boat type or whether sculling or sweeping, should feel and look simple. This means there are certain effective requirements of a stroke but all too often there are too many extras. These extras take up time and have a detrimental effect on the run of the hull. I guess it is up to each coach to determine what is an extra and what is necessary.

While having a clear picture in my head of how I want my crews to row gives me confidence; so too does the acknowledgement that experimentation will find new and better ways for each and every crew. When I look at a new crew I try to start from scratch and see what will work for them. What is the make-up of that crew and do they look like they want to row? From there I can map out a plan and start my direction. Firstly, getting them comfortable and then coaching them to synchronise their efforts in both directions will lead to an appreciation of what the hull can and will do as a result of their combined effort.

Specific technical training

To my mind all training is technical or has a technical aspect to it – but how much you focus on it is up to you. I have a technical aspect to all my training. I try to incorporate technique sessions with a strong T2 (or UT2/1) paddle to follow – 40min technique followed by 40min T2 on speed. I have up to two sessions per week out of twelve doing this and always in the small boat (usually a morning session before work). In a recovery week though this can increase to four or even five water sessions. When in the technique part of a session though I have a rule – if you are in a drill then you must paddle as firmly as you can, given any limitations such as one arm rowing etc. My main technical rule and best drill of all is 'best possible paddling' as it incorporates all the drills ever used. I even call it 'Best Possible Paddling', especially when I want deep concentration on that particular segment of the session. I also ask my crews to show the effect of the drill just used in the paddling directly after. If they are paddling square blade, then I want to see evidence of a square release or a more direct 'hooked' placement. All too often a crew will paddle, do a drill then go back to where they were before the drill. Why do the drill in the first place?

Most coaches have their favourite drills and I certainly go back to some more than others. If I list three, then I am going to start off by cheating – as mentioned earlier I like to remind my crews that good paddling is the best drill of all and without listing that as a drill I want them to think this way. That said, the more traditional drills I go to are as follows:

DRILL 1: Feet out – holding connection through the stretcher is vital. I often talk about two-directional pressure and by this I mean the pressures an athlete can create through the drive. One is in the direction of the stern through the stretcher or footplate and one is in the direction of the bow via the oar handle. All too often the pressure on the handle can be greater than the pressure we maintain through the footplate and especially so when the legs are flat. This is why people struggle with feet out – the pressure they create on the handle forces them off the back of the seat. However, if they can continue to press into the stretcher through the latter part of the drive phase and equal the pressure on the handle then they can remain on the stretcher (and seat). Variations on this drill can be one foot out, which dilutes the demanding nature of feet out. You know you are good enough at this drill when you can row firm pressure with some rate (maybe up to rate 24 or even 26) and the coach cannot tell you have your feet out.

DRILL 2: Checks during the recovery – all the checks have a purpose but the ones I go to most are at the finish and at quarter slide. It is here that you can really feel the hull run on. Stillness is key so the crew must drive the stroke to a point of stillness on the release. If we can retain elements of body stillness while racing the efficiency of the crew will be that much higher.

For the quarter slide check I first get my crews to sit at the catch in their best position with blade flat on the water. Then, without coming out of this posture, straighten their legs to one-quarter slide. Their elbows should be above the knees. The drill then reminds each athlete of this 'set' position.

DRILL 3: Legs only + legs & body – getting the drive sequence right especially when at firm pressure is crucial for speed and efficiency. Often I see athletes and crews changing direction prior to placing the blade and then 'pulling' on the handle before connecting. Legs only drills focus the athlete to separate the initial part of the drive. Variations on this can be the use of roll-ups (from a set position on the recovery, usually the finish, roll up to the front end and place the blade into the water then stopping or pausing before griping and pushing) then applying legs only.

Presently I am working with a crew that enjoys two unusual drills. The first is 'Follow my leader' whereby stroke must listen or rather feel the run on the boat and decide for herself what drill would be useful and start it without comment or indication. Her partner and bow seat must also listen and see if they too can hear the same signatures and then also determine the same drill. When they are really in tune with each other and the boat they will start the same drill at the same time. This brings about deep and targeted thinking as to what the hull is actually doing and will bring the crew together very quickly. It is also good fun to do and watch.

The other 'drill' is to play with the full range of stroke in terms of length and effective arc. Going deep on the catch then shallow through the square off and then deep again at the finish and all the other variables we can think of. Working the hand skills and grip in the drive as well as the recovery is always beneficial.

Part 3

Technique and Drills

Rowing Technique Robin Williams, GB Rowing, London, UK

Robin Williams rowed for the University of London Boat Club and represented Great Britain for the first time in 1981, an international career that lasted 10 years until 1991. He won a gold medal at the Match des Seniors (World Under-23 Rowing Championships) in 1981 and silver and bronze at the 1988 and 1989 World Rowing Championships. He has also won three Henley Royal regatta medals and five Lucerne Regatta medals.

In 1994 he became coach to the Cambridge University Boat Club where his crews won the Boat Race seven times in 10 years. From 2005 until 2009 he coached the men's lightweight crews for Team GB winning gold at the World Championships in 2007. In July 2010 he began coaching Helen Glover and Heather Stanning in the women's coxless pair who won silver at the 2010 and 2011 World Rowing Championships. In 2012 they won gold at the London Olympics and since then have been unbeaten, setting a new world record time at the 2014 World Championships and winning gold again at the Rio Olympics.

Williams was appointed Member of the Order of the British Empire (MBE) in the 2013 New Year Honours for services to rowing.

The subject of rowing technique could easily fill a whole book, but the aim of this chapter is to cover the most important elements of good technique, the problems you face and some remedies and ideas to correct them. It cannot cover everything, of course, so it also tries to give the rower some ways to help him or herself to self-coach. An original thought is always more powerful than one that's been handed down, so the key is to grasp some of the important concepts and principles behind boat moving and then explore them for oneself. Good coaching can certainly help but the rower needs to take responsibility for him or herself and learn actively, not passively.

Like many other sports rowing is at the same time both simple and complicated. The basic mechanics are straightforward but making the whole ensemble work at speed with rhythm, synchronicity and power is a wonderful challenge that gives many of us a lifetime of elation and frustration. What is the appeal of rowing? Compared to the length of a running stride or a swimming stroke, one full body movement in rowing takes you not 2 or 3 metres but 10 or 11, rather like jumping on the Moon in zero gravity. It is a thrilling feeling even if it is sometimes hard for the average spectator to appreciate. Getting the best out of yourself as the power source and the boat and oars is quite an art and while some parts of technique can be measured and coached scientifically, other parts just need to be felt and learned first-hand. It is not just about the individual either – the rower's technique needs to fit in with other rowers and therefore the coach needs to balance up one individual's goals with those of the crew.

Rowing is a demanding sport *physically* and will get you fitter than almost any other sporting activity. If physical power is the 'engine' then technique is the 'gearbox'. Initially, the lack of technique will hold the rower back because he or she won't have the skills to make proper use of their physiology, but once the basic technique is grasped many rowers find that better fitness is what brings success. This may be true for a while – juniors who have had their growth spurt or who are advanced for their age often win races because of that early maturity and senior crews training six days a week will likely beat those training on three days. Nevertheless, it is a mistake to let this impression stick in your mind because when you and your opponents are equally mature physically, mentally as tough and equally powerful, the key difference is often technique. This is especially true with lightweight rowers who are all the same size. Physical capacity has limits but arguably technique has none.

A common theory to do with skill acquisition is that it takes 10,000 repetitions of an action to fully entrain it. In training a rower can easily make 2000 strokes per session, 12,000 per week or half a million per year, so there is huge scope for perfecting poor technique as well as good. A fact of life therefore is that skills have to be learned, unlearned and relearned all the time and we will look at this cycle further on. How long does it actually take to become a good rower? Well if you have never done much sport and are unfit then the physiological development takes some time, probably in the range of 2–4 years. If you are transferring from another sport, then you may have some useful strength and aerobic capacity already and it may happen faster. Acquiring the technical skills *can* be quick but generally isn't; the keenest learners and those with good body awareness can enjoy success quickly but many get so far and then plateau.

How you THINK is the key to unlocking your potential so I urge you to read the next section. It explains why some people improve more quickly than others. Coaches too need to understand how the athlete ticks and many will be familiar with what follows.

PRINCIPLES OF LEARNING

1. Sports are often described as being 'open' or 'closed' skilled. Open means you only have partial control of what happens, things change quickly and your actions have to adapt and respond accordingly. In a tennis match you have an opponent opposite you, so 50 per cent of your decisions depend in part on the shot he or she makes, not you. Rugby, soccer and field sports are similar. A discus throw on the

other hand is a closed skill because you prepare yourself and make your throw on your own terms, in your own time with full control.

2. There are overlaps between the two and rowing is an interesting example because you have your own boat and racing lane – closed skilled – but, being a predominantly crew sport, people have to synchronise, balance and move together plus there are wind and waves, steering and other external factors to contend with all of which make it partly reactive or open skilled. Either way, it is an outdoor sport with plenty of variables including weather so technique has to hold up in all situations and the rower has to take charge of it.

3. Another principle involves the stages of learning. The first stage is 'cognitive': everything is unfamiliar so your brain has to think about every movement and finds it difficult to grasp more than one instruction at a time let alone execute multiple subtle movements in the space of two seconds or one rowing stroke. Think about learning to drive a car. To start with you look at the foot pedals, the gear lever, array of switches and lights and there seems to be too much to cope with. You deal with single pieces of information. Yet millions of people drive and obviously do learn the technique with a few lessons. Rowing is learnable in the same way as this. The next phase is 'associative': when your brain has learned some cause and effect and how to interpret actions. One example of this would be hand heights: if I balance my blade off the water I have room to square it and enter properly. The third stage is the 'autonomous' one where you can row (or drive a car) with intuition and can cope with multiple movements and skills simultaneously.

4. The third principle, the Teaching-Learning cycle, was mentioned earlier. It goes like this:

    A. The coach explains to the athlete what he wants him/her to do.

    B. The athlete attempts to do it.

    C. The coach gives feedback and corrections.

    D. The athlete then repeats and improves.

    E. The coach gives positive reinforcement (praise).

    F. The athlete repeats again to show it wasn't a fluke and keeps practising until the skill is fully and reliably embedded (autonomous).

Having this basic understanding about how we learn things allows us to set about rowing training with more body awareness and a sense that it is not a haphazard process but one with common sense stages to it. This is the first part of getting the mindset right and part of being a good athlete is being able to coach yourself and understand how to learn. Getting things wrong is also part of the process, so don't be fearful of making some mistakes.

Rowers frequently get to the autonomous stage only to find that the moment circumstances change it all reverts and becomes cognitive again. Examples might be switching position in the boat, changing boat class, headwind versus tail conditions or making a technical change the coach asks for. Once you've made the change reliable and permanent then it will feel automatic again. We feel comfortable when things feel 'normal' and uncomfortable when they don't, so you have to get used to dealing with change, risk and vulnerability as you work at your technique. Experienced coaches will understand this process very clearly and be mindful of these phases over the months of the training year.

COACHING AND COMMUNICATION

With many sports the coach can be on the field of play with the athlete and can demonstrate what is wanted. In rowing the coach is usually on the bank or maybe in a coach boat but either way is several metres away from the rower and everything has to be described in words. It's easy enough to convey the physical training: 'Go firm for 10 strokes'. This is a clear and evident command, but technique requires more description, more words, more time. Demonstration is harder for the coach on a bike or while steering a motorboat and sound doesn't travel well with the noises from the rowing so the learning environment is compromised. Shouting loudly is not great because it can imply tension and anger. A loud hailer is better but broadcasts the coach's comments for the whole world to hear and is impersonal, so I personally recommend a radio system. You can talk with natural volume and voice expression, plus if the crew gets a long way from you it is better for safety. Of course, giving a clear briefing before the crew even takes to the water is the simplest way to set out objectives and is time well spent; talking face to face when the crew has a fluid break or is turning the boat around is also useful. Remember also that while rowing the rower will absorb less of what the coach says because the brain's processing speed drops during physical activity, so it is harder to hear and respond compared to when at rest. Clear and simple commands work best and work on one thing at a time, not a whole list. Off the water it pays to hold regular technique reviews, use video examples and discuss methods of feedback. Some people learn through visual stimulus, others are better aurally or kinaesthetically (feeling), so work out what kind of learning style is preferred. A good tip for public speaking is to talk at a rate of three words per second and this is useful for coaching too.

MINDSET

The best technical rowers seem to have an inbuilt curiosity, a real hunger and an urgency to improve, all the time. They strive to grasp the message and thought process behind the coach's comment, not just the comment itself. In other words, they try to interpret the message and see it in context. Others just take it at face value, try to make the change but rely on the coach completely to tell them if they've been successful. Even then they may not be able to repeat it because they have not fundamentally understood so the next day they are back to square one. Mindset is vital for proper technical improvement. Be an active learner, not a passive one. Top coaches make sessions enjoyable, varied and stimulating to fuel the rower's own curiosity and hunger to improve and they ask questions to make sure there has been proper understanding.

One of the best bits of advice for rowers AND coaches is to smile when you arrive for training. Smiling is a trigger to your muscles, body and mind to relax and is connected to the production of 'positive' hormones too. If rowers start training in a positive mood then you will be receptive when being coached – coaching is not done to you, you participate in it and need to enjoy being critiqued, finding flaws which you can correct and therefore get better. Quick learners *want* to be coached, they don't shy away from or fear criticism. Too many rowers see coaching as a threat and pray that they'll get through a session without anything being said to them. This is a barrier to improvement and will slow things down greatly.

Making mistakes is also OK. Things won't be perfect all the time and it is important to know what 'wrong' feels like as much as what feels 'right'. Just occasionally I use this as a coaching tactic with elite level crews, not just novices. For example, we're trying to sharpen the catch so it is millimetre perfect, so go the opposite way first – 'let's *miss* half a metre the catch … OK, now 30cm, now 10cm, now 1cm, now miss nothing at all'. It gives a scale to work with and a sense of progression and the human brain likes this. Just saying day after day 'plus 1cm no, wait, no minus 1cm', can become frustrating and hard to perceive. People like a sense of reward and as legendary British coach Mike Spracklen once said, 'if a rower does not see a *benefit* to making a change, he won't change'.

As you improve and win races your confidence grows and you establish 'Performance Anchors' – 'We did this last time and we won so it must [always] be right'. You rely on what you know, what you have learned, but to get better you often have to let go of these anchors before you can move on again. Ask yourself 'What DON'T I know yet?' rather than relying on learned behaviour. Sir Steven Redgrave won five Olympic gold medals but had to lift his standards all the way through those 20 years, realising that what was good enough today won't be good enough tomorrow. If you think you know it all then you are a moment away from defeat. Rowers and coaches should develop confidence but not be complacent and always keep learning.

So, having understood some learning principles and how you tick as a person, you can turn your attention to your actual rowing technique and how to get the best from yourself.

TECHNIQUE – MECHANICS VS. FEEL

Technique is a big subject so it needs breaking up to understand it better. Coaching comments will fall in to one of two categories: mechanics or kinaesthetics (doing/feeling). The coach might work on mechanical things at certain times and feel at others, particularly when preparing for racing, so seeing technique headings this way can help you to understand the objective for each training session and what the coach wants as an outcome.

Examples of Mechanics

- body positions
- back shape
- sequences of movement
- blade depths
- stroke length
- hand heights
- squaring and feathering
- basic entry/exit timing
- stroke rate
- stroke ratio
- angles
- boat speed

Examples of Feel

- body language
- balance
- fluidity
- blade control
- movement range
- relaxation
- anticipation
- fine timing
- momentum and inertia
- sense of time
- breathing
- boat run
- rhythm
- synchronisation
- poise
- heaviness/lightness

The list of 'mechanical' examples includes things which can be measured and quantified. The coach can usually observe or measure them and in consequence they are often the things coaches coach. The 'feel' list is potentially much longer because it starts to include more subjective aspects like harmony, breathing, anticipation, use of time and these are things that are harder for the coach to see but relatively easy for the athlete to appreciate inside the boat. The ability to feel and understand the stroke, not just do it, is what makes a real boat-mover. There are important basic technical points in rowing but also plenty of artistry too so we can imagine how frustrating a session could be if the coach is talking about a mechanical technique point and the crew are engaged on a kinaesthetic one. For example: 'Reach towards your rigger more ...', 'OK, but if I do that the balance goes wrong'.

Rowers need good mechanics *and* good feel and there is a simple process for working on them: start with a fundamental mechanical movement with an easy skill level and add levels of difficulty to increase the demand on skills. A simple example would be stroke sequences. The stroke needs to unfold in the right way and lack of balance is the thing that often limits good execution.

EXAMPLE DRILL

Stroke Sequences (e.g. hands-body-slide in the recovery)

Stage 1: Sequence practice with blades on the water, boat stationary – *easy!*

Stage 2: As above but blades off, boat moving – *harder!*

Stage 3: Repeat with eyes shut – *challenging!*

Stage 4: Repeat with eyes shut, square blades and at higher speed – *expert!*

Stage 1 could even be made easier by running the sequences on the ergometer or in a rowing tank where balance is no issue at all.

Back in the boat there are always drills you can add to increase both the challenge and the skill level. This is simply taking a cognitive action, practising it until it becomes autonomous and then adding a new challenge, which makes it cognitive again until that becomes easy too, and so on. Racing crews often do over-speed drills to go beyond the movement speeds they will actually need in racing.

The process works in reverse too: if something goes wrong partway through a training session the crew can break down the full movement into something more manageable until they can correct the problem – doing some single strokes to get the finishes together, for instance.

We'll come back to drills and exercises further on but for now let's look at the structure of the stroke. You will find plenty of websites with still photographs or drawings of these sequences, e.g.

GBR – http://www.britishrowing.org/upload/files/CoachingTraining/PerfectStroke Poster.pdf

AUS – http://www.rowingaustralia.com.au/shop/australian-rowing-technique-poster

CAN – http://rowingcanada.org/sites/default/files/rca_technique_final.pdf

FISA – http://www.worldrowing.com/uploads/files/Chapter_3_-_Basic_Rowing_ Te.pdf

They make a very useful reference tool for the mechanics of the stroke and if your coach can take video of you, you can easily compare yourself against these technical models with some interpretation of feel as well. Pictures tell you WHAT to do but not necessarily HOW to do it or how it might FEEL, so try to understand the way the still frames link not just as separate movements.

STROKE SEQUENCE

These picture sequences form the basic structure of the stroke and are a good place to begin defining technique. Here are some simple notes to help describe each one.

The Recovery
In my view there are two main methods for the beginning of the stroke and the debate about which is the best could occupy the whole technique chapter quite easily. One way is for everyone to arrive on the stretcher with blades still out of the water and then enter and drive at the same time; a sort of 'hang and drive technique'. The advantage of this is that it is quite easy to coordinate people's movements and it makes sure that everyone is going in the same direction at the same time. The disadvantage is that you have to accept some deceleration or slip because of the slight pause at the front. The second method is to enter as you arrive with the sense that the entry is the last part of the recovery and the stroke starts under the water with the catch, the whole movement being seamless. I prefer this thinking but it is more technical and needs good execution to work. The important thing is for

1: The finish – the rower keeps legs and trunk 'pressed' until the oar relinquishes its bend or load. This is an important timing point for crews. Everyone is at the same place at the same time and sitting still 'with the boat'. Because rowing is about repeating stroke cycles this 'press point' is the end of the drive phase and also the beginning of the recovery phase and so 'hands away' is the first actual movement in the recovery sequence.

2: As the arms separate from the trunk, they keep extending along the legs and draw the trunk forward in a natural way, not stiffly, into a rocked forward position. There will be a little weight down on the handle to keep the spoon off the water, of course.

All images from page 134–139 are credited to Don Somner

3: shows the rower at about quarter slide by which point the arms are extended, trunk forwards and knees unlocked. She has done most of the preparatory movements for the next stroke already and is in a relaxed and balanced position. From here the boat does the rest.

From 3 to 4: all the rower has done is sit in the same position and allow the travel of the boat under her legs to draw her up the slide until she is nearly fully compressed. This is an important ingredient of boat feel and it is much better for your own mass to be still and the smaller mass of the hull to come to you than the other way around.

5: The Catch, shows that the recovery ends when the rower is fully forward and the blade is back in the water. You cannot move the boat unless the oar is covered so this is a key skill too and needs lots of practice. There is the problem of how to enter the blade when the hull is moving forwards, a process that needs some explanation.

everyone to do the same thing because of the change of direction in mass. In an eight, for instance, one heavy male rower will weigh about the same as the hull itself so if just one person changes direction late, the weight of the boat will momentarily double for the others.

The Drive

The time between arriving in picture 5, entering, catching and loading in pictures 6 and 7 will be approximately 0.2 to 0.3 seconds – in other words it's QUICK! However, it works better if you think EARLY or ANTICIPATE rather than just be 'quick' because it also needs to be flowing and relaxed and thinking 'fast' or 'quick' can communicate tension and anxiety, which usually has the opposite effect and makes it slow and poorly timed.

In summary these pictorial technique guides indicate WHAT to do but only scratch the surface of HOW to do it. It takes a lot of detail to describe the nuances of the movements but there are some useful guiding concepts and if the rower follows them he or she can make a lot of sense of these basics.

6: looks almost the same as 5 – the rowers are in the same position but their muscles have now engaged pressure. Instant feet pressure anchors the spoon against the water and the fingers around the handle. Without foot pressure AND handle pressure there is no connection and no reason for the boat to move so the back and arms have to hold on as the legs produce the force.

7: shows what happens soon *after* the catch because the rest of the load can now be applied. The full weight of the rowers and some of their power is used to fully bend the oar and this creates drive on the hull via the pin. You have to be careful here that the force is well connected from feet right through the body to the handle because it is common for the hull to keep slowing here due to leg pressure against the stretcher. The connection should not be rigid or stiff; it is similar to starting a lawnmower or an outboard engine.

8: Up to this point the stroke has been largely leg-based with the trunk working firmly to transfer the leg movement to the oar but without it giving up much of its own angle. However, the trunk now needs to actively extend away from the legs so the mid-stroke is a combination of pushing *and* pulling whereas the first part was pushing and bracing. When the oar is about 15 degrees before the orthogonal this is where peak handle force has been reached and the sensation is that things really speed up from here. It takes approximately 0.4 seconds from catch to peak handle force assuming firm pressure. The remainder of the stroke will take roughly 0.3 seconds or less so we can see that the first part of the stroke takes longer than the second because of the need to load the oar, the rower's weight and allow some reaction time for the hull to gain speed. The latter part of the stroke happens very quickly if the hull is moving fast.

CONCEPTS OF TECHNIQUE

1. BOAT SPEED is the combination of both drive AND recovery phases so gliding is just as important as working and should be practised.
2. POWER: Use muscles in order of strength, starting with the legs then trunk, then arms.
3. MOVEMENT: Each movement can only be made *once* so if the back opens too early, for instance, it cannot repeat the movement later when it is actually needed.
4. CONNECTION: The legs are strong but not directly connected to the oar so the limitation is how well your trunk and arms can hang on.
5. SMOOTHNESS: The hull moves smoothly through the water so you need to make smooth movements as well, not abrupt ones.
6. LIGHTNESS: The boat is light – you are heavy, so if the stroke feels heavy – it's YOU!
7. BODY WEIGHT: Use your body weight to help move the boat.
8. TIMING: Timing comes from the boat. There may be up to nine people in the boat but there is only ONE boat so if you have good boat feel you will automatically synchronise together.
9. LEVERAGE: Lever the boat past the spoon; don't pull the oar through the water.

9: shows the mid-stroke hip extension continuing as the back angle opens and this feels much like a squat jump you might make off the floor. Remember, the legs push all the way through, the trunk begins to open just before the square off point and then it too continues to the end; the shoulders retract once the trunk has overtaken the seat and finally the arms join in to complete the process.

10: shows the rowers almost at the press point again. Here the rowers have *almost* completed the stroke but still try to keep their hips 'up' so that their body weight is kept on the oar and only returns to the seat fully at the very end. This is achieved by pushing the legs out fully and drawing the arms in fully via the hip and back extension.

10. CATCH is *under* the water. You cannot move the boat with air!

11. LENGTH: *Effective* length is better than *absolute* length. There is little point rowing very long if you are not strong enough in that position or if it interferes with timing.

12. BASICS: If you produce more *power*, more *length*, more *strokes*, more *boat run*, than your opponents you will win. You may not need all of these, however – some crews win using less rate, some using more, so it is a recipe for you to create.

13. RACING: Races are often won by the crew which slows down the least, especially in the second half!

14. TRAINING: Most training is done at steady rates so make sure you train the technique you want to race with, especially the entry and the catch.

15. RHYTHM: An accelerated stroke will generate time in the recovery which in turn creates a feeling of rhythm.

16. TENSION: Muscle tension masks feel. Try to make the stroke powerful in an elastic way not rigid.

Have a think about some of these concepts and refer back to the picture sequence – it should give a sense of HOW to make a good stroke and not just WHAT it is.

BIOMECHANICS

A quick word about biomechanics might help at this stage. We have covered some principles of learning, some technical sequences to give structure to the stroke, some concepts to guide our thinking but some basic science will also help understand why we do certain things to move the boat. Take a look at the force-time curve below. When a rower takes a stroke you can measure the production of force against the time it takes to produce it. The y-axis shows the amount of force generated, the x-axis shows the time or angle used to produce it. Each part of the stroke is labelled and you can see that at the catch you are able to generate force quickly so the graph rises steeply. Force is high (y-axis) but nothing has moved so not much time or angle has been used (x-axis). As the boat starts to move the force climbs less quickly and eventually levels out just before the oar is opposite the pin. This is the point of peak handle force. From this point the boat is moving away rapidly from the pressure in the spoon so the load (force) drops but the handle speed increases. You can push against a brick wall and generate lots of force but it won't move; only if the object moves is power being generated and, of course, that's what we want in a boat. So, to generate initial force (or load) we use the legs, hence the concept of PUSH then PULL. As the legs begin to use up their knee angle the trunk is opened to add a contribution to force and power production. The arms help to complete the process. You can see this on many rowing ergometers which have a power curve display function and a simple drill to practise is to row legs only, then legs plus trunk, then legs, trunk, arms and see how the curve develops with each segment added. The load can be applied very quickly but the key question is 'how much load?' If you load too hard you get a steep curve (lots of force) but you

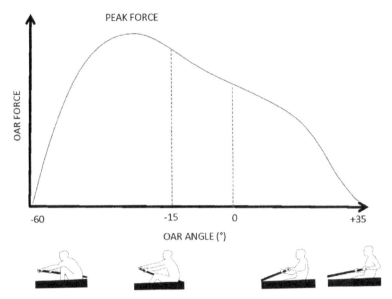

Figure 1: Force angle curve for the drive phase during sweep rowing. *Credit for silhouettes: Suz Riley*

may not get much movement from the system (hull plus crew) so the stroke will feel heavy. Too soft and you get slippage, i.e. too little force so the spoon does not anchor itself sufficiently. Try experimenting with a fast light beginning, a fast hard one, slow hard, slow light and see how it feels. Handle acceleration simply means that it finishes the stroke faster than it starts so you need to decide how much load to create in the first place and then see if you can move and accelerate it.

What changes when we race? During firm steady training the drive time might last 0.9 seconds and the recovery 2.1 seconds: that makes 3.0 seconds per stroke cycle or 20 strokes per minute. At sprint rate the drive might take 0.7 seconds and the recovery 0.8 seconds so the recovery time reduces much more than the drive time. The recovery skills and the ability to change direction at the beginning and end of the stroke therefore become increasingly important as the speed and rate go up. These skills can be practised any time and if you don't want to do high rate bursts or efforts, you can find other ways to train the system. In his book *Assault on Lake Cassitas*, the American rower Brad Lewis recounts how he and his doubles partner, Paul Enquist, spent hours 'shadow rowing' in front of a mirror (no load at all) to prepare for the 1984 Olympics for just this purpose. They won gold! There are many other drills you can do to practise and a few are listed in the final section of the chapter.

Rhythm

How does all of this feel in terms of rhythm? Rowers talk about rhythm a lot and attribute success to good rhythm and defeat to bad rhythm but often cannot really explain what it is or how to make it better. It just *is*. There are certain elements of rhythm that we can define, however. Good rhythm will have a feeling through the drive that there is strong acceleration. Acceleration in the drive gives a sense of time in the recovery; time allows you to be relaxed and being relaxed allows you to have control, particularly the skill areas of blade entry and exit. Conversely a poor rhythm is associated with a heavy feel in the drive phase, the handle and hull not wanting to respond to your effort; this leads to lack of time to complete the recovery movements so this part feels rushed. You are always playing catch up and that creates tension, which undermines motor skills. So the simple elements of good rhythm are: acceleration creating recovery, time allowing smoothness and control around the entry and finish. There are also ways out of a bad rhythm: you can add work to create more acceleration and try to improve the ratio of drive time to recovery. Crews call pushes for this reason sometimes. They realise the stroke feels a bit dead. The danger is that if you are already badly fatigued it may make matters worse. Another way is to tackle the recovery and non-work parts of the stroke. Relax, calm down, give the boat some time to glide, stop rushing the slide. Press the finish cleaner and organise the recovery movements so as to be better balanced with the travel of the hull. The trouble here is that it is counter intuitive during mid-race because the crew often feel they will lose rate and slow even more. You can try a bit of both: some crews call a 're-start' mid-race and sit up a little for two strokes so that they are in a strong position and able to generate more handle speed, then let the hull speed draw them out to length again.

The ENTRY and the FINISH are important because these are the points where you change direction and it is easy to over-run the hull or fall behind it. For the entry you should aim to be balanced and under control by half slide or sooner. That means the upper body momentum being under control and then having control on the slide. The slide is interesting – a rush forward means you use pressure on the stretcher like a footbrake to regain body control but this also puts weight against the direction of travel and slows the hull. It is better to slide freely with the hull speed but balanced on it. In other words, you can have too much as well as too little slide control. As the seat arrives smoothly the upper body is balanced on the lower body and the lower body is balanced on the hull (feet). When the wheels stop moving you are a moment from applying power and a common fault is for the hands to still be dealing with the entry when the legs have already begun to move away. In other words, you are out of time with yourself.

At the finish the most common faults are to 'pancake' the spoon (feather too early), to wash out, or to lean away to get the blade out cleanly. These errors all have the same cause: the pressure on the face of the blade is being lost and the water is catching on the back of the blade. The cure is to hold the pressure *better* to the finish and at the moment the oar goes slack in your fingers and toes then use that time window to slip it out of the water.

A useful tip for coaches regarding rhythm is that if the stroke rate looks lower than it is the rhythm is usually good. If it is the opposite it means the crew are rushing to keep rate.

SKILLS AND DRILLS

We've looked at some of the important aspects of good technique, but what about when they go wrong or when you are simply trying to master them? It always helps to break down a complicated thing into smaller easy-to-understand components, and this is where drills come in. You can tackle a bit of the stroke or a certain skill and then reintroduce it to the whole and get some genuine improvements to your stroke. Most of these drills use the progressions already mentioned, so they have basic, intermediate and skilled or advanced level of difficulty.

1. Balance
You can't do much without a steady platform under you, so an unbalanced boat is a problem. Balance comes mostly from how you sit and partly from how you carry the oar.

DRILL 1 – Finish dips: boat stationary; sit at back stops, dipping the blades in and out of the water. Once you are happy that the balance stays put then add an arms-away movement. Once you can do both of these add the body lean and then start to put in some slide until you can get all the way to front stops balanced.

DRILL 2 – Entry dips: similar to above sitting at front stops and dipping. This establishes stability in the trunk and shoulders plus good hand control. Add difficulty by sliding in from half slide or holding a pause with the blades out of the water at front stops.

DRILL 3 – Pauses: boat moving, choose different parts of the recovery for a pause. Either do single strokes repeatedly or insert one pause every 3–5 strokes. Start with pauses at the finish or hands away and progress to pauses at various slide lengths all the way to front stops.

DRILL 4 – Inside/outside hand changes: take one hand off during the recovery and see if you can still 'centre' yourself even though the weight in the handle will feel different to normal. Usually the danger zones for balance are just after the hands-away when you rock over your hips as this shifts a lot of body mass or when you arrive over the front because your handle(s) are out towards the side of the hull and your upper body weight is furthest away from the centre line of the hull.

2. Sequences

DRILL 1 – Recovery pauses: pauses work for sequences as well as for balance. Check your posture and organisation of movements in each position through the recovery.

DRILL 2 – Back end build-up: the classic sequence starts with arms-only rowing, then with trunk, then progresses by adding the slide.

DRILL 3 – Front end build-up: start rowing from the catch with legs only, then legs plus trunk, then plus half arms, then the full stroke.

DRILL 4 – Double recovery ('Cutting the cake'): insert an arms only 'air stroke' after each normal finish. Variations include doing this with trunk rock over and any amount of slide length up to full. Unloaded movements (i.e. air strokes) allow you to choose your movement more than loaded ones but also test your control well.

3. Entry

A good entry needs the rower to be balanced, under control, well positioned and well timed.

DRILL 1 – Entry dips: sit at front stops and dip the blade repeatedly. This allows you to sit still without the upper body lunging or going off balance and keeps the handle control in the hands. You can feel the weight of the oar leave the hands and find the buoyancy point.

DRILL 2 – Roll-up: from back stops simply go through the whole recovery, ending at front stops and the blade covered. Time the blade entry to your wheels, i.e. arrive at front stops and in the water together. The recovery ends when the blade is covered, not when you stop sliding.

DRILL 3 – Roll-up: get the boat moving with one or two strokes then pause at back stops and then roll-up to the entry. Because the hull is moving forwards the timing and speed of the entry need to be accurate.

DRILL 4 – Speed roll-ups: higher rate adds difficulty because the spoon and handle have much more momentum. This will challenge your upper body control at front stops.

4. Finishes

In rowing we deliberately create momentum in our bodies to the finish in order to accelerate the boat. At the end of the stroke this momentum needs to be controlled so you can change direction again and go back for another stroke.

DRILL 1 – Dips: sit at back-stops with good body posture and dip the handle up and down to get a feel for the handle weight and height. This helps define where the finish actually is.

DRILL 2 – Square blade rowing: some of the crew can balance the boat or, if you can cope with balance, do it with the whole crew. This drill encourages a clean finish and good blade skills.

DRILL 3 – Short arms: rowing with just half the arm draw. This keeps the puddle tight and avoids pressure drifting off towards the end of the stroke. Produces a clean end point to the pressure and avoids collapsing in the hips, elbows, or pancaking (premature feathering). Gradually increase the arm draw until full again but keeping contact with your pressure.

DRILL 4 – Square blades, feet out: this drill forces you to 'recover off your blade pressure'. In other words, you feel contact with the face of the spoon right to the end of the stroke and it teaches you not to tip over the rear of the seat. Be careful not to pull shoulders in over the handle.

5. Connection and muscle chain

Creating a good connection to the blade is vital if you are going to move the boat well. You need to fix the spoon to the water and also attach your mass to it. Boat, rower and blade all connected.

DRILL 1 – Reversals: back the boat down from half slide to front stops keeping the blade covered. As you reach front stops the pressure in the spoon will change from the back of it to the face and you will feel the spoon 'fill up' with pressure. Try to feel which muscles you engage to brace against this resistance. Go back and forth in each direction feeling the oar engage with pressure and release.

DRILL 2 – Suspensions: roll up to the water and 'stand' on the spoon where you enter the water. Hang off your arms. Hips should be suspended 2cm off the seat and still be at front stops.

DRILL 3 – Nudges: like a stand up but instead of passively hanging off the handle you actively make a horizontal connection to the handle when you press your feet, so instead of being lifted off the seat, with the boat stationary, you nudge the hull forwards a few centimetres. It should make you feel the spoon is locked and your muscle chain is engaged from feet through your legs, back, arms, all the way to the handle.

DRILL 4 – Speed nudges: try rowing full length at a steady rate and pick one stroke to just do a nudge stroke. This is a challenge to see if you can really time and react to your entry, making a connection early in the stroke.

6. Acceleration and power

The drive phase needs to build hull speed. As long as you are well connected the increase in handle speed will reflect the increase in hull speed, but BEWARE: a fast moving handle at the catch or fast moving legs CAN mean you have simply failed to make a connection and are slipping, so fast handle/legs are only good if the rower is connected to the water.

DRILL 1 – Light catch, firm finish: acceleration is merely the difference between the handle speed at the beginning and the end of the stroke. If you begin with low handle speed you will feel acceleration.

DRILL 2 – Low rate firm (also known as 'Power strokes'): sometimes done with added resistance of a bungee around the hull or tow a rope, bottle, towel. Good for practicing the loading phase from catch to mid-stroke and for bracing with the trunk. Add difficulty by doing rate bursts with a bungee or even bungee starts.

DRILL 3 – Legs only: the legs are the base source of rhythm and hull speed. Rowing legs only at different rates lets you feel the behaviour and response of the hull during the first 30 degrees of oar arc.

DRILL 4 – Legs plus trunk: this just uses the earlier sequence drill but for building up the power chain. Remember if the trunk joins in too soon it will actually slow down the leg drive.

DRILL 5 – Quarter slide rate lifts: the short slide means the load on the oar is low so the movement will be fast. Use little slide but all the trunk and arms. Try to keep the bladework clean and tidy, avoiding swiping at the entry and tearing at the finish.

7. Speed drills

Any of the previous drills can be done with rate increases to make them more challenging and this helps develop the motor skills to cope with high hull speeds. But you can also do specific speed sessions.

DRILL 1 – Racing starts: starts are not just for getting off the blocks quickly. They also work for speed training per se. You don't have much time to think about it, you just do it. They are powerful, dynamic and the best ones are also relaxed and balanced.

DRILL 2 – Over rate bursts: at quarter slide you can rate over 60spm, and at full slide crews can touch 50spm. This is well above your actual race rate so when you come back to, say, 35spm your body feels well able to cope with the time available for the entry/catch, foot speed, finish etc.

Indeed, almost all of the headings under the section Mechanics vs. feel and Concepts of techniques can be worked on with drills. Could you come up with a drill for breathing control for instance? Or blade depths? There are hundreds of drills and variations and they fit in well with training. The first part of a session is for warming-up so drills for balance, control and sequencing fit well. This gets the basic structure of the stroke in place. As you enter the work phase of the session you can do drills, which don't interrupt the physical work, such as acceleration and power development drills or feet out rowing. Even turning the boat is an opportunity for someone to row square blades and improve their handling skills. The key thing is to do them for a purpose – remember the points at the beginning about how we learn and seeing benefits in what we do. The people who become technically excellent do so because they are explorers and reach their own inner understanding of how a boat moves well.

ADVANCED ROWING

You might expect the very fastest Olympic rowers to display *perfect* technique because they have had years to make it right but not all of them would be technical role models – they have merely developed the most *effective* technique for them. The single scull event sees the most individual techniques whereas the larger crew boats need high levels of synchronisation. The crews we use as examples for educating good technique in others have some admirable qualities, of course and there is a selection of these listed below.

I have followed these principles successfully with Cambridge Boat Race crews, World and Olympic rowers, whether heavyweight or lightweight, male or female.

They make it look easy – this is because they are efficient movers and do not waste energy. They work when they need to and relax when they can. We don't see their bodies locking up with tension, nor the boat behaving erratically so the stroke rate often looks lower than it actually is.

Time – they appear to have more time available than others because they have finely tuned motor skills. For instance, they can allow the hull to run under their feet right up to the last centimetre of the recovery because they have better balance, control and hand skills with the oar. They can filter out imperfections before they become mistakes.

Timing – they understand that the hull motion and speed wave itself creates a sense of timing so at the entry, for instance, the hull draws them forwards to a poised apex on the stretcher and the momentum of the blade helps them into the water. The bow seat of an 8+ or 4x is fantastic for this feeling.

Timing of force – they are the best at producing the right pressure at the right point in the stroke, degree by degree as they work through the stroke arc. Too much pressure too early and the system locks up; too little and the boat goes dead.

Consistency – they deliver stroke after stroke, race after race with great reliability. Their technique does not break down under extreme pressure because they have practised over thousands of kilometres to engrain it in all conditions at all stroke rates.

Body awareness – their muscle chain from feet through legs, hips, trunk shoulders, arms is well connected and without weak links so you don't see an arm wrench, for instance, to make up for a lack of connection somewhere else. This is one reason why they do weight training and trunk strength work so their bodies will physically support their technique.

Rhythm – the overall effect of the points above is that they produce the best rhythm. They are able to create lots of acceleration and momentum forwards, which gives fantastic recovery time (ratio) and the ability to get their momentum under control again before arriving to take the next stroke.

Efficiency – remember that technique is the gearbox. The advanced crews are able to get the most out of their physiology because every bit of power and fitness they have is put to moving the boat with minimal loss through inefficiency.

SUMMARY

Technique for rowing is like a recipe of ingredients and you can combine them in multiple ways to make a fast crew. Hopefully this chapter has given you some ideas about ways we learn, how important mindset is, the interplay of the mechanics and feel, the structure of a typical stroke and some drills and concepts to explore for yourself. Remember, there has never been a perfect rowing stroke but that shouldn't stop us trying.

Training Intensity for Rowing Dr Charles Simpson
and Professor Steve Seiler

Dr Charles (Charlie) Simpson is a Senior Lecturer in Sport and Exercise Science at Oxford Brookes University in the UK. He is a former recipient of British Rowing's Coach of the Year award and provides sport science consultancy to junior and senior rowing clubs in the UK. He is particularly interested in helping coaches, athletes and support staff make better use of sport science research.

Professor Steve Seiler is Vice Rector for Research and Innovation at the University of Agder Kristiansand, Norway. He is also a Senior Research Consultant for the Norwegian Olympic Federation and a member of the Executive Board of Directors at the European College of Sport Science. He is passionate about exercise physiology and training adaptations, particularly to endurance training.

When elite rowers are asked to explain what is necessary to reach the highest levels of competitive rowing, they often point to the importance of completing 'lots of hard training'. Clearly, success in international rowing requires substantial investment of time, effort and motivation in training, but what do they mean when they say 'hard training'? Perhaps it means making significant personal and professional sacrifice to make time for rowing training; that can be hard. Perhaps it has something to do with waking up early and spending several sessions each day performing hours of rowing in cold, wet and windy weather; early starts, frequent sessions and rowing in horrible weather certainly make training hard. Hard training can also refer to the intensity of effort needed to make ever-smaller improvements in stroke technique. Of course, all of these features of preparation are likely to be in the minds of elite rowers when they have to give simple answers to a complicated question. In such situations, the potential for misunderstanding and misinterpretation is high.

It is impossible to know exactly how many aspiring rowers and coaches may have misinterpreted what the phrase 'lots of hard training' really means to an elite athlete. However, it is also clear that many developing rowers include excessive amounts of intensity in their training, perhaps influenced by mistakenly assuming that the hard training referred to by champion rowers means training at maximal and near maximal aerobic or anaerobic power. In fact, an important feature of rowing training programmes at the elite level is actually the very limited use of sessions that push the limits of a rower's aerobic or anaerobic power. Nevertheless, many rowers and coaches are understandably guided by their intuition about how to balance the volume and intensity of training sessions. Yet, there has been great progress in the last 20 years about how to optimise training intensity to stimulate aerobic and anaerobic adaptations. This progress is underpinned by direct observations about how elite rowers and other endurance athletes actually train in addition to well-controlled scientific experiments that compare training approaches. This chapter draws on both sources of information in order to outline what constitutes an effective distribution of exercise intensity during training for rowing competition. Ultimately, training gains are likely to be best when there is careful and restrained use of moderate and high intensity rowing as part of an annual training approach that prioritises high volumes of low intensity training.

UNDERSTANDING THE USE OF TRAINING INTENSITY ZONES

Fundamentally, training gains are the product of the volume and intensity of each specific session. Training volume can be quantified in terms of kilometres or hours of rowing. However, quantifying training intensity is much harder and there are currently many proxies for exercise intensity used by rowers including stroke rate, 500m split time, heart rate, blood lactate, ratings of perceived exertion and most recently stroke power, measured using force transducers embedded in oars and gates. Each measure can be usefully applied to create intensity bands or zones for rowers.

Clearly, there are various concerns and considerations when choosing a marker for training intensity, however, for the purpose of this chapter we will use blood lactate to define intensity zones. This approach is consistent with the training practices of top international rowers (as presented in previous sections of this book). It is also consistent with wider practices in endurance training and reflects the way that scientists develop research studies to examine the effectiveness of aerobic training programmes. In practical terms, we acknowledge that the use of heart rate and blood lactate to categorise training zones necessitates the use of specialist technology. However, the availability of this equipment is now widespread and relatively affordable. Coaches and athletes also have to consider how they will monitor adherence to a prescribed training programme, something that is especially challenging when working with large teams. We are keenly aware that monitoring requires time and effort. But new tools, especially smartphones and smartwatches, can help simplify monitoring by recording and sharing data with software applications that automate the process of categorising training data into discrete training zones. This gives a good picture of training volume and intensity patterns in real time and across phases of training. Our experience suggests that monitoring a few variables accurately and consistently can really help improve athlete-coach communication, and ultimately, team performance.

The five intensity zone model appears to be the most popular for rowing. There is no international consensus about the exact target range for each zone. The differences that do exist between schemes are likely to be smaller than the accuracy of most heart rate and lactate measurements once day-to-day variability and sampling error are considered. Table 1 presents a representative five-zone model used by rowers in various countries.

Table 1: Example of a five-zone intensity classification system used in rowing

	% Maximum Heart Rate	Blood lactate (mmol/L)
Utilisation 2 (Zone 1)	55 to 70	<1.5
Utilisation 1 (Zone 2)	70 to 80	1.5 to 2.5
Anaerobic Threshold (Zone 3)	80 to 85	2.5 to 4.0
Transportation (Zone 4)	85 to 95	4.0 to 6.0
Anaerobic (Zone 5)	95 to 100	>6.0

Many sport scientists prefer to use a three-zone intensity model, which often requires more extensive physiological testing that include monitoring the expired air composition of athletes during step tests to determine ventilatory thresholds. The specific details of the three-zone model and the physiological testing procedures underpinning it are largely unimportant for the readers of this chapter, but many sport scientists have chosen to use only three physiological distinguishable zones to more easily document training programmes in published investigations. To help prepare readers to understand this content, we offer the following brief explanation of the three-zone model and how it relates to the more familiar five-zone approach. Broadly, the delineation between the zones occurs at blood lactate levels near to the 2 and 4mmol/L values (see Figure 1). As such, we can compress a typical five-zone model into a three-zone model by combining zones 1 and 2 (to make Zone 1) and combining zones 4 and 5 (to make Zone 3).

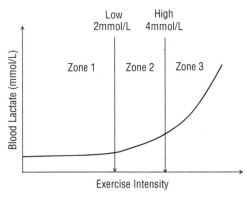

Figure 1: A three intensity zone model using blood lactate divisions at 2 and 4mmol/L

Whether exercise intensities are prescribed in three or five zones, there are limitations when using this type of generalised intensity scale. For example, it does not account for the expected variation in the blood lactate to heart rate relationship, either for an individual or for the type of exercise (e.g. ergometer or on-water rowing). Also, the specific physiological effects of training do not neatly fit into arbitrary zones and there is considerable overlap of training effects across multiple zones. Nevertheless, these possible sources of error and problems of specifying boundaries for training benefits are outweighed by the enhanced communication that is made possible between coaches and rowers when a common intensity scheme is used, especially when real-time heart rate monitoring is used in daily training. If rowers and coaches do not have a common framework for agreeing what each intensity zone means and should feel like in training, it will be very hard to match training prescription to training practice. Thus, the specific number of intensity zones and their respective target ranges for heart rate and blood lactate are far less important than having a shared understanding between coach and athlete as to what training intensity means.

DEFINING EXERCISE INTENSITY TERMINOLOGY

We will use the terms 'low intensity training', 'threshold training' and 'high intensity training' throughout the chapter. These intensities are set according to the blood lactate levels in Table 2.

Table 2: Training intensity terminology

- Low intensity training: exercise performed at a stable blood lactate concentration of <2.0 mmol/L.
- Threshold training: exercise performed at a blood lactate concentration of between 2.0 and 4.0 mmol/L.
- High intensity training: exercise performed at a blood lactate concentration of >4 mmol/L.

Many readers are likely to be familiar with the use of blood lactate measurements, especially those who perform routine blood sampling using handheld devices such as the Lactate Pro or Lactate Scout. Essentially, blood lactate concentration is a biochemical indicator that provides useful insight about rate of muscle glycogen use by working muscles. During very light rowing, muscle glycogen stores are hardly used. When rowers increase their paddling speed towards the low intensity zone, muscle glycogen starts to make a meaningful contribution to the body's fuel requirements and so the reservoir of carbohydrate in the rowing muscles starts to decrease, albeit rather slowly.

Most of the muscle glycogen used to fuel low intensity rowing will be converted to water and carbon dioxide, however, a small amount is converted to lactate and released from the muscle into the circulating blood where lactate analysers can measure the concentrations (typically between 1 and 2mmol/L). This is a very efficient way to use muscle glycogen and it will take many hours of low intensity exercise before a rower fatigues due to exhaustion of glycogen stores. However, when the rower exercises at threshold intensity, the rate of muscle glycogen use accelerates and blood lactate concentrations increase to values between 2 and 4mmol/L. Now if the rower was to exercise at the lower end of this zone, then he or she could take 60 to 90 minutes before becoming fatigued and the likely cause of this fatigue would be depletion of muscle glycogen stores. However, if the rower was to exercise at the upper end of the threshold training zone, then fatigue would occur much sooner, perhaps within 45 to 60 minutes or so. Now the cause of fatigue during upper end threshold intensity training, assuming the rower is well fed, is closely related to increases in muscle acidity and metabolites that interfere with the energy production pathways. Threshold training also causes a sustained increase in circulating hormones, especially the catecholamines epinephrine and nor-epinephrine. There is good evidence to show that prolonged increases in catecholamine levels lead to staleness and overtraining symptoms. Of course, high intensity training (>4mmol/L) also substantially increases muscle acidity, accelerates muscle glycogen use and increases circulating catecholamine levels, but even well-trained athletes can only tolerate high intensity training for short periods before rest is required, so the risk of overtraining through excessive use of high intensity is limited. In comparison, elite rowers are very capable of accumulating large amounts of training time in the threshold intensity zone, substantially increasing their risk of overtraining.

Despite the growing popularity of blood lactate testing, it is important to note that its usefulness depends on the training status of a rower. Novice rowers (i.e. untrained) often exceed the 2mmol/L blood lactate boundary for low intensity training at very low workloads, making the prescription of training intensity using this approach a frustrating and costly effort. However, once a rower has achieved a reasonable basic endurance training volume, blood lactate monitoring is a useful and popular approach that is widely used to guide training prescription and monitor session compliance. The use of blood lactate measurements at fixed work rates (watts) also provide a robust indicator of an athlete's endurance training status, independent of the effects of motivation and conscious control. Blood lactate measurements can also be used to limit the risk of overtraining by informing coaches about the type of metabolic stress experienced when training at certain intensities.

HOW DO ADVANCED ROWERS TRAIN?

There are plenty of training programmes available to help develop rowing performance. Indeed, many national teams and governing bodies, including FISA, publish yearlong training schedules for advanced rowers. A key feature found in the majority of these plans is the dominance of low intensity training throughout the training year. Presently, elite rowers who compete at World or Olympic Championships can expect to spend between 75 and 95 per cent of their annual (rowing specific) training time performing low intensity rowing (i.e. at blood lactate concentrations below 2mmol/L). What remains less clear, however, is whether advanced rowers really do achieve the high proportion of low intensity training that is commonly prescribed in training programmes. It is quite possible that highly motivated rowers allow their enthusiasm and desire for rapid progress to escalate the actual training intensity to the point that a planned low intensity session is actually performed as threshold or even high intensity training. This problem can get out of hand in highly competitive team environments where there are continuous selection pressures for seats and where objective measures of relative training intensity (e.g. heart rate monitoring) are not used. It is perhaps reasonable to speculate that the risk of unplanned training intensity escalation may be greatest in groups of development athletes (e.g. junior and under-23 age group rowers), especially where athletes have less experience and understanding of the effects of overtraining. Moreover, young athletes will often avoid reporting difficulties to their coach about absorbing a training dose because they are afraid such honesty may cost them a seat in a boat. Before considering the problems of repeated encroachments into the threshold and high intensity training domains, we will begin by describing the available published research that documents the actual distribution of training intensity used by advanced national and international level rowers.

One of the first attempts to quantify the annual training intensity distribution of elite rowers was made by Ulrich Hartmann and colleagues in the former West German republic (1990). They obtained blood lactate and heart-rate measurements of 40 international oarsmen during all phases of training between 1985 and 1988. These authors estimated that low intensity rowing accounted for approximately 90 per cent of specific training in the preparation period (autumn, winter and spring), which decreased to approximately 75 per cent in the summer competitive period. They also highlighted that the observed practices of these elite rowers conflicted with the prevailing training advice of the period. At that time, there was a widespread belief among coaches and scientists that endurance training was most effective when performed at threshold intensities (i.e. between 2 and 4mmol/L). However, in the sample of West German rowers, threshold intensity training accounted for less than 10 per cent of specific training in the preparation period and approximately 20 per cent of training during the competitive period.

The West German training study described above is also noteworthy because it is one of the earliest examples of where heart rate monitors were successfully used to capture the actual stress of rowing training in a large group of athletes. Of course, the ability to systematically record and review heart rate changes during training is now taken for granted. Yet, the use of heart rate monitors to help gauge and control training intensity really only become popular with rowers in the 1990s. It is worth considering the possible effects of this significant development on our understanding of effective training practice. This technology made it possible to systematically record the physiological stress of daily rowing training, as measured in terms of per cent of maximum heart rate for each rower (i.e. cardiovascular stress). Now it was possible for coaches and rowers to describe their training in terms of the *internal* physiological stresses, rather than *external* measures such as stroke rate and boat speed. The results of the West German training monitoring study were published in the FISA *Coach* magazine in 1990 and thus, the information was widely available to rowers throughout the world. While most contemporary rowers now appreciate that effective training for rowing requires large volumes of low intensity rowing, this was not always the case. It can be argued that the training practices of today's rowers owe much to the introduction of heart rate technology, as well as the subsequent widespread dissemination of the objective training approaches of top rowers. Both are important factors that have contributed to the evolution of rowing training across recent decades.

The advances in understanding about how to optimise rowing training are perhaps best captured in a study of elite Norwegian rowers since 1970. Fiskerstrand and Seiler (2004) performed a retrospective analysis of the training practices of Norwegian medal winners at World or Olympic Championships between the 1970s and the 1990s. They used questionnaires, training diaries and physiological test data from 27 elite rowers to estimate how the training approaches in Norway evolved across these three decades. Importantly, elite Norwegian rowers in the 1990s were of similar height and weight to the rowers in 1970s, yet they had VO$_2$max values that were 12 per cent higher and ergometer rowing performances that were 10 per cent better. The notable changes in training practices over this period included the following (most of which occurred in the 1970s and 1980s):

- Total training volume increased by around 20 per cent (from approximately 900 hours per year in 1970s to approximately 1100 hours per year in 1990s).
- Low intensity rowing increased from approximately 38 hours per month (1970s) to approximately 60 hours per month (1990s).
- High intensity rowing decreased from approximately 40 hours per month (1970s) to approximately 28 hours per month (1990s).
- The low–high intensity ratio of training time shifted from approximately 50:50 (1970s) to approximately 75:25 (1990s).

The important conclusion from this study was that elite Norwegian rowers developed training approaches that increased annual training volumes, while simultaneously increasing the relative amount of low intensity training and reducing the relative amount of high intensity training.

Juergen Steinacker and colleagues in Germany also reviewed the training approaches of elite German, Dutch, Danish and Norwegian rowers in the last three decades of the 20th century (Steinacker et al., 1998). Similar to the results of Fiskerstrand and Seiler, the absolute volume of training time dedicated to low intensity rowing had increased towards 90 per cent, with the remaining time emphasising high intensity rowing. This finding is also consistent with a reduction in the amount of training time performed in the threshold training zone. Accordingly, the training intensity distribution of elite rowers can be described as having a 'polarised' distribution where most of the training is performed towards either the low or high intensity areas while minimising the amount of threshold training (training in the middle zone; see Figure 2 Polarised training model). Furthermore, there was an increase in total training time of approximately 20 per cent, mostly as cross-training activity. They reasoned that

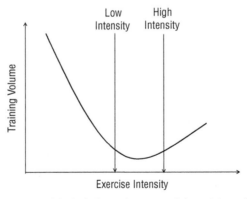

Figure 2: Polarised Training Model which shows that most of the training volume is performed at low intensity with a small amount of high intensity. Very little training volume is performed at threshold intensity. Thus, a polarised training distribution is one where training volumes are skewed towards low and high intensity 'poles'.

these changes enhanced training loads and reduced the risk of overtraining due to biochemical and hormonal imbalance while also ensuring that dietary energy intake, particularly carbohydrate, would be sufficient to support training demands.

Sport science research owes a great debt, on many fronts, to the openness and willingness of researchers connected with the Australian Institute of Sport to share the training and performance data of elite Australian rowers. Indeed, perhaps the best data currently available on the training intensity profiles of elite rowers is contained in a research report published in the *International Journal of Sports Performance and Physiology* by Jacqueline Tran and colleagues (2015). These researchers monitored the training practices of elite Australian rowers, including 14 members of the heavyweight men's rowing team, many of whom competed at the London 2012 Olympic regatta. Data collection began in October with ergometer based physiological step tests to establish training zones based on heart rate and lactate responses. Thereafter, each athlete recorded heart rate and GPS logs at all training sessions for the next 25 weeks using wristwatches before travelling to Europe for the start of the international regatta season. The step tests were repeated at the middle and end of the 25-week monitoring period and the results of all physiological tests enabled the researchers to accurately quantify how much training time was actually spent in each intensity zone. So what did this project reveal about the intensity distribution of elite Australian rowers?

The data showed that the total distance rowed each week (on-water and ergometer) was approximately 140km per week (October to December) and 125km per week (January to March), but when changes in intensity and training mode was included, there was a modest increase in the rowing specific training load across the 25 weeks. The authors calculated the amount of low, threshold and high intensity training using the same categorisation scheme that we outlined earlier in this chapter and identified the following:

- Rowing at low intensity was performed for 82 to 83 per cent of training time.
- Rowing at threshold intensity was performed for 15 to 16 per cent of training time.
- Rowing at high intensity was performed for 1 to 4 per cent of training time.

Tran and colleagues noted that although this intensity distribution did not follow the polarised pattern that is often described in studies of elite endurance athletes, they did suggest that further performance gains might be possible by reducing the amount of threshold training time and redistributing this load into the low and high intensity zones.

Similar to the previous survey of Australian rowers, Dan Plews and colleagues (2014) reported the training intensity distribution of nine elite male and female New Zealand rowers (heavyweight) during 26 weeks of training before the 2012 Olympic regatta. Training data was recorded using heart rate logs and categorised according to time spent in low, threshold and high intensity zones based on blood lactate profiles obtained from physiological step test that was performed at the start of the monitoring period. Average weekly aerobic training time was approximately 18 hours and we are told that training prescription was based on stroke rate and not heart rate per se. The distribution by intensity category was as follows:

- Rowing at low intensity was performed for approximately 77 per cent of training time.
- Rowing at threshold intensity was performed for approximately 17 per cent of training time.
- Rowing at high intensity was performed for approximately 6 per cent of training time.

Clearly, the training intensity distribution of the elite New Zealand rowers is very similar in proportion to that reported for the Australian rowers during the same training period. However, neither distribution can be defined as 'polarised' per se. However, Plews and colleagues noted that the categorisation of training time based on heart rate logs is likely to result in an overestimate of the proportion of time spent in the threshold zone and an underestimate of time spent in the high intensity zone due to heart rate lag. For example, consider that during a high intensity 1000m interval lasting 180 seconds, it may take perhaps between 30 and 60 seconds for heart rate to increase through the threshold zone into the high intensity zone. This reflects an inherent limitation to the approach of categorising training intensity using the length of time in a specified heart rate zone. Specifically, external power output, as measured at the handle, can be rapidly increased into the high intensity zone, but heart rate may take up to 60 seconds or more to achieve a value that represents the high intensity zone. In time, we think this issue may be solved by developing new tools for monitoring training loads in ways that best reflect the underlying signals

Elite rowers in New Zealand spend most of their rowing time in the low-intensity zone (i.e. <2mmol/L blood lactate). *Credit: Steve McArthur*

within the body that are responsible for creating physiological training adaptations. Ultimately, such tools are likely to incorporate a combination of the elements that athletes currently record in training diaries including:

1. External work achieved (e.g. distance rowed and average power sustained).
2. Internal physiological effects of a session (e.g. per cent of maximum heart rate)
3. The main goal of a training session (e.g. a low, threshold or high intensity session plus a self-reported variable that indicates the overall difficulty of a session such as a 1 to 10 scale).

In summary, there are now various investigations that have carefully documented the actual training practices of elite rowers during training seasons. These reports provide excellent insight into the quantity of rowing training needed to compete at the highest international levels. Elite rowers are likely to accomplish 120–200km per week of rowing specific training (combined ergometer and water training), in addition to significant amounts of non-specific training (alternative aerobic exercise such as cycling and cross-country skiing as well as strength training). The reports have also indicated the proportions of rowing specific training time that are performed at low, threshold and high intensities based on the individual lactate profiles of elite rowers. The results confirmed that low intensity rowing is the dominant feature of an elite rower's training and typically accounts for between 75 to 95 per cent of rowing specific training time. When the distribution of training intensity across all three intensity zones is considered, the patterns that emerge often, but not always, show a polarised distribution whereby training time tends towards either the low or high intensity zone (poles), while restricting the amount of threshold 'in the middle' training time.

The tendency to use polarised training programmes in rowing along with large training volumes is consistent with other studies of elite endurance athletes who participate in cross-country skiing, running and cycling. Still, there remains uncertainty about what represents the optimal distribution of training intensity for moderate and high training volumes. Certainly, high training volumes are only possible when low intensity training is dominant. However, the available data from the training records of elite rowers does not specify how best to distribute the remaining proportion of training time to optimise rowing performance (i.e. the approximately 25 per cent of training time performed in the threshold and high intensity zones). The final section of this chapter will review this issue and consider the potential to optimise training adaptions and competition performance through the use of a polarised training distribution.

THE EFFECTIVENESS OF POLARISED TRAINING APPROACHES FOR ROWING

Consider the following thought experiment. Imagine that a group of 100 advanced male rowers have volunteered as subjects for a training study at the beginning of a training year. We next run a series of tests, including rowing performance tests such as 2000m ergometer and on-water single sculling trials as well as a range of standard fitness tests (e.g. lactate threshold, VO_2max, mechanical efficiency). Then, the rowers are matched into pairs based on their similarity to one another in all possible measures (such as rowing experience, height, muscle mass, rowing performance and fitness tests). We randomly allocate one rower from each pair into a 'polarised training group' and the other rower into a non-polarised 'pyramid' group (where the base of the pyramid consists of low intensity, the middle is threshold intensity and the top is high intensity).

All rowers then complete training programmes that average 160km per week of rowing. Each week, several training sessions are adjusted so that the rowers accumulate different amounts of threshold and high intensity rowing. For example, during a single session in the competitive period, the polarised group perform 4 x 2000m intervals at best pace (which coincides with the high intensity zone), whereas the pyramid group perform 4 x 4000m intervals at best pace (which coincides with the threshold intensity zone). Importantly, the rowers in both groups perform these sessions to the best of their ability and with good pacing strategies. The difference in pace between a best effort 2000m and 4000m interval is relatively small, but they result in blood lactate levels of around 3 to 4mmol/L (4 x 4000m session) to around 6 to 8mmol/L (4 x 2000m session), especially when brief rest intervals are used. By the end of the session, both groups will have given equivalent effort, but the metabolic and hormonal responses will differ according to whether the session was performed in the threshold or high intensity zone. The remainder of the week's sessions are adjusted until the proportions (per cent) of training time in the low-threshold-high zones are 79-7-22 (polarised) and 79-14-7 (pyramid). All training data is carefully logged and athletes are regularly assessed for blood lactate during training and laboratory step tests to ensure adherence to the training prescription and to help standardise the training loads between groups as best possible.

At the end of the season, both groups have improved their rowing performance. However, the pyramid group improved their 2000m time by 3 per cent (i.e. 7:20 to 7:07) whereas the polarised group improved their 2000m time by 5 per cent (i.e. 7:20 to 6:58). These idealised 2000m performance results would provide a convincing case for the benefits of a polarised training intensity distribution and the various fitness results and training records could be scrutinised to help explain why this distribution works best.

These hypothetical results represent a best guess about what might happen were such a study ever conducted with rowers. The predictions are based on results from a growing number of studies where recreational or well-trained endurance athletes were allocated to set training groups based on different approaches to training intensity distribution. The athletes in these studies were typically runners, cyclists or triathletes. However, there are several notable studies that compared training responses in rowers when training intensity was manipulated in some way. These studies are described next. Thereafter, we will highlight the results of several well designed experiments that show the effects of intensity manipulations in the training of endurance athletes (non-rowers).

EXPERIMENTS THAT SHOW THE EFFECTS OF DIFFERENT TRAINING INTENSITY INTERVENTIONS IN ROWING

Steve Ingham and colleagues (2008) at Loughborough University in the UK, recruited 18 well-trained male rowers (club and university level) to participate in a study that compared training intensity distribution at the start of a rowing season using two different approaches. The rowers were matched into equal pairs according to baseline fitness from rowing ergometer and laboratory tests. Thereafter, the paired rowers were randomly separated into one of two possible training groups:

- Low intensity group: 98 per cent of recorded training time was low intensity and 2 per cent was performed at high intensity.
- Mixed intensity group: 72 per cent of recorded training time was low intensity and 28 per cent was performed at high intensity (mostly between 84 and 93 per cent VO_2max which is likely to cause blood lactate levels of between 4 and 6mmol/L). The high intensity sessions were performed on three days each week as interval sessions.

The 12-week training programme was prescribed in advance and the planned intensity for each session was provided to each rower using intensity zones mapped to ergometer power, 500m split and heart rate (for use during on-water sessions). Rowers submitted training diaries at the end of the study to enable the researchers to check the volume and relative intensity distribution. It is important to note that the researchers had to estimate the proportions of low and high intensity that each rower achieved from written records rather than electronic records of boat speed or heart rate. This is likely to have limited the accuracy of categorising the training into individual zones. Nevertheless, we are told that the volume of rowing achieved at the end of the 12 weeks was averaged 1140km of rowing (approximately 95 km/week) in both groups.

Most rowers achieved personal best performances on the 2000m ergometer test at the end of the training period, but the researchers failed to find any statistically significant differences between the improved performances of the low and mixed intensity groups. Training improved average 2000m performance by approximately 2.0 per cent in the low intensity group (397 to 389sec) and by approximately 1.4 per cent in the mixed intensity group (401 to 395sec). The change in ergometer performance was closely associated with the peak power produced during the VO_2max testing, which increased by approximately 11 per cent in both groups. However, lactate threshold (expressed as power at 4mmol/L blood lactate) increased more in the low intensity group (approximately 14 per cent) versus the mixed intensity group (approximately 5 per cent). Overall, Ingham and colleagues found no difference in ergometer performance gain during 12 weeks of rowing, irrespective of whether rowing training was performed almost entirely at low intensity or with the inclusion of a significant proportion of high intensity interval training. The most notable difference was the better improvement in lactate threshold in the low intensity training group. The results of this study are consistent with the belief that maximal aerobic power (a central adaptation) is a primary determinant of rowing performance, while lactate threshold gains (a peripheral adaptation) may not immediately translate into improved rowing performance. However, lactate threshold is still an important measure for rowing since it reflects the aerobic capacity of the trained muscles. Also, rowers who have a high lactate threshold are better able to mobilise fat stores to support the energy demands of training (in preference to mobilising carbohydrate stores). This likely makes athletes with high lactate threshold better able to cope with high volume training. This study was conducted at the start of a training year and confirms the benefits of initiating a new training season with a block of extensive low intensity rowing. The favourable peripheral adaptations from low intensity training may help support developing rowers transition from the moderate volumes in this study (approximately 95km/week) towards the high volumes of elite rowers (120 to 200km/week).

Both training groups in this study used polarised intensity distributions, but at relative extremes. The low intensity group (with 98 per cent low intensity and 2 per cent high intensity training) had a polarised approach that was extremely skewed to the low intensity 'pole', while the mixed group (with 72 per cent low intensity and 28 per cent high intensity training), had a relatively modest skew towards the high intensity pole, in comparison to observed distributions in elite rowers. Based on current understanding about how to maximise the benefits of polarised training, which tends towards 80 per cent of training being low intensity, neither training group provided an optimal test of polarised training. Indeed, the proportion of low intensity training in each group was 18 per cent above the 80 per cent target (low intensity group) or 8 per cent below the 80 per cent target (mixed intensity group). This may partly explain the failure to find any statistical differences in ergometer performance or peak power at VO_2max between the groups. If this study had included a third training group with polarised distribution where low intensity training accounted for 80 per cent of training time, then perhaps more substantial gains in performance would have been observed.

Several other small-scale research studies have also compared short-term training responses in moderate and well-trained rowers when the training intensity distribution is made more polarised by the addition of interval training. For example, Matthew Driller and colleagues (2009) at the Tasmanian Institute of Sport compared training responses during 2 x 4-week training periods that included two sessions per week on a rowing ergometer of either:

- High intensity training (8 x 2.5min intervals) at a pace equivalent to blood lactate of 10mmol/L.
- Continuous rowing training at a pace equivalent to blood lactate of 2 to 3mmol/L (i.e. threshold intensity).

Subjects were 10 well-trained male and female lightweight rowers and the study appears to have been completed during the competitive rowing season. All subjects repeated both four-week training interventions in a crossover design (i.e. five subjects completed the high intensity training in their first four weeks while the other five subjects completed the continuous training first before both groups swapped to the alternative training method for the final four weeks). The researchers then averaged the performance data for all rowers according to the allocated training group, regardless of the order in which the four-week blocks were completed. The high intensity and continuous training sessions were matched for total work. Additionally, training records suggest that there was no difference in the total weekly training stimulus for rowers, apart from the high intensity or threshold training. The four weeks of high intensity training improved 2000m ergometer time by 1.9 per cent (437 to 429sec), whereas four weeks of continuous training at threshold pace had a 0.5 per cent influence on 2000m time (434 to 432sec). Interestingly, the high intensity group achieved significantly greater improvements in VO_2max compared to the continuous training (7 per cent vs. -1 per cent, respectively), but both groups had similar changes in lactate threshold (approximately 5 per cent). We cannot describe the extent to which the addition of interval training must have created a more polarised distribution because the complete training data was not provided. However, the addition of high intensity intervals as described must have shifted the training intensity distribution towards a polarised approach. Accordingly, this study provides meaningful evidence in support of polarised training distributions.

Similar to the Tasmanian study, Alexander Stevens and colleagues (2015) found that the inclusion of 10 sessions of 4 to 6 'all-out' 60-sec intervals distributed across four weeks improved 2000m ergometer performance in Canadian university oarsmen (415 to 411sec; 1.0 per cent gain) versus a standard training approach (413 to 411sec; 0.4 per cent gain). Researchers randomly split the oarsmen into two training groups and began the intervention immediately after all rowers had completed six months of typical rowing training. The weekly training programme for the interval training group certainly exhibited a far more polarised approach to training intensity distribution and appears to have largely avoided training in the threshold region based on blood lactate (i.e. 2 to 4mmol/L), whereas the standard training group used the full range of training intensities, including an average of 15min per week at or above 2000m race pace. However, various other training features differed between the groups including the use of strength training and total training time (the interval training group completed only 55 per cent of standard group's training time). This makes it impossible to isolate the effects of the interval training alone, although it is interesting to note the tendency towards better performance improvements in the more polarised group (interval group), despite a substantially reduced accumulation of training minutes.

In 2016 researchers in Ireland (Ni Cheilleachair et al., 2016) compared the effects of introducing two sessions per week of either threshold or high intensity interval training in two independent groups of randomly allocated moderately trained male and female rowers (n=19 N.B: the letter 'n' is used to indicate the number of subjects in the study). The study was performed during the preparation phase of the season and lasted eight weeks. Although much of the training data was not provided in the study, it is clear that all rowers completed 10 rowing sessions per week (mixed water and ergometer) including:

- Eight low intensity sessions and
- Two interval sessions that differed between experimental groups as follows:

- High intensity group: 6 to 8 x 2.5min at high intensity (blood lactate >5mmol/L)
- Threshold group: 3 x 10min at threshold intensity (blood lactate 2 to 4mmol/L)

Thus, 80 per cent of training sessions were low intensity, while 20 per cent of sessions were either high intensity or threshold intensity. After eight weeks, only the high intensity group significantly improved 2000m rowing performance (407 to 400sec; P=0.01; 1.7 per cent improvement) whereas the threshold group had no significant change (416 to 411; P=0.24; 1.1 per cent improvement). The physiological data captured immediately before and after the eight-week interval section showed that only the high intensity group increased VO_2max (approximately 6 per cent) and that blood lactate profiles experienced a rightward shift in both groups, with a trend towards greater improvements in the high intensity group. Although the overall training loads were likely to be similar in the two groups, it was the high intensity group that received the greater benefit of training. These results are consistent with the theme that training in the middle 'threshold' intensity zone is less effective than training in the 'high intensity' zone (i.e. a polarised approach).

Sylvie Richer and colleagues at the University of Western Ontario published a study in 2016 that compared an 11-day training block of interval training to the rower's standard training approach for this phase of winter training. All the rowers had completed at least eight weeks of standard training before the study commenced. Sixteen highly trained male and female rowers were randomly allocated to either the 'supramaximal interval training' group (n=8) or the 'continuous group' (who just followed the standard plan offered by the team coaches; n=8). The supramaximal interval group added six sessions of very short burst ergometer rowing across the 11 days and each session was performed as follows (excluding warm-up and cool down):

- seven hard strokes at 40 strokes per minute followed by two light strokes at 24 strokes per minute (which was equivalent to 10sec hard rowing and 5sec light rowing)
- repeat the above sequence 10 times
- eight minutes recovery
- repeat above until six sets completed

The total duration of intervals in this session was 15 minutes (10min of hard rowing and 5min of active recovery). A novel aspect of this interval approach was that the extremely brief two stroke recoveries were too short to allow oxygen consumption to decrease, such that the majority of the 2.5 minute intervals elicited VO_2 values at, or near to, VO_2max. Also, blood lactate was substantially elevated to approximately 10mmol/L at the end of each set. Clearly, this workout places high demands on both the aerobic and anaerobic pathways.

Table 3 presents the training intensity distribution for each group during the 11-day intervention, both as absolute time and relative to total training time grouped according to the chapter definitions of low, threshold and high intensity. Clearly, the supramaximal interval group completed a more polarised training intensity distribution, with the least absolute and relative time spent in the threshold zone.

Table 3: Distribution of training time in High, Threshold and Low intensity zones during 11-day intervention (data from Richer et al., 2016).

	Training minutes			
	Low	Threshold	High	Total
Continuous group (n=8)	610	210	155	975
Supramaximal intensity group (n=8)	888	75	90	1053
	Training time (as per cent of total time)			
	Low	Threshold	High	
Continuous group (n=8)	63%	22%	16%	
Supramaximal intensity group (n=8)	84%	7%	9%	

The effectiveness of training was assessed via laboratory tests for aerobic power and functional performance measures derived from a 3-minute 'all-out' ergometer test where rowers were asked to row as hard as possible from the start to finish of the test. The results of this test are too complex to present here in detail, however, the power achieved at the end of a laboratory based step test were similar between groups before and after the 11-day training, with no changes during the training period. Likewise, aerobic power did not change for either group. However, other measures of functional rowing power obtained during the 3-minute all-out effort such as peak power during the first 10 seconds and sustained power were improved in the supramaximal interval group.

Richer and colleagues have offered an interesting alternative approach to rowing training. This study was performed in February, after an eight-week period of winter training in a highly competitive Canadian university rowing team. We do not have details of the rest of the rower's training prescription, except that rowers in both groups were also performing a core strength training programme. However, there must have been additional sessions of low intensity rowing during the study in order to achieve the large amount of total training time. So, although the supramaximal interval group did use a polarised distribution of training intensity, the use of repeated days of high intensity intervals during their winter training represents a considerable departure from conventional rowing training. Also, the researchers were unable to measure 2000m rowing performance shortly before and after the 11-day training. Nevertheless, the results do provide some limited support for a polarised training approach and opens up the possibility that a similar study design could be used to examine longer periods of more conventional rowing training with polarised intensity distributions.

This section examined the available research in moderate and well-trained rowers where it was possible to identify distinct comparisons between the effects of low, threshold and high intensity training zones during intervention periods lasting approximately 2 to 12 weeks. Although there are clearly many limitations in the comparisons offered above, including issues such as variations in total training load, training zone classification systems used and objective monitoring of actual training sessions to validate the proportions of time in zones, we believe the results are consistent with the belief that polarised training approaches offer the greatest chance to optimise training benefits and enhance rowing performance. We believe these observations help move coaches and rowers beyond simply developing training programmes that emphasise a high proportion of low intensity training and a much smaller proportion of threshold and high intensity training. After accounting for the necessity to include large amounts of low intensity training time, rowing coaches should consider distributing their remaining training time allocation to favour the use of high intensity training to a greater extent than threshold intensity training. In order to help validate this claim further, as well as to help indicate suitable proportions of training time within each zone, we will end the chapter by presenting several excellent studies of endurance athletes (non-rowers) where polarised training approaches have been compared. We recognise the limitations of making such comparisons, but believe it is the best approach having exhausted the available evidence with specific studies of rowers.

POLARISED TRAINING APPROACHES – LEARNING FROM OTHER ENDURANCE SPORTS

The effectiveness of polarised training approaches for enhancing endurance training adaptations is widely accepted by international calibre athletes in swimming, cycling, cross-country skiing and running. Undoubtedly, the popularity of polarised training in these sports, especially at the elite level, is influenced by well-controlled research studies. We have selected two such influential studies to help elucidate the value of polarised training approaches. The first study was conducted in Scotland with moderately training cyclists (club level) and the second study was conducted in Germany with moderately training athletes from a range of aerobic sports (cross-country skiing, running, cycling and triathlon).

Craig Neal and colleagues (2013) at Stirling University in Scotland observed training and performance responses of 11 club-level cyclists (approximately 8 hours of training per week) who completed six-week training bouts in both of the following training intensity distributions:

- Threshold training: 57 per cent of training time was low intensity and 43 per cent of training time was threshold intensity (so 0 per cent of training was high intensity).
- Polarised training: 80 per cent of training time was low intensity and 20 per cent of training time was high intensity (so 0 per cent of training time was threshold intensity).

A remarkable and extremely challenging feature of this study was that the trained subjects completed a four-week 'detraining period' then a six-week training block (on either the threshold or polarised training approach) before repeating another four-week detraining period followed by a six-week training block (using the alternative intensity approach). This design allowed the athletes to be randomly allocated to the threshold or polarised approach for six-weeks first before being 'crossed over' into the alternative training approach. Half the subjects were initially allocated to the threshold group with the remaining subjects initially allocated to the polarised group. The training time and distribution by low, threshold and high intensity zones is presented in Table 4. The researchers attempted to keep low intensity training time in each group as similar as possible (although it was ultimately slightly higher in the polarised group). When cyclists were allocated to the threshold group they incorporated three sessions per week of 60-minute 'hard rides' (threshold zone of approximately 2 to 4mmol/L blood lactate). Similarly, when cyclists were allocated to the polarised group they incorporated three sessions per week of 6 x 4-minute high intensity intervals (high intensity zone of ≥ 4mmol/L blood lactate) separated by 2-minute recoveries. The researchers monitored these sessions, and where necessary, increased exercise intensity to preserve training in the prescribed zone. The balance of training time in both groups consisted of three sessions of low-intensity exercise. All weekly sessions were recorded and checked to ensure compliance (which was ≥96 per cent per week).

Both groups increased their cycling performance and physiological capabilities, however, the greatest improvements were in the polarised group (see Table 5). Clear gains were made in short high intensity efforts (e.g. time to exhaustion at 95 per cent peak power) and lactate threshold, as well suggestions of improved performance during prolonged efforts (i.e. 40km time trial performance). The design of this study compared two interventions that represent relatively extreme differences in training intensity distributions. Despite reasonably similar amounts of training minutes in the low intensity domain between groups, there were clearly greater training benefits when cyclists used a polarised approach that totally avoided any threshold training. These gains occurred despite the polarised group completing approximately one hour per week less of total training and most of this time emphasised low intensity

Table 4: Overview of training intensity distribution according to low, threshold or high intensity zones for subjects allocated to the Threshold or Polarised groups (data from Neal et al. 2013).

	% of training time		Total training time (min/week)	
	Threshold	Polarised	Threshold	Polarised
Low intensity	57	80	261	305
Threshold intensity	43	0	197	0
High intensity	0	20	0	76
Total time	100	100	458	381

Table 5: Relative change (% relative to baseline) in performance and power measures for subjects allocated to the Threshold or Polarised groups (data from Neal et al. 2013).

	Per cent change after 6 weeks of training			
	40 km time trial (mins) performance	Ride to exhaustion (secs) at 95% of peak power (from baseline step test)	Power (W) at lactate threshold	Peak power (W) obtained in final stage of step test
Threshold Group	4%	37%	2%	3%
Polarised Group	8%	85%	9%	8%

Note: Statistically significant differences existed between groups for all variables except 40 km time-trial performance cycling with just a small amount of high intensity training. These results may seem counterintuitive, but confirm our earlier comment that spending lots of training time exercising in the 'middle' threshold intensity zone does not optimise training gains, despite the obvious difficulty and discomfort encountered by athletes who attempt this type of training. Instead, considerably better training results are achieved when the majority of training time is low intensity and supplemented with several sessions per week of high quality, high intensity training.

All of the studies that we have reviewed so far have included relatively small numbers of athletes and compared just two interventions. However, Thomas Stöggl and Billy Sperlich (2014) successfully completed a comparison of four different training intensity distributions with 41 elite Austrian endurance athletes in Salzburg, Austria. Most of the athletes were either cyclists or runners and all had just completed six months of training (10 to 20 hours/week of training) that consisted of predominantly low intensity-high volume endurance activities with a limited amount of threshold intensity (limited to no more than two sessions per week). At the start of the study, all athletes completed several days of laboratory testing (incremental step tests) to establish baseline fitness and performance capacities. Athletes were then randomly allocated to four different training groups that were equivalent in baseline aerobic fitness and proportions of cyclists and runners and completed nine weeks of controlled training. All four groups were designed to have similar total training loads (after accounting for both volume and intensity), but to differ in the proportion of training time allocated to low, threshold and high intensity training (terminology note: the term definition of 'threshold' training used in this study was defined as exercise sessions that elicited blood lactate between 3 and 5mmol/L, which is slightly different to the definition of threshold intensity 2 to 4mmol/L that we have used throughout this chapter). Table 6 displays each group's total training time and the percentage of training sessions (rather than time in zone) dedicated to the three intensity zones.

Most of the training sessions and all of the laboratory testing used either cycling or running as the activity of choice. Individualised training intensity zones were prescribed using the initial laboratory tests and athletes used heart rate monitors to help achieve their prescribed training intensity distribution. The researchers were able

Table 6: Overview of allocated training volume and intensity distribution during a 9 week training intervention where aerobically trained subjects were allocated to one of four intensity distribution conditions (data from Stöggl and Sperlich, 2014).

	High Volume Group	Threshold Group	High Intensity Interval Group	Polarised Group
Total hours of training in 9 weeks	102	84	66	104
Total number of sessions in 9 weeks	58	49	47	54
% of sessions at low intensity (Blood lactate: <2 mmol/L)	83	46	43	68
% of sessions at threshold intensity (Blood lactate of 3 to 5 mmol/L)	16	54	0	6
% of sessions at high intensity (Blood lactate >5 mmol/L)	1	0	57	26

Table 7: Selected results from Salzburg study (data from Stöggl and Sperlich, 2014)

	High Volume Group	Threshold Group	High Intensity Interval Group	Polarised Group
% gain in absolute VO$_2$max	+3	-4	+5	+12
% gain in time to exhaustion during step test	+8	+6	+9	+17
% gain in lactate threshold (power/velocity at 2 mmol/L)	+1	+2	+12	+9
% gain in peak power/velocity achieved during step test	-2	+2	+4	+5

to verify that overall compliance to the assigned training groups was approximately 96 per cent. The specific training sessions and pattern of weekly training are complex but are free to view within this research study hosted on the Frontiers in Physiology journal web page (see: http://journal.frontiersin.org/). Briefly, all four groups included low intensity sessions each week (e.g. 90–240min easy cycling or running). The high volume group also included a small amount of threshold intensity sessions (e.g. 3 x 15min at threshold intensity with 3min recovery). The threshold group also included similar threshold type sessions (i.e. 3 x 15min) as well as other threshold session such as 75min of Fartlek training and 6 x 8min threshold pace intervals. The high intensity group excluded any threshold intensity activities, and instead shifted their training towards high intensity using sessions (e.g. 4 x 4min at 90–95 per cent of peak heart rate with 3min recovery). Finally, the polarised group added two sessions per week of high intensity training (e.g. 4 x 4min at 90–95 per cent of peak heart rate with 3min recovery) as well as short explosive 5-sec bursts of speed (6–8 x 5sec maximal sprints) included within two of the low intensity sessions.

The key results from the Salzburg study are summarised in Table 7 and provide strong support for the benefits of polarised training approaches. Overall, the results were most favourable for the polarised group and least favourable for the threshold group. Furthermore, the relatively limited gains in fitness achieved by the high volume group likely reflect that all subjects began this study after having recently completed six months of high volume-low intensity preparation phase training. Although the study did not include any rowers, it is worth remembering that lactate threshold, and especially VO$_2$max, are well correlated with 2000m rowing performance. Therefore, the results of this study lend support for the idea that the most effective training programmes for rowers are likely to be those that emphasise polarised intensity distributions and include good variation of training approaches to avoid monotony.

CLOSING REMARKS

This chapter has attempted to persuade rowers and coaches that a training programme dominated by high volume-low intensity training can be further enhanced by introducing a polarised intensity distribution that places more emphasis on high intensity training in preference to threshold training. The importance of low intensity training for rowing is well established, but far less is known about how to effectively distribute the remaining balance of training time at higher intensities. We have made a case that the least amount of training time should be dedicated to threshold type training. Indeed, it may be perfectly reasonable to completely avoid threshold type training in order to maximise metabolic adaptations and enhance tolerance and responses to training, especially when multiple sessions per day are included. Accordingly, if we allocate an initial value of 80 per cent of training to low intensity rowing, then the recommended amount of threshold training would range between 0 and 9 per cent, with high intensity training making up the 11 to 20 per cent balance of training time.

Various issues regarding the effectiveness of polarised training for advanced rowers remain outstanding. These include the need for better evidence of the underlying physiological mechanisms to explain the benefits of polarised training, as well as direct comparisons of a range of polarised approaches in elite rowers. Additionally, there is very limited basis to make any recommendations about how to apply polarised distributions at different phases in the rowing season. However, in this respect, it is noteworthy that the training programme for New Zealand's rowers during preparations for the 2016 Rio Games had the following targets:

- Baseline phase (early season): training intensity should consist almost entirely of low intensity training.
- General conditioning phase (mid-season preparation for competitive period): approximately 75 per cent of training should be low intensity; 20 per cent of training should be threshold intensity; 5 per cent of training should be high intensity.
- Specific conditioning (competition period): approximately 80 per cent of training should be low intensity and 20 per cent of training should be high intensity.

Thus, the approach to polarisation taken by New Zealand rowing to intensity distribution reveals a broad shift from a near exclusive focus on low intensity training at the start of the season, to a non-polarised middle phase still dominated by low intensity training before entering the final highly polarised training phase that avoids threshold intensity. Readers may be interested to notice that the specific non-polarised distribution in the general conditioning phase while preparing for the 2016 Olympics was almost identical to that which was used before the 2012 Olympics (as described earlier in this chapter in the study by Plews and colleagues). Perhaps this accumulation of real-world training and performance data across annual and quadrennial cycles will help direct further refinements in polarised training approaches and support future advances in rowing performance.

SUMMARY

- An 80–20 ratio (low intensity – threshold/high intensity) of training time appears to be the dominant approach of successful rowers.

- Extensive amounts of low intensity training (i.e. < 2mmol/L blood lactate) are especially helpful for developing physiological adaptations and are likely optimised for rowers within the range of 120 to 200km per week of rowing.
- Excessive use of elite threshold intensity training (i.e. between 2 and 4mmol/L blood lactate) increases the risk of hormonal and biochemical dysfunction in athletes, restricts the physiological benefits of training and can disrupt progress.
- Successful rowers need to include high intensity training, rather than threshold training, to maximise training responses, especially in the competitive period.
- The ideal polarisation pattern for rowers has yet to be established and may change depending upon the phase of training and training status of the athlete.
- Polarised training intensity distributions are highly effective for elite athletes and also provide substantial training and performance benefits at the sub-elite and even recreational level, in comparison to pyramid-type intensity distributions which include large proportions of threshold intensity training.
- Ideally, consistent monitoring, with a combination of a physiological measure such as heart rate, with some form of perceived exertion scale for each training session may help athletes and coaches fine tune their communication and optimise the daily training prescription over time.
- In order to simplify the monitoring process, it may be useful to categorise entire sessions as predominantly low intensity, threshold intensity, or high intensity in focus in order to better understand the stress load encountered by the athletes and how they are coping.

REFERENCES

Driller, M. W., Fell, J. W., Gregory, J. R., Shing, C. M., & Williams, A. D. (2009). 'The effects of high-intensity interval training in well-trained rowers', *Int J Sports Physiol Perform*, 4(1), 110–121.

Fiskerstrand, A., & Seiler, K. S. (2004). 'Training and performance characteristics among Norwegian international rowers 1970–2001', *Scand J Med Sci Sports*, 14(5), 303–310. doi:10.1046/j.1600-0838.2003.370.x

Hartmann, U., Mader, A., & Hollmann, W. (1990). 'Heart rate and lactate during endurance training programs in rowing and its relation to the duration of exercise by top elite rowers', *FISA Coach*, 1(1), 1–4.

Ingham, S. A., Carter, H., Whyte, G. P., & Doust, J. H. (2008). 'Physiological and performance effects of low- versus mixed-intensity rowing training',. *Med Sci Sports Exerc*, 40(3), 579–584. doi:10.1249/MSS.0b013e31815ecc6a

Neal, C. M., Hunter, A. M., Brennan, L., O'Sullivan, A., Hamilton, D. L., De Vito, G., & Galloway, S. D. (2013). 'Six weeks of a polarized training-intensity distribution leads to greater physiological and performance adaptations than a threshold model in trained cyclists', *J Appl Physiol (1985)*, 114(4), 461–471. doi:10.1152/japplphysiol.00652.2012

Ni Cheilleachair, N. J., Harrison, A. J., & Warrington, G. D. (2016). 'HIIT enhances endurance performance and aerobic characteristics more than high-volume training in trained rowers', *J Sports Sci*, 1–7. doi:10.1080/02640414.2016.1209539

Plews, D. J., Laursen, P. B., Kilding, A. E., & Buchheit, M. (2014). 'Heart-rate variability and training-intensity distribution in elite rowers', *Int J Sports Physiol Perform*, 9(6), 1026–1032. doi:10.1123/ijspp.2013-0497

Richer, S. D., Nolte, V. W., Bechard, D. J., & Belfry, G. R. (2016). 'Effects of Novel Supramaximal Interval Training Versus Continuous Training on Performance in Collegiate, National, and International Class Rowers', *J Strength Cond Res*, 30(6), 1752–1762. Doi:10.1519/JSC.0000000000001274

Steinacker, J. M., Lormes, W., Lehmann, M., & Altenburg, D. (1998). 'Training of rowers before world championships', *Med Sci Sports Exerc*, 30(7), 1158–1163.

Stevens, A. W., Olver, T. D., & Lemon, P. W. (2015). 'Incorporating sprint training with endurance training improves anaerobic capacity and 2,000m Erg performance in trained oarsmen', *J Strength Cond Res*, 29(1), 22–28. doi:10.1519/JSC.0000000000000593

Stöggl, T., & Sperlich, B. (2014). 'Polarized training has greater impact on key endurance variables than threshold, high intensity, or high volume training', *Front Physiol*, 5, 33. doi:10.3389/fphys.2014.00033

Tran, J., Rice, A. J., Main, L. C., & Gastin, P. B. (2015). 'Profiling the training practices and performances of elite rowers', *Int J Sports Physiol Perform*, 10(5), 572–580. doi:10.1123/ijspp.2014-0295

Strength and Conditioning

Dr Trent Lawton High Performance Sport New Zealand

Trent Lawton is a world-class expert in strength and conditioning with over 21 years' experience coaching Olympic and world champions. He is currently the National Strength and Conditioning Lead for Rowing New Zealand. Through High Performance Sport New Zealand (HPSNZ), Trent's role is to support national rowing coaches by ensuring targeted crews are engaged in competitive strength training environments, receive superior technical tuition, effective programme integration and the achievement of individual performance targets. His doctoral thesis, completed in 2012, examined the *Strength Testing and Training of Elite Rowers*. Trent has previously been Senior Strength and Conditioning Coach at the Australian Institute of Sport (1999–2004), and Strength and Conditioning Coordinator at the ACT Academy of Sport in Canberra (1992–1998).

I still remember my first weight-training circuit. Each 30 repetition station was searing strength from my muscles. Halfway through the circuit, with my lungs heaving, it took all my personal resolve to get up and start the next exercise. And I won't ever forget that delayed muscle soreness, almost 24 hours later to the minute. It felt like a pack of razor blades had been inserted into every single muscle, slicing every nerve-ending no matter how little I moved.

I was far from 'hooked'. But I felt my strength improve quickly and my rowing too. As my back got stronger it ached less; as my upper-body endurance improved I could hold the pressure at rating, and slowly, there was some shape forming on my fatless and slender frame. Those initial gains on- and off-water came easy. Three years later it all seemed to stall and I had to fight hard to get even the smallest of gains. So on turning to this chapter, it would not surprise me if you were a rower or coach who is ambivalent about weight training. After all, you didn't take up rowing because you wanted to weight train. So why consider it as part of your preparations?

THE AMBIGUITY OF WEIGHT TRAINING

When it comes to the rationale for weight training, most arguments seemed to draw on testimonial experience. Often the advocates' propositions don't resonate with your own mentor's advice. You may then choose to align your views with schools of common thought.

Even the results of research studies on weight training for rowing seem unclear, and rarely do those projects examine the importance of weight training for high-performance rowers. Possibly the most common challenge to the use of weight training in a rowing training programme is in the knowledge that 80 per cent of the energy needed for a 2000m race is delivered by the aerobic system, so why invest in the 20 per cent that is delivered anaerobically using weight training?

As you might guess, the available scientific evidence supporting the appointment of a strength and conditioning coach would appear dubious. Nonetheless, practical experience from around the globe indicates there may be good reason to incorporate strength training and testing in rowing. All I will say is that my somewhat tenuous appointment in 2009 to New Zealand rowing provided great incentive for me to ensure any weight training I did assign helped rowers and coaches to make the boats go faster.

It is my intention in this chapter to provide you with my take on the plausible benefits attainable with the inclusion of weight training as part of rowing preparations. A significant proportion of this chapter is based on research that I have reviewed or personally conducted as part of my career as a strength and conditioning coach. Other insights are based on my day-to-day experiences of working with elite rowers.

However, I appreciate that my experience of common-sense practice in developing successful rowers is likely to differ from yours. Nevertheless, medical practitioners, physical therapists and allied health professionals make judgements about suitable treatments and interventions that are informed by research as well as their personal and professional experience. I hope that the ideas and evidence that I share in this chapter will help you decide how best to use weight training in your overall training approach.

WHAT ARE THE BENEFITS OF WEIGHT TRAINING FOR ROWERS?

When we meet with other rowers or coaches, it is not uncommon that we benchmark our programmes by comparing prognostic measures such as a 500m time trial. Good prognostics serve as useful predictors of 2000m performance. However, the extent to which changes in a rower's strength and power can be considered a 'good prognostic' of 2000m on-water performance among the rowing community is less clear. If there is doubt about the specific performance benefits gained from strength development, then coaches and rowers are right to be hesitant to use such methods.

Therefore, in the quest to maximise stroke-power during 2000m racing, we explored the role of muscular strength and power testing and training. Significantly, we completed a series of experiments with our national team rowers that gave excellent insights into the real value of strength and power development for enhancing on-water rowing performance.

We started our experiments after the 2009 World Championships. At that time, it was apparent that few scientists had recruited internationally successful rowers for their training interventions. In contrast, our experiments were designed to be part of an 18-month selection, training and assessment programme for New Zealand's international rowing teams.

We included target groups of elite rowers who are less commonly researched (i.e. junior elite and senior elite women), for whom the appropriate applications of weight training, testing and benchmarks for strength, were especially lacking. By encompassing a longer-term framework, we were able to clarify the performance benefits attributable to weight training, as the training experiences preceding each intervention were more uniformly controlled.

In the table below, I have outlined the most important benefits we have gained by inclusion of weight training.

Table 1: Weight Training: Framework of Objectives

To increase...	Assessments
1. Absolute leg-drive strength to sustain the desired 2000m boat speed.	1. 6RM Leg Press (>250kg/180kg)*
2. Effective total-body muscle mass (cross sectional area) recruitment to optimise anaerobic stroke-power.	2. 1RM Power Clean (110kg/85kg), 6RM Prone Bench Row (110kg/85kg) , and 100-m rowing ergometer time trial.
3. Absolute upper-body muscle-endurance to ensure rowers are capable of elite endurance-training volumes, in particular during periods of injury, rehabilitation or cross-training (i.e. cycling)	3. Max reps in 1 or 2min using 85% (>15) or 70% (>30) of 6RM Prone Bench Row
4. General soft tissue-resilience to tolerate high training loads	4. Frequency of physiotherapy appointments
5. Address muscle imbalances or dysfunction to reduce training time lost to injury	5. Training days lost to injury
*Benchmark kilogram targets for heavyweight males and females, respectively.	

Boosting the leg-drive

It became clear from our observations that the limiting factor to the quantity or quality of rowing training was upper-body muscle strength and endurance. However, given that more than half the total propulsive power in 2000m racing is developed by the leg-drive, it was not surprising that our research found that rowers with superior leg strength (about 10 per cent greater) performed better (faster) as a crew.

We assessed leg strength development by recording the average work performed over a five repetition maximum using a Concept2 Dyno. The advantage of measuring work is that it includes both the 'length and strength (or force)' generated while leg-pressing. This means taller rowers who may be weaker (greater length – less strength), can produce a work score equal to or greater than a shorter rower who may be stronger (less length – greater strength).

In summary, in 2009 we suggested to the national centre for rowing excellence that lower-body weight training be incorporated as part of regional preparations for selection trials. At that time, believe it or not, very few NZ rowers performed any weight training.

Since then, and with the regular monitoring and review of data collected over seven years, we have learned much more about the benefits of weight training for elite rowers as simplified in Table 1. The differences observed during our initial short-term studies become more obvious with continued application. Our results at international

Stephen Jones from the New Zealand men's eight performing a strength and conditioning session.
Credit: Trent Lawton

competition certainly have not suffered, and have indeed improved, since integrating weight training.

THE CASE FOR WEIGHT TRAINING

Even though we established benchmarks for leg-strength testing, our coaches and rowers still needed to be convinced that the attainment of such targets (or at least 80 per cent of the benchmark) had good odds of improving rowing performance. It may be that strength can be steadily acquired over a number of years, as endurance training volumes gradually rise. In other circumstances though, where there is less time available, weight training may need to be emphasised to boost muscular strength or power.

In such cases, a common concern is that there may be a risk of compromising aerobic capacity, or an undesirable gain in body mass. As a result, some coaches prefer specific strategies, such as towing ropes in the water (to increase the drag acting on the boat), to develop strength, or more specifically the leg-drive.

To investigate these concerns, we developed two controlled intervention studies to compare adaptations attained from (on-water) rowing alone, to rowing with the addition of weight training in the build-up to competition.

In the first study, participants were assigned to rowing only 250–270km a week or rowing 190–210km plus four weight training sessions (two strength: 4–6 exercises, 4 x 6–15 reps; and two muscular endurance: 6–8 exercises, 3 x 25–40 reps) a week during the off-season.

After eight weeks, there was no compromise in aerobic capacity or undesirable gains in body mass. However, only rowers who performed weight training improved their lower-body leg strength and muscular-endurance.

Our second study assessed the gains in lower-body leg strength over 14 weeks, with and without weight training, during a repeated intensive pre-competition programme incorporating resisted rowing (i.e. two sessions of 'towing-ropes', 8 x 3min).

We observed that at best without weight training, leg strength was maintained.

In summary, while success in rowing is clearly dependent on a multitude of factors, we have found that among other things weight training can be used to boost leg-strength better than just rowing. We also found that the assumed negatives, such as losses in aerobic condition or undesirable excessive gains in lean body mass, were easily mitigated.

Other researchers have attempted to explain why strength development provides performance benefits for elite (aerobic-trained) endurance athletes. It is believed that improvements in running and cycling economy, time trial 'speed' and time spent at maximal effort to exhaustion are improved after increasing strength as fewer cells are required to attain the same muscle work output. As the muscle has greater mechanical efficiency and reserve, greater physiological economy, work capacity and power can be realised. For our NZ rowers, this economy is particularly important and not just to sustain boat speed over the middle 1000m, but for the final leg-drive burst required to win a 2000m race.

INTEGRATING WEIGHT TRAINING

Before addressing the important issue of programme design, here are a few tips on how to ensure that weight training is successfully integrated into a training week.

Scheduling

Firstly, as part of a training week, weight training need not be too time-consuming. Most critically, weight training sessions should be scheduled after sufficient recovery from any preceding endurance exercise (e.g. 3–4 hours' rest). This is not difficult to plan, as I advocate only two sessions each week to develop muscle strength or power, 72 hours apart (e.g. Monday and Thursday).

However, for two sessions a week to be effective, rowers should persist with it year-round, at least within practical limits. This approach can avoid losses in strength and power and saves wasted time and frustration retraining for strength at the start of each training year.

I find rowers remain focused and energised by the diversity and high intensity exercise offered in the gym. Rather than squeeze it around on-water and ergometer work, we make it a stand-alone session for the afternoon, dedicating the morning to rowing.

This can be more difficult to achieve if three or more weight training sessions are assigned each week, unless a reduction in other training units is programmed. During such phases, for example from October to January, I like to mix-up our approach to strength training by using a circuit format or, by integrating other team-based strength challenges like pushing a truck up a hill.

Individualisation

Secondly, I use low-repetition strength tests to evaluate individual strength training needs. I am a strong believer that to evaluate weight training success there first needs to be a clear rationale and context provided on integration (i.e. training phase goals or the development stage of a rower). As an example from Table 1, younger rowers who have lesser leg strength (6RM leg press) may need to focus on the lower-body in weight training, to ensure they can sustain the faster boat speeds achieved by senior crews.

We have also found from performance modelling, that the amount of weight lifted (kg) for a 6RM prone bench pull and a 1RM power clean, are strong determinants of peak stroke-power (watts) or 500m ergometer performance (seconds). So I recommend these exercises form part of weight training or are included as part of testing every three or four months; but only if injury free or where lifting technique permits.

Perceived exertion

Finally, as part of my weekly athlete tracking I monitor low repetition exercises, such as the amount of weight progressively used with good form for six repetitions during a leg press exercise (i.e. a six repetition maximum, RM). Lower repetition exercises offer greater precision, as it is easier to adjust the weight by small increments each set. The re-test reliability of low-repetition exercise is also much better as an assessment, so I can track progress knowing that the weight used for a set will differ by less than 2.5 per cent if a rower were to attempt it again the next week. This means I can precisely assign loads for each training session, ask for feedback using a rating of perceived exertion, and then adjust the progressive overload the following week.

I have found caution is required when monitoring high-repetition weight training, common in many rowing programmes (e.g. the maximum repetitions attained performing a 50kg bench row). When high-repetition exercises are repeated on separate days, the scores can vary by more than 15 per cent (or >10 reps for an original test score of 67 reps). This doesn't allow me to evaluate, to refine or to effectively progress a rower's weight training programme. Ideally, any high-repetition tests are performed only when large training gains are anticipated. For example, a rower who has injured their lower-back and re-commences training on a bike using the weights for upper-body muscular endurance (discussed later in this chapter).

PROGRAMMING AND PERIODISATION

We can now discuss weight training programme design, overload and periodisation.

Planning training windows

The actual time required for the achievement of each training objectives varies.

Many development training objectives can be quickly acquired (e.g. 4–6 weeks) while others may take some time (e.g. more than 24–36 months). Rather than allocate a set block emphasising weight training and then ceasing, my suggestion is that you should persist with weight training year-round, compounding gains as much as possible.

My golden rule is that 10 per cent matters. It may be that injury or travel sets your competitor back and you are able to leap ahead of them. With travel and tapering for competition, you may find 2–3 months each year of disrupted training time. Remember, I only advocate two sessions a week if you are persistent year-round.

Reverse step loading

As a training year progresses, I like to decrease the volume of weight training exercise and increase the intensity (meaning the weights get heavier), as this helps to manage muscle fatigue, as the demands of rowing training become progressively greater (see Table 2 below and Figure 1 on the following page).

Notice that the volume of weight (kg) is progressively decreased and stepped, not unlike an endurance training template but in reverse. This is because for advanced rowers, who should be more familiar with selecting RM loads, I assign greater volumes (i.e. total repetitions) in the weight room when endurance volumes are less.

In general, I repeat these 12-week phases over the year but at greater loads (i.e. weights) as strength is increased.

Table 2: a 12-week example of sets of repetitions and the approximate intensity assigned (as a percentage of an individuals' 6RM determined by testing) to develop muscular strength and power.

Week:	1	2	3	4	5	6	7	8	9	10	11	12
set 1	15	15	8	6	15	10	6	6	10	6	3	6
set 2	15	12	8	6	12	10	6	6	10	6	3	6
set 3	15	10	8	6	10	10	3-3-3	4	10	6	3	3-3-3
set 4	15	8	10	4	8	12	3-3-3	4	12	4	6	-
set 5	-	-	-	4	6	-	-	6	-	4	6	-
Intensity (%6RM)												
set 1	70%	70%	90%	85%	70%	90%	80%	90%	90%	85%	90%	80%
set 2	70%	80%	90%	90%	80%	90%	90%	95%	90%	90%	95%	90%
set 3	70%	85%	90%	95%	85%	90%	100%	100%	90%	95%	100%	100%
set 4	70%	90%	90%	100%	90%	90%	100%	105%	90%	100%	105%	-
set 5	-	-	-	105%	95%	-	-	100%	-	105%	110%	-
Intensity (average)	70%	81%	90%	95%	84%	90%	93%	98%	90%	95%	100%	90%
Training Load (kg)	42.0	36.6	30.6	24.7	42.8	37.8	27.8	25.5	37.8	24.7	21.0	18.9

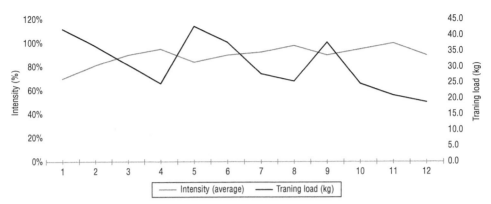

Figure 1: The training load volume (i.e. total repetitions multiplied by average intensity, expressed in kilograms) is reduced each week as the average (and maximum) intensity assigned increase.

I can make this 12-week template longer, (e.g. 16 weeks), by repeating the greater volume of weeks 1–4 to focus on building muscle cross sectional area, increasing absolute (lactate) work capacity and strength.

Alternatively, closer to competition, I may choose to repeat the greater intensities of weeks 9–12, to focus on a rower's ability to recruit muscle fibres concurrently (as well as the neuromuscular coordination required between groups of muscles working together), increasing their (a-lactic) peak power and maximal strength, without remarkable gains in body mass.

Typically, two divergent schools of thought arise when overload is discussed in the context of weight training for rowing – some support the use of low loads (50–60 per cent of 6RM) but highly repetitious efforts (e.g. 25–50 plus reps), while others prefer heavy loads (70–100 per cent of 6RM) and low number of repetitions (e.g. 6–15 reps).

Ultimately, the most useful overload is a reflection of the programme objective, the types of activities selected and the muscular adaptations sought. As you can see in my approach, the two main adaptations I seek to improve rowing performance through resistance weight training are an increase in muscular strength and power.

Strength is defined by and progressively overloaded by an increase in weight for a desired number of repetitions, where the rate (or speed) and range of motion of each repetition performed is relatively constant.

In general, the number of repetitions I use to develop muscle strength and power is between 6 and 15; however, this does not negate the use of lower repetitions (for example, 3 or 4 reps). Lower repetitions and heavier loads may assist advanced weight-trained rowers with specific goals such as an increase in peak stroke-power, where additional muscle mass may be undesirable (as may be the case for some lightweight rowers). Fewer repetitions (e.g. 3 or 4) at an equivalent intensity (e.g. 90 per cent of 6RM) may also be more appropriate to the nature of activity selected (e.g. a power clean), even if more repetitions are possible with the assigned loads (e.g. 6 or 8).

Power is defined by the rate at which work can be performed, and is the product of both movement speed and the load (or weight) lifted – that is, power = speed × strength. There is an inverse relationship between speed and strength – as speed increases, the load that can be lifted decreases and subsequently mechanical power will change.

Power can be developed by using lighter loads and greater movement speeds (e.g. with loads between 50 and 60 per cent of the 6RM ability) – exercises like this are often referred to as high-velocity weight training. Explosive exercises allow a greater acceleration phase and can be performed safely at faster speeds by eliminating issues associated with momentum of the resistance load. As an example, when the same light weight is used, a prone bench pull is a more powerful exercise than a traditional seated cable row.

Overload to develop the rate at which muscles generate peak forces (or impulse) should also be considered as part of exercise selection. An impulse is the change in momentum of an object (or mass) as a result of the force applied over an interval of time. Generally, a rower has less than 0.7 seconds to apply force to an oar. All other things being equal on-water, a greater impulse (or the force developed over that time) will result in faster boat speeds (or momentum).

Impulse training involves progressively increasing the mass lifted for an activity where the contraction time is relatively constant and similar to rowing (e.g. power

Table 3: Sample Weight-Training Programmes for Rowing

In-common Preparation (warm up)		
10 x Overhead Squat 10 x 3-point kneel thoracic rotations 5 x Cat/camel/Prayer stretch 30s Wide-kneel sit back hip stretch	30 x Air Squat in Sumo Stance 10 x Hindu Push Ups 10 x prone alternate arm/leg raises 2m Skipping	
Programme 1: Basic Strength	Programme 2: Advanced Strength	Programme 3: Upper-Body Endurance Circuit
(90/60kg)* RDL or 32/24kg KB Swings (250/180kg) Leg Press	(90/60kg) Snatch Pulls 60cm Box Jump Ups	60 x Seated Cord Rows (35/25mm width) 30 x Incline Bench DB Alternating Press (10/7kg) 30 x Prone Bench Rows (50/40kg)
(90/60kg) Seated Cable Rows (80/50kg) Bench Press	(90/60kg) Power Cleans (160/120kg) BB Hip Thrust	15 x Clap Press Ups 10 x Chin Ups with Kipping 5 x Burpees
(40/28kg) 1-arm DB rows (90/70kg) 1-leg leg press	1-leg squats onto a box (40cm) (+30kg/BW) Chin Ups	
Notes:		
*Benchmark target 6 Repetition Maximums (RM) loads (kilograms) for males and females respectively, in parenthesis. Your actual 6RM will differ depending on your training experience and testing results.		
KB = Kettlebell, DB = Dumbell, BW = Bodyweight, BB = Barbell.		

Table 4: Examples of training weeks incorporating weight training

Example 1: Two sessions a week		Example 2: Three sessions a week (emphasising weights)	
(refer Table 2 for sets and reps)		(refer Table 2 for sets and reps)	
Day 1		**Day 1**	
7am: Row 16km		7am: Row 24km	
3pm: Hard Weight Session (RPE 7-8/10)		3pm: Hard Weight Session (RPE 7-8/10)	
	Basic Strength (Programme 1)		Advanced Strength (Programme 2)
e.g. week 1:	4 sets	e.g. week 8	5 sets
	15 reps each set		4-6 reps each set
	70% of 6RM		Increase load by ~5% each set from 90-105% of 6RM (see Table 2)
Days 2-3: Endurance rowing		**Day 2: Endurance rowing**	
Day 4		**Day 3**	
7am: Row 14km		7am: Rowing prognostics, 3x5000-m at fixed rating.	
3pm: Moderate Weight Session (RPE 6-7/10)		1pm: Moderate Weight Session (RPE 6-7/10)	
e.g.	Basic Strength (Programme 1)		Advanced Strength (Programme 2)
	3 sets		4 sets
	15 reps each set		6 reps each set
	70% of 6RM		90% of 6RM
Days 5-6: Endurance rowing		**Day 4: Endurance rowing**	
		Day 5	
		7am: Row 20km	
		1pm: Light Weight Session (RPE 5/10)	
			Basic Strength (Programme 1)
			5 sets
			4-6 reps each set
			Increase load by ~5% each set from 90-105% of 6RM (see Table 2)
		4pm: Technique Row (6-8km)	
		Day 6: Endurance rowing	

clean). While in both approaches the rate of muscle contraction is extremely high, the intensity as a proportion of the maximum load is much greater (e.g. 85–100 per cent of a 6RM) in a high-velocity weight training exercise.

As you can see in Table 3, knowing which exercises to select is one of the key arts to reaching specific rowing training objectives. My advice is to use weight training sessions primarily to develop muscle strength and power. Narrow down your objectives and assign the least number of strength and conditioning exercises to attain that outcome.

Clustering and inter-repetition rest

Please be aware that in my research and gym, I do not allow rowers to reach exhaustion (or repetition-failure) during a typical exercise. This approach is intended to preserve movement technique and repetition speed (or power) throughout a training session (e.g. instead of six consecutive repetition using a 6RM load, three repetitions are performed, then after 30 seconds rest, an additional two sets of three repetitions). (For an example of scheduled clustering, see week 7 in Table 2)

Over the week, the loads assigned to each session are managed by adjusting the volume (sets or repetitions) and average weight lifted as a proportion of the assigned RM (or intensity). (See examples in Table 4: weight-training week examples 1 and 2.)

However, if rowers are looking fatigued, then I will ask that they break for up to 30 seconds for a rest during any assigned set of repetitions if the movement stalls (i.e. by almost half). I want to preserve the volume achieved at the assigned RM percentage, and to maximise mechanical power. Research indicates we can achieve training adaptations of greater relevance to sports performance using such methods.

SELECTING WEIGHT TRAINING ACTIVITIES

You may be tempted to just pick up the 12-weeks training phases and programme examples I have provided in Tables 2–4 above. Admittedly, they are not the most complex of programmes and require little technical skill. However, activities selected for a weight training programme must be relevant to the objectives and take into consideration the experience, movement competency and injury profile of the rower. I am not at all opposed to using low-skill exercises with senior rowers. Ultimately, each task performed must assist in improving a rower's performance on-water.

I highly recommend asking yourself this simple question: If I could only prescribe three exercises for the weight-training programme to meet my training objectives, what would they be?

Of course, if your rowers have good access to a medical team, these individuals may also have a repertoire of exercises assigned to rehabilitate or reduce the severity or likelihood of injury. However, refocus on rowing performance – what is it that will contribute to the shorter and longer-term performance?

Rather than perform a hit and miss template approach, this exercise will quickly refocus your attention on what really matters when you hit the weight room. It is easy to let an exercise, set or repetition slip here and there if you are unclear which activities are critical to your needs. Even strength coaches struggle with this challenge: everyone always wants to add more 'just in case' or to 'cover another base'.

Messages get lost when there is too much information. Think of how much information is lost given that a rower must focus on form and technique, remembering different cues for each exercise, adjusting loads and working around other people. And if you are not there to reinforce the regime, what really will be happening? Start small and there may be benefits to keeping it focussed rather than adding more activities over time.

COACHING EXERCISE TECHNIQUE

To avoid injury due to poor form or excessive loading on the spine, the repertoire of exercises should only be advanced once a technical level of proficiency is demonstrated. I can't see any reason why time cannot be assigned during each session for technique development for more advanced activities, like a deadlift or power clean.

Screening movement

I have provided a suite of activities as an in-common preparation for the weight room session (see Tables 1–4 weight training programme examples on pages 173–180). I have found these drills useful because if a rower's spine or hips are restricted in movement it may force them to adopt techniques less favourable to developing power or enduring work. If you use these drills, pay close attention to individual changes in movement freedom. You can compare rowers to each other, but ideally track changes observed in each individual.

With regard to injury risk, one benefit claimed and readily observed from weight training is an improvement in the general 'resilience' or 'robustness' of rowers. Quite simply, there are benefits in performing basic movements through larger ranges of motions and in postures dissimilar to rowing. Any office worker can attest to the effect of endless hours seated in front of a keyboard.

We have also observed that the number of training days lost to injury can be reduced when rowers train to keep their general posture and muscle balance (length and strength of opposing segments). That is, they bounce back from injury more quickly, feel more robust and seek treatment less often for rowing niggles. Of course, this reduction must be taken in context of the intent of the weight-training programme and also other allied health support they receive, such as massage.

On the occasion when a rower gets injured, you may need to adjust their programme to enable a soft tissue injury to subside (e.g. in the lower back). To reduce the risk of harm it is important to seek guidelines from a medical practitioner or allied health professional.

My primary objective as a strength and conditioning expert is to keep a rower training on-water. However, while the balance of training objectives may be temporarily reviewed, where possible an injured rower should be kept on performance target for a phase of training. Look always for what a rower can do, rather than focus solely on what they can't do.

What about muscular endurance?

Our research clarified that upper-body muscular endurance is developed effectively from endurance rowing. Therefore, high-repetition muscular endurance weight training is best used when combined with cross-training such as cycling, or in place of rowing in the case of injury (e.g. lower back) or inclement weather.

I think running and cycling up mountains are more refreshing ways to develop muscular endurance. Because of this, I would target upper-body endurance in the gym, particularly if your rower has a low back injury. For example, you might consider allocating twice the volume of exercise to the upper-body (4–6 exercises) than lower-body (2–3 exercises). For an example, see Table 3 (on page 179).

In general, muscular endurance is developed when between 25 and 50 repetitions are performed within one set of an exercise; often a given interval of time is assigned. However, I believe muscular endurance can be progressed better when multiple sets of fewer repetitions are performed, but with shorter rest intervals between repeated bouts (for example, 10 reps press-ups, followed by 10 reps pull-ups and the pattern repeated 5 times). This is a particularly effective training method where more powerful activities have been prescribed and a drop off in reps or movement speed is undesirable such as jumping or an Olympic weightlifting exercise or derivative (e.g. power snatch).

In my opinion, because muscular endurance loads are of lower intensity (e.g. 50–60 per cent of 6RM) and the repetition movement speed is thus faster, it is another form of high-velocity weight training. Therefore, if I manage muscle fatigue and recovery carefully by clustering repetitions, assigning inter-repetition rest and alternating exercises, I can ensure my rowers' gain an increase in muscle endurance at greater (but not peak) average muscle power.

HOW MUCH STRENGTH IS ENOUGH?

At some stage, the question of how much gym strength is enough will arise, particularly as there are many activities where the level of skill required is low (e.g. leg press) and the ability to lift heavy weights (e.g. double to triple body weight) for numerous repetitions is easily attainable. My reaction to that question is to ask one of my own: are rowers more capable of developing superior strength than weightlifters? I doubt a rower is going to surpass their potential capability in strength when performing only two or three sessions a week, when a weightlifter spends as many sessions in the gym as a rower spends on endurance training.

Perhaps this question could refocus on rowers who are seen performing very heavy and slow movements in the gym. As a guide and in my opinion, for senior rowers who are strong (i.e. who have surpassed any suggested benchmarks), is that when the speed of repetitions (or concentric contraction) during any strength exercise (e.g. leg press) is very slow (over 3 seconds) and that contraction takes significantly longer than the drive phase during rowing, it may be more suitable to focus training on exercises that require a greater impulse (e.g. power clean) or are more explosive (e.g. jump squat).

Emma Twigg, World Champion in Women's single scull in 2014, initiating a lift in training. *Credit: Trent Lawton*

EVALUATING STRENGTH TRAINING METHODS

In the first instance, strength testing should be used to assist periodically with the assignment of loads for weight training. For example, after a period of accustoming to exercise (e.g. three weeks), rowers should determine appropriate training loads for prescribed repetition maximums (e.g. 6RM).

However, you may notice that I am recommending quite a high repetition maximum. This is because the testing should be related to the training zone assigned in order to prove useful. Additionally, given that elite rowers demonstrate a unique ability to perform large volumes of work at high intensities, it is not uncommon for a peak strength measure (1RM), when a comparison is made to a more anaerobically trained athlete, to be quite unremarkable. (An example of suggested intensities and repetitions after warming up can be seen in Table 2a, week 11, on page 177.)

The more like training a test is, the more it will reflect the changes (adaptations) attained. As we did in our research, strength testing can be used to explore differences in muscle adaptations and rowing performance. This can be particularly important if diversity in training methods exists (e.g. trying a new type of strength-training circuit like CrossFit). Strength training methods that lead to greater rates of change or greater efficacy are highly desirable. (Remember, we observed that a difference of around 10 per cent in lower-body strength was associated with greater boat speed.) I hope the training objectives and assessments provided in this chapter help you to evaluate your own strength and power methods to improve rowing performance.

SUMMARY

Success in rowing is very multi-factorial and a training programme should address each physical capacity in turn to optimise on-water rowing performance. By no means should you feel that weight training is 'compulsory', and on reading this chapter you may see there appears to be no disadvantage to its inclusion, or no good reason to exclude it.

However, our experiences of using weight training to develop muscular strength, power and endurance in New Zealand's elite rowers has proved fruitful. I hope that giving you some insight into our systematic and practical research approach to training has helped you to reach some provisional conclusions about the possible performance benefits associated with weight training.

Nonetheless, you may wish to gather your own evidence (empirical or research) to establish whether there is a plausible relationship between rowing performance and a weight training programme or strength measure. In the interim, perhaps you may consider the more general benefits mentioned in this chapter, such as improved posture, bounce-back from injury or well-being, which are all important outside of the sport of rowing too.

In summary, I believe that best practice in weight training is to assign objectives and targets according to each individual's need and anticipated rate of progress. The ensuing programme of overload and activities should be appropriate to the experience of each rower, and in context to the calendar of competition. In particular, consider persisting with a small element of strength and conditioning all year – rowers that do this are more likely to gain a competitive advantage.

The success of a weight-training strategy should be measured against the specific reasons that it was included in the overall training scheme. Given weight-training objectives, targets and anticipated rates of progress should vary for individuals, there is no magical one-size-fits-all approach to advance rowing performance.

Nutrition for Advanced Rowing

Dr Charles Simpson Senior Lecturer in Sport and Exercise Science, Oxford Brookes University, UK.

Dr Charles (Charlie) Simpson is the course leader for the MSc in Sport and Exercise Nutrition at Oxford Brookes University. He is an Academic Associate of the Sport and Exercise Nutrition Register (SENr) and is a former recipient of British Rowing's Coach of the Year award. He provides sport nutrition consultancy to junior and senior rowing clubs in the UK.

The food and drink choices of a rower can have a major effect on rowing performance. This is surely a claim that few would disagree with, yet nutrition is a topic that often struggles for attention in rowing circles. Most magazines and coaches' conferences give comparatively little information on the matter, especially when compared to subjects such as training, technique and psychology. Perhaps it is something about which rowers and coaches don't believe they need much tuition. Surely rowers are capable of finding out for themselves if they train better after having eaten breakfast or whether drinking during training makes any difference to their performance. Perhaps the majority of rowers and coaches already believe they are sufficiently experienced in this area and that adding more information might just confuse matters. Either way, the importance of nutrition for rowing performance doesn't appear to be reflected in the amount of attention it gets.

People often view nutrition in the same way as they view driving a car. As long as they know how to put fuel in the tank so they can drive wherever they want, it doesn't really matter to them where the fuel comes from. Yet, anyone who has ever suffered the misfortune of filling up a diesel engine with standard petroleum gets an expensive lesson about the importance of making careful fuel choices. That is obviously an extreme case, and the human engine can run very well on a diverse range of food 'fuels'. Furthermore, a car's performance gets worse the more it is used. In contrast, a rower's performance gets better through regular use and the improvement almost always occurs regardless of whether he eats an optimal or sub-optimal diet. This may be the biggest challenge to getting rowers and coaches to take more interest in nutrition. Rowers can make their own dietary choices, which appear perfectly adequate to support impressive training gains. But, how would they ever know if their unique approach just works reasonably well or whether the benefits of their training gains could have been much more impressive had the athlete made different dietary choices?

To be fair, most rowers would probably be willing to make some sort of adjustment to what they eat and drink if they really believed that a particular change would help improve their competitive performance. There are certain groups of rowers, such as lightweights and coxes, who are usually very interested in improving their understanding of the effects of dietary adjustments. However, just having an interest in nutrition and concern for calorie consumption doesn't necessary lead to good dietary decisions. What most rowers seek when offered the opportunity to discuss nutrition, regardless of their starting level of interest, is clear direction. They want to know what they should eat and drink; that is an obvious concern. But rowers often mention that they are unclear about who is responsible for guiding the nutrition decisions of both them and their teammates. It seems that many rowing teams, even at the elite level, offer very little in the way of structured guidance about nutrition. Essentially, rowers are left to work it out for themselves. Yet, some teams clearly do recognise the importance of nutrition for performance and see this as an area where they can gain competitive advantage. These teams take nutrition very seriously and would not think to leave something so important to chance.

Whatever your interest level or knowledge of this topic, I hope to at least raise awareness about the untapped potential to advance rowing performance through the effects of diet. This is not the place for a discussion of the difference between a vitamin and a mineral or simple versus complex carbohydrates. There are plenty of textbooks for such matters. Instead, I would like to offer coaches and rowers a direction and purpose for their nutrition decisions. The first section begins with an overview of several key issues that affect our ideas and perceptions about nutrition for rowing. These are worth mentioning because making changes in the diet of individual rowers or an entire team will be extremely difficult unless there is some level of shared agreement about who is responsible for directing the dietary strategies. All readers will have at least a minimum level of understanding about the essentials of appropriate nutrition and might even have some established expectations about the balance of responsibility between coach and athlete. But how much common agreement on this topic could we expect to find within a team? Indeed, is it even a problem if the coach and athlete disagree about nutrition? Does it matter if members of the same crew hold very different beliefs about their nutrition? Clearly, disagreements between coaches and athletes and within crews can cause major difficulties and there is no sport that has a greater connection between individual contribution and team performance. So, before making any decisions about how to help rowers improve their nutrition choices, it is worth gaining better understanding about the likely resistance to any possible changes. Not every coach or rower will be keen to engage with this topic, so I want to bring a wider perspective of the typical issues that can arise when efforts are made to changes nutrition habits within a team.

ENGAGING ROWERS IN A CONVERSATION ABOUT NUTRITION

Some people believe that rowers can eat as they wish, whereas others are very prescriptive and suggest that rowers choose foods according to their nutrient content (e.g. carbohydrate, iron), amounts and timing in relation to training activities. At first, this range of opinions may seem unimportant and simply a matter of personal choice and understanding. But what if you discovered that the rowers in your crew hold very different opinions about nutrition? Does it matter if some rowers are very relaxed about what they eat, while others in the crew are especially attentive to diet? Even if everyone managed to keep their views private, there is no practical way to hide eating behaviours from teammates who train, travel, compete and socialise together. This can lead some rowers to make unwelcome comments about the commitment of other crew members and their willingness to make personal sacrifices for the sake of the crew's performance. Far from being a hypothetical example, most coxes actually know this situation already and quickly learn to adjust their eating in the days before a major competition, often by eating privately or not eating at all in order to avoid unwanted comments from teammates about carrying 'extra weight'. Surely the range of personal opinions about nutrition for rowing and the strength with which these are held creates great potential to affect team harmony. Knowing what to eat to help support the nutrient and fuel needs for rowing training is the obvious nutrition concern of most rowers and coaches. The part of the story that is rarely considered is that the shared beliefs of a crew are also important. In rowing, the personal beliefs and dietary habits of one crew member can easily become a cause for concern for everyone else, and this is an issue that I will return to shortly.

I am also conscious that readers of this chapter will have a wide range of acceptance about the extent to which nutrition is likely to have a direct effect on training adaptations and competitive performance. Even for those readers who are quick to agree to proclamations that nutrition is important for rowing, many won't have much else to say on the matter, and this happens at the elite and sub-elite levels. Sometimes this is because people are uninterested, unconvinced or just genuinely unaware about the potential for diet to affect rowing performance. But even when there is good acceptance and knowledge about the benefits of nutrition, coaches and rowers often prioritise other important goals such as improving stroke technique and optimising the rig of the boat. There are only so many hours in a day and nutrition considerations are especially easy to push to one side, in part, because all rowers have to deal with nutrition in some way. There is no sustainable option whereby rowers can avoid eating. Perhaps another reason why nutrition fails to inspire wider interest is that much of what a rower does eat and drink is unseen by the coach and so presents less opportunity for comment. Rowers don't usually eat three-course meals midway through a training session. However, stroke technique and training effort are much more in the coach's line of sight and what gets seen likely gets the greatest attention. Yet, there are time-efficient ways for teams to exploit the performance enhancing benefits of well-chosen nutrition strategies.

Interestingly, the performance benefits from many nutrition strategies only really appear once rowers reach a moderate to highly demanding training programme (e.g. >80km of rowing training per week), at which point, changing eating behaviours and individual attitudes is likely to be extremely difficult. This is why teaching good nutrition habits to new rowers is an important inclusion in an effective long-term athlete development programme, especially for young rowers who may have recently moved out of the family home into university residences or self-catered private accommodation.

GETTING AN APPETITE FOR BETTER TEAM NUTRITION

There are understandable reasons why many rowing teams fail to consider the advantages available from tackling the nutrition practices of its members, many of which will persist regardless of the scale of advantage available. Simply highlighting more opportunities to optimise the health and performance of rowers through nutrition strategies will do little to help teams where there are bigger problems to address first. Thus, it makes practical sense to begin with a discussion of the wider problems that rowing teams often face when seeking to influence the nutrition practices within the group.

One of the biggest problems to consider is how to adjust the delivery of nutrition strategies to cope with the range of knowledge, experience and opinions that exist within a rowing team. Clearly, everyone will have many years of experience in making nutrition decisions as part of everyday life, as well as having accumulated at least some familiarity with key concepts in nutrition through information sources (e.g. school, TV and internet, family members). At the other extreme, there may also be rowers who are especially well educated and interested in nutrition, but even for these individuals there is often a failure to convert good understanding and enthusiasm into effective daily eating choices and practices. Unsurprisingly, presenting basic everyday healthy nutrition information to groups of rowers where there is a wide range of background understanding does little to enthuse rowers with a desire to learn more about nutrition and may even be counterproductive. In team settings, there is an important need to evaluate the knowledge and ability of the members before targeting improvements.

While some rowers begin to experiment with their nutrition based on information presented on television or an internet source, it is far more common that rowers change their eating habits based on advice from people they know. Many people have lost weight or experienced other health benefits from making self-selected changes in their eating habits and want to share this information with others. Some of these personal testimonies are often very appealing to rowers, especially when they come from trusted friends and family whom the rower believes has their best interests at heart. So, often rowers are keen to at least give these ideas a try simply because they may sound reasonable and were offered with the best of intentions. Much of this advice can be helpful, but much of it can be inappropriate to the needs of an athlete. When bad advice comes from a trusted and friendly source, it often becomes harder for coaches and nutritionists to make subsequent corrections. In team settings, promoting effective changes in the nutrition choices requires both an appreciation for the amount of appropriate and inappropriate knowledge that exists, as well as sensitivity for the wide range of personal beliefs that likely exist. Predictably, the scale of this problem grows in proportion to the size of the team. The bigger the team, the greater the risk that an individual member will tune out from messages about nutrition which are perceived as unintelligible, boring and that may conflict with personal opinions.

Coaches are particularly aware of the importance of preserving team harmony and may think nutrition is simply a topic that is loaded with potential for conflict. This view may further restrict interest in studying the benefits of nutrition for performance since the very act of dispensing an opinion may cause upset in teams where there are many existing opinions. There are also coaches and rowers who begin with an enthusiastic interest in learning about specific nutrition practices that can improve rowing performance. However, they can quickly become disheartened by the apparent complexity of the topic and the lack of straightforward answers. Even a simple and perfectly reasonable question such as, 'what should I eat and drink to help the boat go faster?' is not easy to answer. Nutrition is a topic that is especially crowded with opinions, personal experiences and marketing hype. The simple truth is that there are few points of widely agreed consensus about what rowers should consume. Even reasonable questions are often difficult to answer without courting controversy.

Despite the ambiguity, complexity and challenges inherent in sports nutrition, it is nevertheless still a problem that many teams willingly seek to address. Most coaches and athletes can reasonably accept that diet is important for enhancing training and competitive performance, but who should lead the conversation? Is it really fair to expect the team coach to be responsible for considering the nutrition needs and requirements of the rowers, giving effective advice about improvements, not to mention doing so in ways that avoid creating offense or belittling the beliefs and understanding of all team members?

DO COACHES HAVE A RESPONSIBILITY TO EDUCATE ROWERS ABOUT THEIR NUTRITION?

Coaches are the obvious 'go to' source of information for rowers on all sorts of important matters connected to competitive performance including technique, training, rigging, equipment purchase and race tactics. But should coaches also be expected to give information and advice on nutrition? This question does not appear to have a simple answer. Certainly, lots of coaches make comments to rowers about the need to improve diet. Understandably, athletes are often receptive to such comments, irrespective of the coach's scientific credentials. Athletes, especially those in the early stages of their career, have usually experienced the benefits of learning to trust their coach's advice and this often extends beyond training and skill development to wider issues such as sleep, time management and lifestyle. Athletes value the wide range of expertise offered by an experienced coach, so it can feel perfectly natural for an athlete to also seek opinions about diet. Many rowers certainly welcome the input of a coach on matters of nutrition, regardless of whether the coach perceives this as part of their job.

On the other hand, many athletes are far less interested in the coach's views on nutrition and may simply ignore any offered advice. Coaches shouldn't be disheartened by these athletes. Every new rower arrives at their very first practice with many years of eating experience. They have their own taste preferences, habits and opinions. This is very different to most other areas of coaching advice. New rowers begin the sport with no specific knowledge about how to balance a boat or adjust oar length and are extremely willing to take advice. So, coaches who have been frustrated by past experiences of working with athletes who seem unreceptive to diet guidance might do well to reconsider their approach. These athletes are rarely uninterested in nutrition; it may just be that they base their nutrition decisions more strongly on their personal experience than other team members. The important point in this discussion is to highlight to coaches who are willing to tackle the topic of nutrition that when advice is presented to athletes in a way that is similar to how the coach might present information in other areas of importance, such as technique, many athletes are likely to appear uninterested and unwilling to make changes. This leads to frustration for both athletes and coaches, and is likely to be a key explanation as to why many coaches and rowers ignore talking to one another about nutrition.

We also need to remember that many coaches have good reasons to avoid giving specific nutrition advice. They may not feel sufficiently qualified or even interested. Also, there are usually major time pressures on team coaches, and entire days can be lost to important tasks that need attending to within the boathouse. Nevertheless, these coaches may still want their athletes to benefit from changes in diet that can enhance training and race performance. It is also perfectly understandable that a coach may not believe it is their duty to discuss specific aspects of nutrition with their athletes. Much about our food choices are influenced by our private beliefs and a coach may not want to tread on what might be regarded as personal matters. Consider the coach who wants to encourage the team to eat more protein to help support muscle repair and recovery from weight training. If the coach suggests that the team should consume more milk and meat to achieve this goal, could this directive offend any vegetarians in the group and produce a pressure to conform?

Resolving these issues is not impossible, but the best solution is likely to be one where both coaches and athletes formally recognise the importance of making dietary adjustments. Ultimately, it is the athlete's responsibility to decide what to eat, but wise coaches still need to communicate this clearly so that all athletes, regardless of their personal expectations of a coach, can make progress in their dietary practices.

BRINGING IN SPECIALISTS

Personally, I think that it is unfair to expect most rowing coaches to take lead responsibility for providing athletes with specific nutrition guidance. However, I also think that leaving athletes to sort this issue out on their own is likely to reduce the possible benefits and may even be counter-productive for some rowers. In reality, nutrition is likely to be a topic best handled by a suitably qualified sport nutritionist who can advise both the coach and team about effective approaches. This already happens in many high performance teams (see pages 171 (New Zealand), 31 (Norway) and 95 (Texas)), but even in these situations, the gains are often reduced because the coach essentially outsources all responsibility for diet matters to the nutritionist. But changing a person's lifetime behaviour is much harder than changing their blade handling ability. Even the best sport nutritionists are limited in what they can achieve without the active support of a coach.

In team settings, nutrition specialists usually only have a short time to work with individual athletes and each occasion may be separated by many months. This is where coaches can substantially enhance each athlete's progress by reminding and reinforcing nutrition recommendations, especially those initially explained by the team's sport nutritionist. Recent developments in phone apps and smartwatches are very helpful for reminding athletes to perform an action at a specific time. For example, an athlete's watch might vibrate one hour before a scheduled workout to remind him/her to drink two glasses of water. However, wearable technology has no inherent power to motivate change. In contrast, a coach that reminds athletes to drink water shortly before training through a medium such as social media (e.g. Twitter, Facebook etc.) or verbally adds a significant element of persuasiveness. Most athletes are highly motivated to respond to what the coach asks and will likely feel some level of compulsion to act in the interests of the group. When a coach reminds their athletes about the importance of diet for team performance, he/she also sends out a powerful message to everyone that such changes are important.

At the highest competitive levels, and ironically often in situations where there is professional nutrition support, many athletes fail to make sustained progress in diet and performance when their coach seems uninterested in discussing the topic. This frequently happens when coaches are sceptical about the merits of change or are simply under informed about nutrition. The next section discusses reasons why many coaches and athletes are unwilling to adopt the advice of a sport nutritionist. Even readers who already appreciate the importance of instilling good nutrition practices may find this section useful to better understand why other team members are often less interested in making dietary changes.

WHY MANY ROWERS AND COACHES IGNORE WHAT THEY KNOW TO BE IMPORTANT (AND WHY THEY MIGHT WANT TO RECONSIDER)

Rowers need to eat more food and drink more fluid than the average person. In the case of high-performance international rowers, the increased food consumption provides the extra energy needed to sustain between 100 and 250km of rowing each week, while the extra fluid intake helps rowers restore body water that is lost as sweat during training and competition. Indeed, if anyone attempted these demanding training loads while eating and drinking the amounts typically consumed by non-athletes, they would quickly get plenty of signals from the body to make changes. Hunger and thirst alone would give such a person a strong message to increase their food and drink intake.

Sometimes athletes will argue that they just need to listen to their body when making decisions about their diet. They believe that the same biological systems that provide prompts to eat and drink when hungry and thirsty are also sufficient to help make ideal diet choices for rowing training. This idea has obvious appeal – why think about something that seems to have a pretty good auto-pilot setting. However, this would be a very short-sighted approach for rowers with high performance aspirations. Consider, for example, that these evolved appetite stimulating processes really don't work nearly as well as we might like to think. Try asking any overweight coach or rower [politely] how well those innate appetite regulating behaviours are working for them. The signals that tell the brain to eat when hungry are not equally well matched by signals to stop eating once the body has achieved its essential requirements. Overweight individuals, whether athletic or not, need a considerable amount of motivation and conscious effort to successfully make dietary adjustments to regain a 'normal' weight. Leaving athletes to make dietary decisions on the basis of their self-awareness and ability to listen to internal biological cues is a poor strategy for individuals seeking to make the most of their physiology. Evolution has provided humans with effective ways to avoid the health risks of starvation, but survival instincts are not concerned with maximising 2000m boat speed.

Rowers may also ignore the benefits of diet because they have limited understanding or confidence in their own nutrition knowledge. These issues are made worse when rowers have little practical ability in food preparation and cooking, as well as limited time and financial resources. The financial problem of eating to support rowing training is a particularly tricky issue to solve. High-performance rowers require approximately twice as many calories as non-athletic individuals, and this is likely to double the weekly shopping bill. Many of the better-funded rowing programmes have addressed this issue by subsidising food costs for their athletes. For example, most collegiate rowing teams in the United States offer comprehensive meal plans to their athletes through buffet-style cafeterias that offer a wide range of food options to suit individual needs. International rowing teams in Britain, Australia and elsewhere have similar approaches and employ full-time chefs that often travel with the team to training camps and major regattas. Yet, for many aspiring rowers around the world, high food costs and limited access to funds are major barriers to improving their nutrition. The real problem for these rowers is being able to access and consume the large quantities of food needed for training. Understandably, it is hard to think about issues of food quality and diversity when just meeting the energy needs of training and daily living is a dominant concern.

Cost cutting ideas to help rowers save money

- avoid shopping on an empty stomach
- prepare and shop from a list (reduces risk of impulse buying)
- buy certain foods in bulk (e.g. rice, pasta, cereals)
- choose dairy produce, especially milk, rather than purchase commercial protein mixes
- use discount coupons, especially ones for reductions on your final bill
- use discount supermarkets and brands (where possible)
- learn to compare cost of products by price per unit (e.g. price per 100g)
- use smartphone apps to track supermarket offers and compare total shopping list costs
- prepare bulk amounts of meals at start of week and freeze portions for later use
- prepare home-made sports drinks from glucose/sucrose and tap water

Of course, there are many top rowing teams where the athletes get plenty of appropriate nutrition advice. These teams invest time and money to bring in qualified professionals to advise their athletes. In Great Britain, for example, the international rowing team has been well supported for many years by a highly qualified and experienced nutritionist, albeit on a part-time basis. However, with upward of 100 athletes and limited time available for consultation, this is still far from an ideal situation.

Lastly, athletes may be unwilling to consider changes to their diet because of a perception that their successes in training and competition thus far were achieved while eating according to their own wishes. Why make changes to something that is apparently working well? It is surely the case that one of the first lessons a person acquires when they begin a new sport, consciously or not, is that excellent progress in training can be achieved without paying significant attention to eating strategies or food choices. Training gains are easiest to notice during the initial months of training. As the training volumes increase, most rowers do make dietary changes, even if this happens too gradually for them to notice. For example, the hunger signals get stronger after long training sessions, which prompts athletes to increase their consumption of food and leads to greater energy and protein intake, both of which are good examples of self-selected dietary changes that help support training gains. I have already highlighted the limits of this approach for athletes who want to optimise their training gains. Nevertheless, it is worth considering that rapid gains in fitness that occur in the early phases of training are both impressive and robust. Large improvements in fitness and performance happen whether or not an athlete follows an optimal diet. One consequence of this is that athletes can legitimately claim that their dietary decisions have got them to a certain level of fitness. The challenge is getting athletes to recognise that better dietary choices can lead to even better progress – something that becomes increasingly important as rowers reach higher levels of competition.

ATHLETES STILL WANT TO KNOW ABOUT NUTRITION

Even in situations where the coach is uninterested in nutrition and there is no access to professional sport nutrition services, athletes often find ways to gain nutrition advice. Some rowers even spend considerable amounts of time discussing nutrition. Unsurprisingly, this group includes most lightweight rowers and coxes. If they cannot get the advice they want from the coach or from a professional, they will find other ways regardless of the quality of the source.

In the case of lightweight rowers at least, there is good data to help identify where these athletes get their information about weight loss before competition. Based on the results of a survey obtained with the input of 100 male and female lightweight competitors at the Australian Rowing Championships, Gary Slater and his research colleagues (2005) found that weight-loss strategies were most influenced by 'other rowers'. Approximately two-thirds of respondents said that other rowers had either a 'high' or 'very high' influence on their own weight-making strategies. The second most important source was 'coaches' (one third of respondents). Interestingly, the influence of a dietician was considered important by approximately half of the female rowers and a quarter of the male rowers, although it is likely that many of the rowers had little or no access to this service. The rowers considered other sources of weight-making advice, such as doctors, physiologists and mass media to be rather unimportant in their personal experience of making weight. The clear message from this study was that the beliefs of an individual rower about how to achieve weight loss are most likely to be influenced by what they are told by other rowers and by their coach.

From an organisational point-of-view, strategies to enhance athlete nutrition that involve significant input from coaches and other athletes are likely to have far greater success in comparison to situations where athletes are not provided with clear direction. It may be helpful to have a nutritionist visit to give a specialist talk to the team, but in isolation, the benefits are likely to be small. Making changes to long established eating behaviour is hardly any easier just because an expert tells them what improvements to make. However, if the input of an expert helps athletes to develop a group consensus about particular nutrition approaches to support training and race performance, then much can be achieved. Furthermore, the coach can improve matters by helping to re-communicate nutrition changes, providing frequent and more specific reminders to athletes and, above all, by showing an interest in the nutrition of all team members, the coach is able to use their special position to indicate change is needed. The engagement of coach and athlete in this more focused way helps everyone on the team, even the sceptical athlete or the athlete with their own strongly held beliefs, to make positive changes. Neither the coach nor athletes need expertise in nutrition, they just have to concentrate on making improvements that have been clearly identified by someone that the team can be confident does have such expertise. This leaves all team members free to focus on supporting each other to make improvements, just as they would if someone was struggling to make improvements in stroke technique or fitness.

GETTING EDUCATED AND THE TROUBLE WITH NUTRITIONISTS

Many athletes have little or no direct support from sport nutrition experts, but good information is available. Most rowing magazines and governing body websites contain at least some information on nutrition and this is usually of a good quality. The final section of this chapter discusses a selection of nutrition matters that will likely be of interest to rowers.

It is important to state that most nutritionists and dieticians believe that a good diet begins with basic nutrition matters and not issues to do with dietary extremism or what supplements to take. Essentially, basic nutrition means that an individual should eat a 'balanced diet' before attending to advanced nutrition matters. In the UK, the National Health Service (NHS) states that a balanced diet, '... means eating a wide variety of foods in the right proportions, and consuming the right amount of food and drink to achieve and maintain a healthy weight' (see Figure 1). However, an expanded discussion of such matters rarely interests rowers and coaches. Nevertheless, all rowers are sensibly encouraged to develop their basic nutrition knowledge and to achieve a balanced diet.

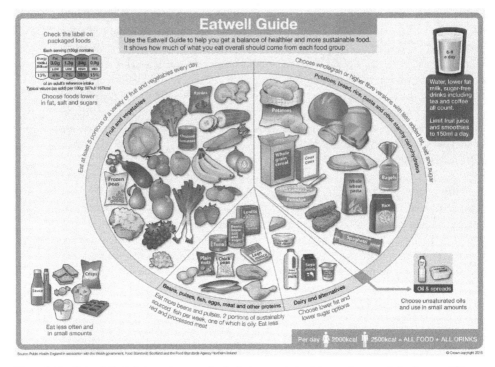

Figure 1: The Eatwell Guide[3] shows how much of what you eat should come from each food group. This includes everything you eat and drink during the day.

There are various excellent resources available on this topic elsewhere and readers are encouraged to develop their understanding of basic nutrition, as appropriate. What many rowers often do lack, however, is information about nutrition that is much closer to the specific needs and interests of high-performance rowers. Many of these rowers already a have a reasonable grasp of what a balanced diet means for the ordinary person, but want to know more about the potential for diet to enhance their training and ultimately their rowing performance. The remainder of this chapter highlights four relevant topics in nutrition that will hopefully interest high performance rowers and stimulate enthusiasm to develop their broader nutrition knowledge beyond this chapter.

SELECTED NUTRITION TOPICS FOR ADVANCED ROWERS

The question about how much a rower should eat is a good starting point for a specific discussion of nutrition for rowing. This is a much less controversial topic than matters such as what types of food to eat or how close to training an athlete can eat.

[3] The Eatwell Guide graphic is subject to Crown copyright protection and reproduced under the terms of the Open Government Licence. Source: Public Health England in association with the Welsh government, Food Standards Scotland and the Food Standards Agency in Northern Ireland.

What are the daily energy requirements of advanced rowers?

If you coach a team, consider asking each member to make an estimate of the total amount of kilocalories that they need for a typical day of training. If this is done on a blank sheet of paper with no guidance whatsoever, the answers can be very revealing. Typically, the estimates are reasonable and we'll consider those in a moment. However, some rowers struggle to make even a basic guess and either leave the paper blank or give a highly improbable value such as 20,000kcal per day. If it seems unfair to drop this question on a team without warning, consider that most breakfast cereal boxes list the typical daily energy requirements for adults on the packaging. For a typical non-athletic adult, the recommended daily intake is 2000kcal for women and 2500kcal for men. So how much more energy than ordinary adults does a rower need in order to support training demands?

In theory, it should be easy to evaluate how much energy rowers need to ingest each day. An athlete simply needs to record all the food and drink that he consumes during a three-day evaluation, including the specific amounts, for example, 200g of cooked fresh pasta. The diet log is then entered into a dietary analysis computer program that contains a database of typical foods and magically, 200g of pasta is converted to approximately 260kcal of energy. The process is repeated for all recorded foods and an average daily energy intake estimate is provided. Essentially, most surveys of rowers use this approach. Yet, when the overall energy intake results are revealed, the values are often much lower than expected, with some athletes apparently eating little more than the average non-athletic adult.

Nutritionists are well aware that using food logs to evaluate a rower's daily diet almost always results in estimates that are lower than the likely truth. Unfortunately, there really isn't much practical alternative on the energy intake side. When people are asked to complete food logs, it's a safe bet that many individuals will accidentally forget to write things down and/or they will change their normal eating habits to give a better impression to the person making the analysis. Interestingly, even professional dieticians change what they eat when asked to complete their own food records to make the results look more favourable. There is also good evidence that the food records of highly motivated rowers almost always produce energy intake estimates well below their likely typical intake. This problem occurs even when rowers are aware of the importance of maintaining their typical eating habits and making accurate, prompt records. In some cases, the food records of rowers provide energy intake values that can be as much as 50 per cent lower than the likely true value.

An alternative approach to answering this question is to estimate how many kilocalories a rower needs based on assessment of body composition alongside activity monitoring using accelerometers and heart rate monitors. Consider that the Concept2 ergometer already presents rowers with a reasonable estimate of how many kilocalories are expended during training. For example, if a rower completes 15km in one hour, this yields a reasonable energy expenditure estimate of 1000kcal on the performance monitor. It's worth knowing that the formula used by the Concept2 performance monitor assumes that the rower is 80kg. If the person was 60kg and completed an identical workout, the energy cost drops to 925 kcal[4]. The accuracy of

[4] See http://www.concept2.co.uk/indoor-rowers/training/calculators/calorie-calculator for more details.

Table 1: Estimated range of daily energy intake for adults and advanced rowers

Category	Estimated daily energy intake target (kcal/day)
Female (~57 kg; 25 yrs), sedentary	2000
Female (~57 kg; 25 yrs), active lifestyle (equivalent to 5km of brisk walking)	2400
International standard lightweight women (~57 to 61 kg)	3000 to 4000
International standard openweight women (~75 kg)	4000 to 5000
Male (~70 kg; 25 yrs), sedentary	2400
Male (~70 kg; 25 yrs), active lifestyle (equivalent to 5km of brisk walking)	3000
International standard lightweight men (~70 to 75 kg)	4000 to 5000
International standard openweight men (~90 kg)	5000 to 6000
Source of data for sedentary and active adults: Dietary guidelines for Americans 2015 to 2020 (http://health.gov/dietaryguidelines/2015/guidelines/)	

24-hour energy estimates is greatly improved when athletes use wearable technology such as the Polar V800 heart-rate watch. Critically, this technology can only give trustworthy estimates of total energy expenditure if heart rate is recorded during all exercise sessions and ideally, if VO$_2$max is also programmed into the settings[5].

The actual energy intakes of elite rowers have been estimated by Wendy Martinson, a trained dietician and nutrition advisor to the British Rowing team. Based on her experience of analysing the diet records of Britain's top international rowers and surveys of rowing related research, she has provided a range of likely daily intakes for rowers (see Table 1). These ranges represent the intake of rowers who typically complete the weekly equivalent of 140 to 200km of rowing and two to three resistance training sessions as well as several sessions of cross-training. The ranges also assume that rowers are not actively attempting to lose or gain significant amounts of body weight. The energy intake of lightweight rowers who are actively attempting to lose weight is likely to be 500 to 1000kcal lower than the values in the table below.

So what can we say about the likely energy needs of adult rowers who are not full-time athletes training and competing within a national team training set-up? A reasonable guess for these athletes, who are likely to be performing about half the amount of training as international standard rowers, is probably midway between the reference non-athletic individual and the closest category of high performance rower. For example, a 70kg female collegiate rower (e.g. NCAA division 1) is likely to need approximately 3000–3500kcal per day (which is midway between the reference 'normal' women and an international female rower). There will also be significant

---

[5] If VO$_2$max is unknown, it can be reasonably estimated by using: http://www.concept2.co.uk/indoor-rowers/training/calculators/vo2max-calculator

differences between athletes in the same club team because the height, weight and body composition will vary much more so than in national team athletes. Also, occupation is worth considering when estimating energy intake, since an athlete that works in a highly active job such as a full-time bike courier or furniture-removal specialist will have daily energy requirements near to the values presented for international athletes.

Ultimately, all rowers will benefit from having an idea about their normal energy intake and daily requirement. This information informs conversations about body weight management and can encourage athletes to better manage food intake during periods of intensified training (e.g. training camps) or enforced rest (e.g. injury). It is especially important for athletes who are training to increase muscle mass, and these individuals may need to add an extra 500kcal per day beyond their established 'weight-stable' energy requirements. For coaches and rowers seeking accurate estimates of daily energy requirements, the best approach is to combine careful use of food records and assessments of body weight/composition. The use of 24-hour activity monitoring via wearable technology that incorporates heart-rate measurements is increasingly being used to estimate energy expenditure with or without the additional information gained by diet and body weight records. Keep in mind that it is the food record that gives insight into how athletes achieve their energy intakes, including the quality and quantity of food and drink that is selected.

Does alcohol reduce the benefits of rowing training?

Many rowers enjoy regular consumption of alcoholic drinks but the typical amounts and pattern of intake is likely diverse. For present purposes, it may help to divide rowers into three broad groups according to their typical alcohol consumption behaviours and with the presumption that all are adults over the age of 18. The first group are the 'non-drinkers' and essentially never drink during the rowing training year. Many coaches expect that their athletes will be part of this group, especially in funded performance system (e.g. high-performance training centres and NCAA varsity rowing programmes). Indeed, many rowing programmes have written policies in place that convey clear messages that athletes should restrict or eliminate alcohol ingestion.

The second group of rowers by alcohol intake behaviours are the light/moderate drinkers. These athletes do consume alcohol, but typically do not exceed the recommendations stated by government health advisories. For clarity, a unit of alcohol (which differs slightly by country) is usually considered to be equivalent to a single shot of an alcoholic spirit (e.g. 25ml of whisky or vodka) while a small glass of wine (150ml) or pint of moderate-strength beer (4 per cent alcohol, 568ml) approximately 2 units. In the UK, the most recent national guidelines (published in January 2016) advise that adults should not exceed 14 units of alcohol per week (with no difference between males and females), that all adults should include at least several alcohol-free days each week, and in cases where an adult is ingesting 14 units, the intake should be spread evenly over three days or more. At present, the alcohol advisories of most other European governments are generally a little more relaxed. However, the health authorities in the UK have recently decided that there is no such thing as a 'safe' level of alcohol intake. So this second group of rowers could best be described as 'restrained drinkers'.

The final group of rowers are the 'moderate/heavy drinkers'. These rowers will regularly exceed national health guidelines either by drinking intakes of >2 units per day on most days of the week or by episodes of binge drinking. It is hard to get good information on the proportion of rowers who fall within this group, but anecdotally it is reasonable to suggest that there are quite a number. There are strong traditions that endorse alcohol intake by athletes in many university and club programmes across the rowing world. Team celebrations, whether formal or informal, frequently include alcohol and, of course, many boathouses have their own bars that offer cheap alcoholic drinks to all club members. Given the likelihood that at least some athletes within a team will be classified as either 'restrained drinkers' or 'moderate/heavy drinkers', many coaches and rowers have growing concerns about the effects of alcohol intake on training benefits.

At present, there is no straightforward answer to whether training gains would be any different between the teetotal, restrained and moderate/heavy drinkers. There is very limited research on this topic and the work that has been published is usually concerned with the immediate effects of alcohol on sleep, hydration and motor skills. Ideally, what would be helpful to our understanding is a study that randomly divided a large rowing team into our three groups at the start of the training year. The teetotal group would promise to avoid all alcohol and would submit to regular and random tests to check for compliance. The restrained group would receive a supply of alcoholic drinks and told to consume these according to a planned schedule. Finally, the moderate/heavy drinkers would be provided with large quantities of alcoholic drinks and asked to participate in regular social gatherings where they would be encouraged to drinks lots of free alcohol. All of the rowers would ensure that they follow the same standard training programme and at the end of the training year we could compare improvements in 2000m performance on rowing machines and in single sculls. If the average gains in land and water rowing performance were high for the teetotal athletes, medium for the restrained drinkers and low for the moderate/heavy drinkers, then we would have our clear answer. Researchers and coaches could then do a better job of explaining why alcohol reduces the benefits of training. The most likely reasons would include detrimental effects of regular alcohol such as higher likelihood of dehydration, sleep disruption, interference with nutrient absorption and undesirable body composition changes due to increased body fat levels and attenuated muscle mass gains and muscle damage recovery. Unfortunately, no one is ever likely to do this sort of study due to the costs and difficulty of completing as well as the challenges of finding willing volunteers (at least for some of the groups).

The suggestion that regular alcohol ingestion 'may' reduce gains from training is speculative and controversial. However, the results of a carefully controlled study by Evelyn Parr, Louise Burke and co-workers (2014) have provided good evidence to show that alcohol does interfere with muscle adaptation. Professor Burke is well known to many Australian national team rowers since she has been the head of sport nutrition at the Australian Institute of Sport for many years. The study examined eight physically active males who completed a training session that consisted of resistance training (8 x 5 leg extensions at 80 per cent of 1 repetition maximum) and aerobic training (30 minutes of moderate intensity cycling) on several occasions. On separate occasions, the subjects consumed one of the following drinks immediately after completing the exercise session and the same drink again four-hours later:

1.   protein drink (no alcohol)
2.   protein drink with approximately 6 units of alcohol
3.   carbohydrate drink with approximately 6 units of alcohol

All subjects ate a carbohydrate rich meal soon after exercise and allowed researchers to take small samples of muscle tissue (from the upper leg) for analysis of muscle protein synthesis. Since all subjects repeated the same training session three times, with only the drink consumed changing, it was possible to make conclusions about the effect of adding a large intake of alcohol after training on short term muscle adaptation (note: the subjects consumed a total of approximately 12 units in four-hours of recovery from training, which was considered as 'moderate/heavy drinking'). Compared to pre-exercise resting values, muscle protein synthesis increased after all three drinks. The smallest increase occurred when subjects consumed the carbohydrate+alcohol drink (+29 per cent) followed by the protein+alcohol drink (+57 per cent), and the greatest gain occurred with the protein only drink (+109 per cent). These results should be treated as provisional until other researchers can confirm the interpretation, and especially in highly trained endurance athletes rather than just physically active subjects. Nevertheless, there are good reasons to think that ingesting large amounts of alcohol after training reduces the potential for muscle growth and repair. When these results and those from other short-term investigations are considered, it is reasonable to suggest that the rowers who we earlier categorised in the hypothetical season-long experiment as 'moderate/heavy drinkers' would perform worse than expected in the end-of-season 2000m races. However, what is of far greater and immediate relevance to most national, university and club rowers is whether 'restrained drinkers' would see any difference in 2000m training gains. Unfortunately, there is just too little information to justify a comment for this group. The most that we can say is that restrained drinking behaviours are highly unlikely to provide physiological or technical benefits to the athlete and, at worst, have potential to reduce training gains and present other health risks. For these reasons, rowers and team coaches seeking to maximise gains in rowing performance may want to consider minimising or removing alcohol from the training diet.

Do sports drinks improve rowing performance?

It seems that almost everyone has their own personal answer to this question, whether they are involved in rowing or not. Sports drinks, which are essentially just carbohydrates (usually glucose) mixed with water, are popular targets for TV programmes and mass media, especially when the main story focuses on national and international obesity trends. To be clear, it is perfectly reasonable that journalists highlight the link between excess sugar consumption and the increasing prevalence of obesity in children and adults. Sports drinks most certainly do contribute to this excess of sugar intake in the wider population, and common sense tells us that the plentiful stock of commercial sports drinks in corner stores, petrol stations and

International rowers drinking before a race. *Credit: Steve McArthur*

supermarkets far exceeds the collective thirst of 'athletes' who use these shops. Of course, this is a very different situation to that of high-performance rowing where the carbohydrate and calorie needs of rowers are among the highest in society. Yet, many rowers and coaches are understandably confused about the use of sports drinks. The mixed messages from magazines and television programmes, which frequently muddle the use of sports drinks by athletic and non-athletic for editorial convenience, help explain much of the confusion. So do sports drinks help rowers perform? The simple answer is 'yes and no'.

First, consider that sports drink companies sponsor many international rowing teams. For example, British rowing teams have enjoyed commercial sponsorship with several companies that sell sports drinks, including SiS and Lucozade brands. Consequently, top rowers throughout the world have plentiful access to sports drinks and many will consume several litres per day. Clearly, vast numbers of rowers at high-performance training centres use sports drinks and when asked, are usually happy to say that doing so helps their training. Perhaps it is surprising to learn that there is actually very little published research on the direct effects of sports drinks on rowing training and performance per se. Researchers have simply not been particularly interested in this topic, at least not with rowing as the focus. On the other hand, the amount of sports drink-related research in other endurance sports, notably distance running and cycling, is impressively large. The headline conclusion from many hundreds of studies is that sports drinks, in comparison to an equivalent volume of placebo (flavoured water), can provide worthwhile benefits to the endurance capacity of both recreational and professional athletes. It is important to note that in this context endurance capacity is usually defined as exercise tasks that last one hour or more and are performed at moderate to vigorous intensity (i.e. between 70 and 95 per cent maximum heart rate). Indeed, the specific details from many of these studies are frequently well known by rowers and coaches and are likely to have helped inform the decisions of international rowing team managers when choosing a commercial sponsorship partner.

The detailed evidence that supports the use of sports drinks by rowers is too extensive to review here. However, it is important to note that the potential benefits of sports drinks are only indirectly related to 2000m performance. In other words, sports drinks help rowers during long training sessions, but there is no suggestion that consuming standard formula sports drinks (i.e. a drink with carbohydrates and electrolytes such as sodium and potassium as the active ingredients) shortly before a 2000m event will be beneficial. Some sports drinks contain caffeine, and there are reasons to expect that this ingredient does contribute small gains in 2000m performance. However, some rowers have experienced gut discomfort and vomiting due to drinking a sizable volume of sports drink shortly before a 2000m maximal effort. Under these circumstances, sports drinks may actually compromise rowing performance, and often rowers who reject the use of sports drinks in all circumstances do so because of single bad episode that looms large in their memory.

The main selling point for sports drinks is that they supply carbohydrate and water in a convenient way during prolonged training. Similar benefits are likely if rowers choose to consume other forms of carbohydrate (e.g. fruits) alongside water. Also, many of the research studies that show benefits from sports drinks do so by ensuring that athletes arrive for testing in a fasted state (approximately 3 to 12 hours after their last meal). The positive benefits for these drinks during prolonged exercise after a recent meal are much harder to demonstrate. So if a rower has consumed a carbohydrate-rich meal or snack shortly before training, they may wish to drink only water in training since the body may already have sufficient access to carbohydrate for fuel from the muscles, liver and gut. Potentially, sports drinks become more useful to high-performance rowers in the hours immediately after a training session, especially if two or three sessions are planned for the day. However, even this statement has become more controversial in recent years. There is growing evidence that performing 'some' prolonged training sessions in a fasted and/or low carbohydrate state may enhance aerobic adaptations within the active muscles.

So, when rowers and coaches decide what advice to follow regarding the use of sports drinks, it must be understood that there are situations where these drinks are unhelpful and unnecessary (e.g. shortly before a 2000m race) and other situations where they contribute to training enhancement, enjoyment and recovery. Perhaps, this helps explain why some of the best rowers in the world are enthusiastic consumers of sports drinks, while others avoid them at all costs. I hope that these brief comments go some way to helping individuals move past the confusing information promoted by both the mass media as well as the marketing strategies of commercial companies. It is highly likely that rowers can win Olympic titles without ever consuming a sports drink, but clearly many top rowers do find acceptable ways to use these products

Table 2: Benefits and risks from the use of sports drinks by rowers

Potential benefits	Potential risks
Provides glucose to active muscles during training	Unwanted weight gain
Enhances immune function	Teeth decay
Reduced risk of low blood sugar in training by sparing liver glycogen	Gastrointestinal upset (including vomiting)
Encourages voluntary drinking, reducing dehydration risk	Costs can be expensive when drinks are not supplied free of charge
Helps athletes achieve total daily carbohydrate intake targets	Some concern that high sugar intakes increase risk of metabolic disorders (e.g. Type 2 diabetes)
May help athletes maintain concentration during long sessions	Adding carbohydrate to a drink reduces rate of fluid transfer from the stomach
May reduce the rate of perceived exertion during long training sessions	Unpleasant taste
Pleasant taste	

to support their training progress and in doing so, are likely to experience indirect benefits to their 2000m rowing performance. Table 2 presents a summary of the potential benefits and risks to the regular use of sports drinks by rowers.

Nutrient manipulation

Perhaps the most exciting of recent developments in sport nutrition is the discovery that it is possible to enhance physiological and performance outcomes in endurance athletes by controlling the amount of fat and carbohydrate they consume before and after training. Various studies since 2005 have established that training in either a fasted state, or when the body's carbohydrate reserves are low (e.g. soon after completing an interval training session), enhances the aerobic adaptations in active muscles. The most important of these improvements is a greater than expected increase in the amount of mitochondria in trained muscles (e.g. in the leg muscles of cyclists). Mitochondria are the machinery within muscle that converts fat and carbohydrate to adenosine triphosphate (ATP) energy, which transports chemical energy within cells for metabolism, as long as oxygen is also available to support the process. Ultimately, the fat and carbohydrate that athletes consume gets delivered to the mitochondria where the chemical bonds within each macronutrient are broken, freeing energy to be used to keep the body functioning and to power muscle contractions. For an endurance athlete, developing large numbers of mitochondria is a great way to improve endurance and increase the body's ability to rely on fat stores for fuel, sparing the limited carbohydrate stores. In theory, increasing the amount of mitochondria in an athlete's muscles should make it easier to perform exercise using energy produced by the aerobic rather than the anaerobic pathways.

Between 2005 and 2016, various research groups found that it was possible to improve aerobic adaptations to endurance training by manipulating the carbohydrate stores of the body. The most popular manipulations included either reducing a person's carbohydrate intake before and after training or by performing repeated training sessions in short succession with a normal carbohydrate intake. Both approaches are designed to create a training situation where the lack of available carbohydrate reserves results in greater use of fat stores and subsequent gains in mitochondria levels. Greater endurance adaptations should, in theory, lead to greater endurance ability. Indeed, some researchers were able to demonstrate enhanced endurance capacity but only in untrained individuals. There was no convincing evidence that manipulating an athlete's carbohydrate stores, either through training or dietary approaches, would enhance sporting performance during relatively short, high intensity efforts (<1 hour) in already well-trained endurance athletes. Even when substantial improvements in aerobic physiological adaptations were achieved, there was often a reduction in high intensity performance due to a decrease in physiological adaptations responsible for the rapid conversion of carbohydrate stores to energy. Essentially, the subjects in these studies improved their ability to perform low-intensity training, but simultaneously compromised their ability to perform high intensity training. Both low and high intensity training are essential to maximise aerobically demanding events such as middle-distance running. Thus, the strategy of training with low carbohydrate stores succeeded in improving aerobic adaptations achieved through low intensity training, but failed to enhance overall performance gains because of a reduced ability to complete high intensity training. The challenge was to find a diet and training approach that could both enhance aerobic adaptations and still allow athletes to maintain the quality of their high intensity sessions.

In 2016, Laurie-Anne Marquet, along with colleagues in France and Australia published a report that appears to have found a way to enhance both physiological gains from training and performance by altering the timing of fat and carbohydrate intake around training. These researchers reasoned that changing the pattern of eating before and after training sessions could enhance the benefits of training, and help transfer the physiological benefits into performance gains.

They recruited 21 triathletes and separated them into two groups. Each group performed the same three-week training programme and consumed approximately 6 to 7g of carbohydrate per kg of body weight each day. There were no differences between groups in training or overall daily diet. Instead, it was the timing of carbohydrate intake during each of the first three days of each week that differed between groups. Essentially, both groups completed an interval training session at approximately 5 p.m. on day 1 of each week. This session consisted of high intensity intervals (6–8 x 5min at high intensity with 1min recovery) and was designed to reduce the muscle glycogen content by approximately 50 per cent of normal values. One group then avoided eating any carbohydrate for the remainder of the evening and overnight (sleep with low muscle glycogen group; sleep-low group). These subjects were fed meals and snacks containing only protein and fat, whereas the subjects in the control group ate a normal mixed diet containing protein, fat and carbohydrate (control group).

The next morning, subjects in the sleep-low group avoided all food and completed a 60-minute session of low intensity cycling in a fasted state, after which, they ate a high carbohydrate breakfast (2.5g/kg of body mass) followed later by a high carbohydrate lunch and afternoon snack. In contrast, the control group ate the high carbohydrate breakfast before the 60-minute low intensity cycle session and then consumed lower quantities of carbohydrate during the day compared to the sleep-low group. So both groups performed the same training sessions and ate the same overall diet components, but the sleep-low group performed the low intensity training in the first three days in a fasted state and then ate their entire day's carbohydrate allocation between 10 a.m. and 5 p.m., where the control group avoided training in a fasted state and ate carbohydrate throughout the full day. This approach meant that both groups had plenty of carbohydrate reserves to perform the high-quality interval training (5 p.m. session) and then the subsequent sleep-low protocol meant that the sleep-low group performed the low intensity session (next morning) with a greater reliance on fat stores, providing a stronger adaptation stimulus. This pattern of eating and training was repeated across three sequential days and then all remaining training each week was performed at low intensity.

The improvements in performance in the sleep-low group were impressive. After three weeks, they improved 10km running time on an indoor track from 40:23 to 39:10 (2.9 per cent improvement), whereas there was almost no change in the control group performance (41:26 to 41:24). High intensity performance was tested through a cycle to exhaustion at 150 per cent of the maximum power achieved during a VO_2max test. The sleep-low group extended their time to exhaustion from 53 to 58 seconds while there was no statistical improvement in the control group's time to exhaustion (58 to 59 seconds). The sleep-low group also experienced favourable changes in body composition (enhanced body fat loss) and cycling efficiency consistent with enhanced physiological adaptations from the sleep-low approach. Strictly speaking, it is not possible to identify whether the enhanced physiological and performance benefits in the sleep-low group were due to the strategy of condensing the entire day's carbohydrate into a narrow period between 10 a.m. and 5 p.m. or whether performing low intensity morning training in a fasted state per se is the important feature responsible for success. In either case, this study provides strong evidence that manipulating macronutrient timing around low and high intensity training sessions can enhance endurance training and performance outcomes. Future studies are clearly needed to confirm these results and better explain the underlying physiological mechanisms of improvement. Nevertheless, these early results justify the prediction that rowers should be able to enhance their training gains and 2000m performance by adjusting their diet and training structures to include periods of low intensity training in a fasted/low carbohydrate state.

SUMMARY

- Many advanced rowers and their coaches are interested in improving their nutrition practices to help support rowing performance, but are often unclear about how to initiate positive changes.
- Rowers gain much of the understanding of sport nutrition from other rowers and coaches, but the quality of this information is highly variable.
- In the first instance, coaches are advised to remove any ambiguity about who is responsible for making changes in a rower's diet by providing clear communication about responsibilities rather than leaving this to chance.

- In most cases, rowing coaches are unlikely to have extensive understanding, knowledge and qualifications in nutrition and are therefore unlikely to provide their athletes with anything beyond general nutrition guidance.

- Rowers should not expect coaches to provide highly specific and individualised nutrition guidance. Instead, dietary recommendations for individual rowers and teams are best led by a well-qualified nutritionist/dietician who has specific training in sport nutrition and experience of working with well-trained endurance athletes.

- Many of the world's best rowers regularly work with professional sport nutritionists and sports dieticians to address the quality of their dietary approach.

- The nutrition choices and eating behaviour of rowers and coxes can be a source of potential conflict in teams. These problems can be minimised within a team when coaches, athletes and sport nutrition specialists engage in a supportive dialogue, especially where this leads to educational strategies for improvement.

- Coaches and rowers are likely to gain better results from the use of specialist sport nutritionists when there is awareness that the services offered normally include an initial focus on healthy eating. Once rowers have a good appreciation of the benefits of eating a balance diet, it is appropriate to target dietary improvements that can support demanding training loads and enhance competitive performance.

- Rowers can benefit from extra support in finding cost-effective ways to ensure that they meet the energy demands of training.

- Although the effects of regular alcohol consumption after training are not yet clear, it is likely that moderate to high intakes will reduce training benefits and compromise competitive performance.

- The use of sports drinks by rowers before, during and after training offer many benefits. However, rowers are advised to be mindful that the benefits of carbohydrate-based drinks are likely greatest during prolonged training sessions. Sports drinks that are consumed shortly before racing are unlikely to enhance performance and may actually decrease competitive performance due to unwanted side effects such as nausea and stomach fullness.

- In future, rowers may seek to enhance training responses by the selective adjustment of dietary carbohydrate intake and/or the use of training and nutrition strategies that promote physiological adaptations without compromising high intensity training capacity.

Selected references

Marquet, L. A., Brisswalter, J., Louis, J., Tiollier, E., Burke, L. M., Hawley, J. A., & Hausswirth, C. (2016). 'Enhanced Endurance Performance by Periodization of Carbohydrate Intake: "Sleep-low" Strategy', *Med Sci Sports Exerc*, 48(4), 663–672. doi:10.1249/MSS.0000000000000823

Parr, E. B., Camera, D. M., Areta, J. L., Burke, L. M., Phillips, S. M., Hawley, J. A., & Coffey, V. G. (2014). 'Alcohol ingestion impairs maximal post-exercise rates of myofibrillar protein synthesis following a single bout of concurrent training', *PLoS One*, 9(2), e88384. doi:10.1371/journal.pone.0088384

Slater, G. J., Rice, A. J., Sharpe, K., Mujika, I., Jenkins, D., & Hahn, A. G. (2005). 'Body-mass management of Australian lightweight rowers prior to and during competition', *Med Sci Sports Exerc*, 37(5), 860–866

Utilising Technology for Advanced Rowing

Dr Conny Draper Biomechanist

Conny Draper has worked as a sports biomechanist within elite sport at a World and Olympic level for several national federations since 1996. She completed her Sports Science degree and master's thesis in Germany and then relocated to Australia, where she was working at the Australian and New South Wales Institute of Sport, having completed her PhD at the University of Sydney in 2006.

Conny's technical expertise as an applied sports biomechanist is focused mainly around rowing and canoe kayak; although she also has wide ranging experiences in advising and delivering biomechanical services to other sports – including diving, swimming, football, and Para-sports – at both provincial and national level.

In 2012, Conny became a FISA member of the Equipment and Technology Commission (an advisory committee including monitoring and control of equipment and technological developments and other issues). Conny is currently living in Switzerland and offers applied sports biomechanical/scientific consulting services internationally – to national rowing federations, university and school rowing programmes.

Until recently, a stopwatch and a video camera were the main tools of the trade for the majority of rowing coaches. While stroke/speed coaches and heart-rate monitors have been standard training monitoring and racing tools for the top teams, GPS tracking and on-water data acquisition systems and phone/tablet-based applications are becoming more attractive to the wider rowing community. Coaches and athletes usually have many questions once they receive data from their training and racing sessions and this is an area that offers an opportunity to optimise and individualise rowing performance.

MODERN INTERNATIONAL REGATTA FEEDBACK

During the Olympic Games in Rio 2016, World Rowing offered the coaches and athletes GPS information for each race. The information for each boat covered the main parameters 'stroke rate' and 'boat velocity' averaged for every 50m. This can be used to analyse the race performance for each competitor and to compare the different race profiles to each other.

The lightweight men's four category is a good example, where very tight racing is expected, especially at the World Championships and Olympics. However, when you look at each of the six boats, you can identify various racing profiles in regards to stroke rates, in particular during the first and last 500m. While the top three LM4-

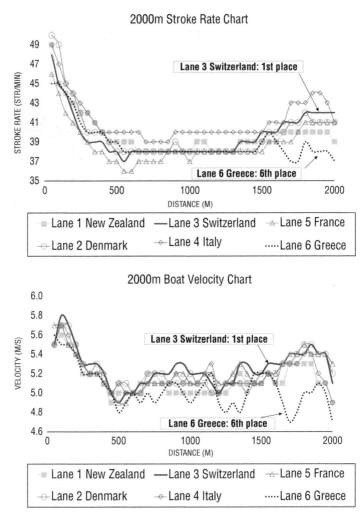

Figure 1: Olympic Rowing Final A: Lightweight Men's Four (LM4-); (a) stroke rate chart, (b) boat velocity chart

boats were within 2.34sec (6:20.51 – 6:22.85) of each other, the boat in sixth place was over 16sec behind (6:36.47). The six different boat velocity profiles gave a clearer understanding where crews gained or lost speed during the race.

A closer look at the boat velocity profile of lane 6 highlights that the fluctuation jumps between the 50m measuring increments were too high. It is almost impossible for international standard crews to race this way. It becomes obvious that the information is faulty and that the data from the lane 6 GPS unit (see bottom line in Boat Velocity chart) possibly carried an error in some way (i.e. a faulty GPS unit or unstable GPS signal etc.). As such, the information for this team should not be analysed or used as feedback. This example serves to highlight the need to critically view data before it is utilised for feedback sessions following training or racing.

COACHING AND FEEDBACK

Coaching and the 'coach's eye' has special significance for instructional and training purposes due to the advantage of quick information feedback (eye observation and acoustic feedback). However, it can lack in precision, as the coach's opinion about a good understanding of an efficient rowing motion and the interpretation of technical faults, can vary – and is often subjective.

The utilisation of biomechanical equipment and applied analyses can be the 'objective coach's eye', due to its advantages of precision (data is measurable) – assuming that the information is correctly measured and analysed, as well as being meaningful and applicable feedback to monitor the athletes' technique and control the development of their performance.

This information combined allows coaches and rowers to examine the different aspects of executing the rowing movement more precisely while allowing for individual differences and comparing it to a 'technical rowing model', which must clearly be defined by parameters that use boat speed (the key performance indicator). It also provides a basis for the development of other physical and psychological requirements.

In addition, the information gathered and provided (in real-time or post-session) needs to be 'applicable (rowing-specific) – coachable (complements the coaching terminology) and trainable (athletes can relate to the information to make technical changes)'.

ROWING SPECIFIC PARAMETERS AND ANALYSIS

Rower, blade, boat and water are in continual interaction during the rowing stroke and must be highly coordinated to achieve medal-winning performances at any rowing level. Its continuous, cyclic and closed skill movement must be repeated more than 220 times in a race at a high strength level. Technical proficiency is essential to achieve an optimal performance, as it is of little value to develop strength, endurance and physiological capabilities if these qualities cannot be transferred into boat speed.

The main parameters that have been widely accepted and proven successful for coaching and training purposes to analyse the rower's technical skill and performance level and development are:

- The main boat-specific parameters:
  - stroke rate
  - boat velocity
  - boat acceleration (propulsive, transverse, vertical direction)
  - boat orientation (pitch, roll and yaw (fishtailing) of the boat)
- The main individual athlete-generated parameters:
  - handle forces (one to multi-dimensional, measured on the oar handle or oarlock)
  - oar angle (horizontal, vertical, roll of the oar, measured on the oar handle or oarlock)
  - footstretcher forces (one to multi-dimensional)
  - handle, seat and trunk velocity and displacement etc.

This technical and detailed performance-related information is best illustrated by graphical displays in combination with derived variables (ie. stroke rate, average boat velocity, individual's power per stroke, stroke length) that allow a comprehensive analysis of the rower/s and crew's technique and their effect on the key performance variable; the boat velocity. Together, both displays complement each other, however, they also have different levels of importance in the feedback process. While the boat velocity information is clearly best described numerically (average boat velocity over distance covered or stroke rate), the boat acceleration curve characteristics describe how and why the intra-stroke boat velocity fluctuates. This detailed information could not be displayed in single numbers.

Due to the continuous cyclic rowing sequence, most boat-specific and athlete-generated parameters are identifiable by characteristic rowing-specific curve

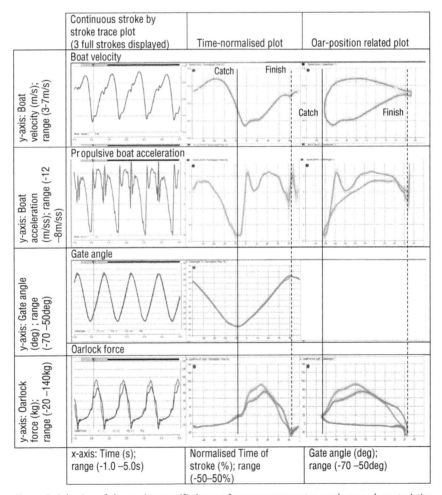

Figure 2: Selection of the rowing specific key performance parameters and curve characteristics

patterns[6]. The four main parameters are displayed in Figure 2 in three different ways – as a:

- continuous stroke by stroke trace plot (three full strokes displayed)
- time-normalised plot and
- oar-position related plot

The data in the time-normalised and oar-position plot (Figure 2) display the stroke by stroke information over the second minute of the 2000m race of an international medal-winning crew. It reveals for all four parameters an extremely high consistency in the stroke by stroke delivery (also individually between the two athletes).

The next example (Figure 3) compares two clearly visible propulsive boat acceleration profiles (boat acceleration versus time/stroke) of two men's double sculls during racing (data taken from 250–750m). However, the left-hand one is from a junior men's double (under-15), the right-hand one from two international medal-winning senior men's athletes. In general, it can always be found that a higher stroke by stroke consistency curve characteristics plot indicates a greater skill and performance level of the athletes and crews.

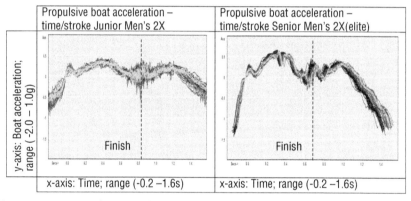

Figure 3: Comparison of two propulsive boat acceleration stroke by stroke profiles (from 250–750m at race pace): junior men's double scull (under-15; left) versus senior men's double scull (international medal-winning athletes)

Examining any of the rowing-specific parameters must be related to the external conditions (temperature, wind direction), the athlete's skill level, gender, the boat type and the rigging set-up as well as to the type of training captured.

More commonly in practice than the stroke by stroke information is the display of average curve profiles, represented by a single stroke over a selected time period (using time-normalised and oar position plots).

---

[6] Detailed biomechanical information about most of the rowing variables can be found in the literature provided at the end of this chapter (see page 221).

However, it is *very* important and strongly recommended that only data of similar stroke rates is averaged (maximum recommended range: approximately +/-2strokes/minute), otherwise 'the averaging process' leads to miscalculation of time-depending movement sequences, which can change the representative curve characteristics and 'realistic absolute' magnitude of the selected technical and/or performance parameters (see Figure 4; i.e. boat acceleration and one individual force profile) and would lead to the wrong technical feedback.

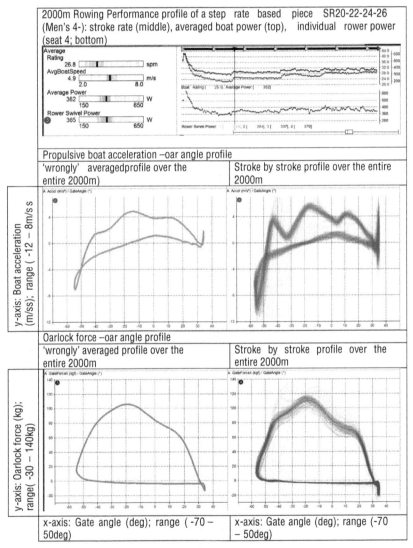

Figure 4: Display of a 2000m step rate piece (SR20-22-24-26); comparison between the 'wrongly' averaged profiles (left) versus the stroke by stroke profiles (right): boat acceleration (middle) and one individual force (bottom)

COACHES AND ROWERS AS TECHNOLOGY OPERATORS

Coaches and rowers often question:

- What type of tools would be useful to assist and benefit my team to get started with biomechanical analysis?
- Which new innovations in biomechanical technology could enhance rowing performance and improve feedback to the athletes?

It is important to look at your coaching and training environment and go through a few logistical questions:

- What level of rowers do I coach, how big is the squad, what are the main boat categories we train in?
- What type of weather and water conditions do we train in (wind affected; salt/fresh water; current, river, busy waterways, etc.)?
- Where are the boats stored (out/indoor)?

Technical questions:

- Can additional technology enhance my coaching and training:
  - as a monitoring, assessment and feedback training tool?
  - by identifying areas for technical improvements?
  - to assist the coaching 'eye' and enhance coaching decisions?
- What elements of the training and racing do I want to quantify?
  - training loads, individual technique, boat performance, etc.
- When and how should I implement it into training?
  - as a monitoring, regular assessment or racing and feedback tool
  - plan to use it during repetitive training session for tracking purposes
- How can I ensure that the information gathered is accurate?
  - always be precise in the hardware set-up, calibration, maintenance procedure and data capture and analysis
  - be aware that data analysis takes time – plan what you want to do
  - don't 'out-gadget' yourself
- What do I need to be aware of while using technology?
  - objective data can only be accurate and meaningful if the operator is very thorough during data collection and analysis
  - be aware of the limitations and the accuracy of the technology
  - trust your instincts and always view the data critically
  - stay focused in your feedback and work to a plan that matches your technical or training focus

ROWING-SPECIFIC TECHNOLOGY

Thanks to a fast growing, accessible and more affordable technology market, several miniaturised user-friendly devices for capturing on-water rowing performance are now available. These tools make it simpler for coaches and athletes at any level to independently gather and analyse information and receive real-time feedback similar to the monitor of a rowing ergometer.

With modern sport trending towards greater specificity and individualisation in equipment design, rowing equipment and materials are also becoming more and more technically sophisticated (boats, oars, riggers, stretchers and seats). Even seat shapes and footstretchers are more individualised and gender or weight-category specific to suit various body types, leg lengths or various specific Para-rowing requirements. As biomechanists, we are often asked to assist high performance athletes and crews to:

- Analyse various pieces of rowing equipment with high-end comprehensive biomechanical on-water acquisition systems (i.e. Peach Innovations or BioRow in combination with other GPS units and/or applications) or vice versa.
- Advise on what technology is suitable for their school/club/college/elite rowing programme dependent on the boat equipment they have available.

To quantify the equipment and any athlete and boat performance comprehensively, rowing-specific technology is necessary to obtain accurate measures. This means that the sensitivity and technical specifications of those devices need to be pre-adjusted for 'the rowing motion and its on-water training demands' to achieve optimal sampling performance. These prerequisites on the technology will ensure that the data analysis of the multitude of technical and performance aspects that describe the rowing movement, can be accurately and reliably delivered.

Currently on the open market, there are various advanced accessible technologies with lightweight non-obtrusive tracking devices incorporating high frequency datalogging, GPS technology and inertial sensors offering a wide range of 'on-water rowing' hardware and software solutions:

- The comprehensive biomechanical on-water acquisition systems (e.g. Peach Innovations or BioRow) can capture and analyse the complex kinematic (time, velocity, acceleration) and dynamic (forces, power) aspects of the athlete's movement on the oar, seat, stretcher and boat rowing motion and performance – for any boat classes from a single scull to a coxed eight boat. These systems are obviously more cost demanding, however deliver the accuracy and reliability required to examine the athlete's and boat's technical performance, and ensure precise assessment and feedback.
- Various lightweight and user-friendly GPS devices (e.g. Catapult MiniMaxX, Spin, AccRow) are perfect for monitoring boat performance (boat velocity and propulsive boat acceleration) during training and racing and additionally for analysing multidimensional boat behaviour (boat rotation and side/vertical boat

displacement). These devices are stand-alone products, however, are often used in combination with systems that offer additional individual athlete information. It is absolutely crucial to point out that not every GPS unit will automatically be useful for analysing the rowing-specific boat motion, and might require a 'rowing-specific' written software application to guarantee the accuracy of the information regarding the boat performance.

- Instrumented oar handles (e.g. smartOar, OarPowerMeter) provide another solution to measure the individual force and power output on the oar in relation to the boat motion. These instrumented handles are easy to mount, wireless and flexible to use during training. However, so far they do not give you any information about the oar angle positions.

- Phone/tablet-based applications are already popular as monitoring tools. These units have mostly built-in GPS technology and inertial sensors incorporated, measuring kinematic parameters (i.e. acceleration, velocity, distance on the boat or oar) continuously and depending on what they aim to measure can be mounted onto the boat (e.g. RowinginMotion) and on the oar (e.g. rowingapp). So far it is hard to find validated information regarding the accuracy for these various rowing-specific parameters gathered within the various software applications. However, there is unlimited potential of combining phone and tablet-based apps with other technologies for training feedback.

Video footage and analysis will always be one of the important coaching and training feedback tools. From stand-alone photo and video cameras to GoPro cameras, drones and phone/tablet based video capture and analysis applications and video goggles etc. – the range of options to provide visual feedback is limitless.

Any type of data analysis will always be enhanced if it can be combined, or ideally synchronised, with video footage.

HARDWARE SET-UP AND CALIBRATION

Utilising these miniaturised technologies and placing the sensors either on the athlete and/or the rowers' equipment (i.e. boat, rigger, oars, seat, footstretcher) is enabling easier and more frequent monitoring of training and racing. Nowadays, most instrumented equipment is so robust to weather and extensive training usage, coaches and athletes tend to leave the rowing-specific equipment on the boat for a period of time.

However, it is essential that special care is taken of the instrumentation, the boat set-up and the calibration. The aim of any measurement is to give objective feedback, which can only be valid when the information is accurate and reliable, otherwise the feedback is misleading to the athlete and can interrupt and even harm the athletes' technical developmental progress and also his/her well-being (i.e. rower's stretcher and rigger position gets wrongly adjusted to an extreme boat set-up due to a calibration error in the oar angle position). This is where the highest chances for mistakes in the data gathering process can occur, especially if the data is logged and not viewed in real-time.

However, most incidents are avoidable by allowing an extra 5–10 minutes before the on-water session to check if all the measuring devices are mounted firmly and correctly, batteries are charged and all rowing-specific information related to the crew or the rower (i.e. rigging details) are correctly stored in the datalogger box (to avoid wrong calculations). Coaches should make sure the athletes are aware when on-water data collection takes place, so no extra rowing gear (e.g. water bottles) accidently interferes with the measuring devices. Another common occurrence is that sensor boxes moved from their original mounted and calibrated point due to wet boat conditions (e.g. the velcro tape moved). Two examples of common accidental errors are displayed below. In example 1, the GPS unit was attached to the boat the wrong way around and in example 2, a gate angle sensor worked lose and moved around the pin before or during the session – in both cases neither the coach nor the athletes noticed the issue – so the faulty data was recorded.

Example 1 (Figure 5): the GPS unit has incorporated multidimensional boat acceleration sensors, measuring the boat motion in the propulsive, transverse, vertical direction. The propulsive boat acceleration sensor measures in the direction of the boat travel (positive, when the hull is accelerating during the main drive phase and up to two-thirds of the recovery). The main deceleration phase during a rowing cycle is from approximately the last third of the recovery phase until after the catch when the blades are covered in the water and start to propel the boat hull again.

If the GPS unit is mounted facing the wrong way around on the boat, the sensor measures the boat movement in the wrong direction and so the information is faulty and cannot be used.

Example 2 (Figure 6): the angle sensor (the silver disc below the oarlock) is integrated into the instrumented oarlock system (in this case, Peach Innovations). The sensor needs to be tightened to the pin via two screws and calibrated in relation to the boat hull to measure the horizontal angle movement and the propulsive oarlock force (in the direction of the boat travel) accurately.

If the screws loosen and the angle sensor moves (e.g. the oarlock gets hit at the pontoon during the boat launching), it affects the absolute oarlock angle and force

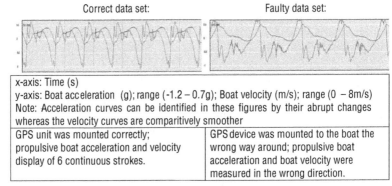

Correct data set:	Faulty data set:

x-axis: Time (s)
y-axis: Boat acceleration (g); range (-1.2 – 0.7g); Boat velocity (m/s); range (0 – 8m/s)
Note: Acceleration curves can be identified in these figures by their abrupt changes whereas the velocity curves are comparitively smoother

GPS unit was mounted correctly; propulsive boat acceleration and velocity display of 6 continuous strokes.	GPS device was mounted to the boat the wrong way around; propulsive boat acceleration and boat velocity were measured in the wrong direction.

Figure 5: Display of two data sets of the continuous boat velocity and boat acceleration trace (correct – middle vs. incorrect – right due to a mounting error of the equipment)

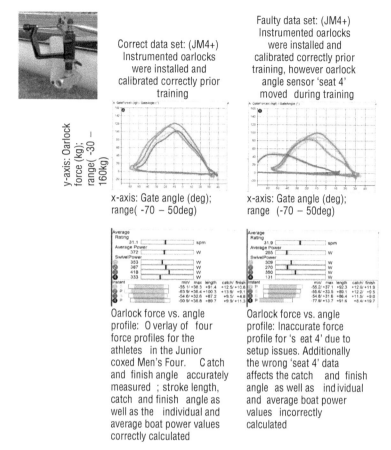

Figure 6: Display of two data sets of the overlay of four average force-angle profiles (correct – middle vs. incorrect – right due to a loose oar angle sensor during the data collection

information. Additionally, the individual as well as the averaged boat power values will be calculated wrongly as a cumulative error, which affects the analysis and feedback for the one athlete as well as the crew.

PLANNING MONITORING AND TRAINING ASSESSMENT

Before coaches and athletes had regular access to their own on-water technology and to information resources, the sport scientist and/or engineer was largely controlling all aspects of the biomechanical on-water data acquisition system, testing design, data collection and analysis aiming to provide high quality detailed yet often delayed (time-consuming) post-training and racing feedback.

Standard testing protocols were designed to evaluate all aspects of the athlete's technical skill level and physical capacity throughout the range of training up to racing stroke rates (including starts) and over longer distances to also cover the effect of the fatigue component on the individual technique and boat speed.

One common typical protocol for elite athletes would be performed as such: (1) 2000m-step rate test (500m @ stroke rate 18–22–26–30/32; for bigger boat starting two stroke rate points higher), 2x 500m simulated race pace stroke rate (one standing start 500m piece, one running 500m piece) and three starts (5 strokes, 10 strokes, 15 strokes). The advantages are that the pieces (1) cover the entire technical skill level under different velocity conditions and stroke rates (SR) and (2) are comparable between the individuals and different testing blocks throughout the seasons. The disadvantages are that the assessment (protocol) is time-consuming and physically quite demanding, especially early in the training season, and definitely not applicable for all levels of rowing. Additionally, the testing protocol results depend on the individual and crew 'day' performances under the given weather conditions.

Looking practically at the limited number and time-restricted training sessions of big university and club rowing programmes, comprehensive protocols like this are not logistically suitable as well as not necessary for the number and different levels of rowers you are considering to evaluate. An adjusted simplified testing protocol (consider 2–3 increasing stroke rates over a selected distance) that can be implemented into your training with repeatable sessions over the season would be an advantage (protocols may vary between teams depending on your access to waterways). Despite a careful preparation, the more consistent the controlled (protocol) biomechanical data measurement can be performed, the more precise you can evaluate the technical skill and performance development of the individual athletes the crews and the squad and the more specifically you can individualise the training.

We always need to remember that rowing is a strength endurance sport (it requires high volumes of training) but technical proficiency is essential to achieve a high performance, as it is of little value to develop strength, endurance and physiological capabilities if these qualities cannot be transferred into boat speed.

Having access to highly accurate training and racing technology and data provides comprehensive monitoring and feedback opportunities in addition to regular assessment sessions. Utilising on one hand the advantages of precision (data is measurable) underlines, however, on the other hand the importance of how data should be thoroughly captured, analysed, presented and stored.

Biomechanical technique and performance analysis and feedback training remain only an aid for coaching and training. The expertise of the coach in carefully and critically implementing objective information into training – is the art of coaching.

'Technology' checklist

This checklist aims to guide and assist coaches, athletes and operators towards becoming confident in the implementation of biomechanical 'on-water' rowing-technology and utilising data during training and racing.

Before training/ racing		Y	N
Equipment and Hardware tools	Have you charged all hardware tools that require batteries (e.g. logger boxes, GPS devices, phones, tablets, cox boxes, heart rate monitors, megaphones etc.)? Does the toolbox have all required tools for any equipment adjustments? Do you have the logbook?		
Quality assurance	Is the system set-up complete, are all attachment points and screws tightened? Are all sensors calibrated and zeroed? Do you need to change seat, oarlock, stretcher set-ups before the session? Is the current rigging set-up (inboard, oar length, span of the oars) recorded in the logger box?		
During the session	Have you, the athletes and the coxswains turned the devices on? Most on-water assessment tools need to be turned on when the boat sits stationary on the water for calibration purposes. Ensure the data that appears on the screens is correct and the boat goes in a straight line before you give 'measured' feedback to the athletes. Have you made a record of the session, including weather conditions?		
After the session	Have you downloaded and saved the files in the appropriate folders? Have you checked the data for quality assurance? Have you marked the pieces of interest from the session (consider carefully which pieces you quantify – try to exclude rowing around corners when evaluating an athlete's oar angle positions)? Have you included session details (boat class, athletes' names, weather conditions, workload)?		
Data management	Have you recorded what type of session it was? Did you include monitoring, assessment/protocol, feedback-training, racing? What analysis/templates have you used for the reports? Have you added pieces and reports to the database?		
Finish	Have you ensured that all devices will be fully operational and charged for the next session?		

Selection of recommended rowing literature for training and coaching

Kleshnev, V., *The Biomechanics of Rowing*, Crowood Press, Ramsbury, UK, 2016

Altenburg D., Mattes K. & Steinacker J., *Manual for Rowing Training: Technique, High Performance and Planning*, Limpert Verlag GmbH, Wibelsheim, 2012

Nolte, V., *Rowing Faster*, Human Kinetics, Champaign, Illinois, 1st edition 2005, 2nd edition 2011

Secher, N. H. & Volianitis, S. (Eds), *Handbook for Sports Medicine and Science, Rowing*, published under the auspices of the International Olympic Committee (IOC), in collaboration with the International Rowing Federation (FISA), Wiley-Blackwell, London, 2007

Smith R. & Loschner C., Biomechanics feedback for rowing, Journal of Sports Sciences, 20, 783-791, 2002

Monthly Rowing Biomechanics Newsletter (www.biorow.com)

On Bullshit Point

Christopher Dodd Journalist, editor, author, and rowing historian

Christopher Dodd covered rowing for the *Guardian* and the *Independent* for 40 years.

He is founding editor of the International Rowing Federation's *World Rowing* magazine and British Rowing's *Regatta* magazine, which he edited for 15 years. He continues to contribute to its successor *Rowing+Regatta* and the blogs Hear the Boat Sing and RowingVoice.

In 1994 he left his day job as an editor in the *Guardian*'s features department to set up the River & Rowing Museum at Henley-on-Thames, where he helped to assemble the collections and is now a vice-president. He has delivered history lectures at several FISA coaching conferences.

He has written nine books, including histories of Henley Regatta, the Boat Race and World Rowing. *Unto the Tideway Born* is the story of 500 years of the Watermen's Company; *Water Boiling Aft* is the story of London RC's 150 years pioneering rowing on the Tideway, and *Bonnie Brave Boat Rowers* is the story of Tyne professionals, boatbuilders and the songwriters who honoured them. Further info can be found at www.doddsworld.org

Dodd's inglorious rowing career gave him brief appearances at Clifton College, Nottingham University, Poplar, the London Irregulars and lengthy ones on FISA pleasure tours.

Pierre de Coubertin, the father of the modern Olympics, asked himself a question about the founding Olympic sport in 1911. Why, he queried, has rowing not died out, given that it is so handicapped, particularly when the idea is to make the least effort possible and when 'the love of publicity and the hatred of discipline are so overtly predominate?' He observed that spectators complain that they only see the finish if they are on the stands, and see nothing at all if they are following along behind. 'If people are lured ... all they really manage to do is catch a few quick glimpses of a spectacle that only the initiated can appreciate.'

He then answered his own question by saying that 'Rowing is a rigorous, tough cult, which is all about obedience and self-denial... Not a single one of its followers has abandoned it. This should give you some idea of its value and endurance'. Some idea, also, of rowing's training environment formed long before Coubertin's Games began in 1896 (yes, there was rowing on the programme, but only one sculler reached the stakeboat in the stormy Bay of Piraeus).

Coubertin would hardly recognise rowing a hundred years later. In his day, FISA held annual European Championships where English was rarely or perhaps never heard, while the Olympic Games was largely a duel between English speaking countries, dominated by Britain and the United States.

I began to follow international rowing as a journalist in 1970, several years after I retired as a humble student oarsman. My beat became the Oxford and Cambridge Boat Race, Henley Regatta, World Championships and the Olympics, with a good smattering of other events in between. The Cold War spiced things up a good deal. Everyone was suspicious of everyone. There were constant rumours of defections from East to West. Suspicion and jealousy of coaching methods and training regimes abounded. Coaches metaphorically kept their arms close to their chests at all times. And there was, of course, frequent allusion to pills and performance enhancing substances.

Another great thing in the 1970s was that rowing teams and national federations did not have press officers or public relations departments. Outside the Eastern bloc, they were lucky if they had a team manager. If they did have a team manager, he or she was responsible for getting people and boats to the Back of Beyond Regatta, finding accommodation, arriving at the start for the right race in the right event, and getting everybody and everything home again. If there was no team manager, guess who was in charge? Coach.

For the correspondents, this was a double-sided coin. Information was difficult to come by until you found people who trusted you, but there were fewer restrictions on where you could go or whom you could talk to.

For a reporter, the first thing to do at a regatta was to find Bullshit Point. Every regatta course has a Bullshit Point, even if it's only a tent with a television screen in it,

International crews racing past Bullshit Point at Lucerne. *Credit: Steve McArthur*

where those coaches who can bear to watch gather to spy on races. They smile slyly to themselves when their charges make a killing spurt, or opponents drag anchors. They mutter excuses when events topsy-turvy their best laid plans.

The Rotsee in Lucerne is a good example. There is a corner near the boating pontoons from where the first 1000 metres is visible, and where crews tend to make their moves as they pass. As a race comes down, coaches behind the reeds at the water's edge cradle stopwatches as if sitting an exam, fending off the prying eye behind the shoulder. Grimaces or grins tell stories. Faces lighting up tells a big story.

As I say, every regatta course has a Bullshit Point, and regattas usually entertain a debate among rowing correspondents as to whether 'bullshit' is one word or two.

Until the Berlin Wall came down in 1989, rowing thrived on mutual suspicion. An example came at the Amsterdam World Championships on the Bosbaan in 1977, when two rumours spread simultaneously. One started when a Soviet crew scratched because of sickness. The other began with hearsay that Schiphol airport's control tower was having interference in Russian during the hours of racing, which implied illegal coaching from the bank.

After hours of clandestine digging by several reporters, neither story stood up. The Soviet sickness was genuine, not a cover for defection (although I believe that an East German defected at the end of those championships). When I called Schiphol's control tower from a public telephone, the duty officer confessed to Russian language interference during the hours of racing, but said it originated from a Moscow radio station and happened regularly in particular atmospheric conditions. It turned out that the Japanese were using ship-to-shore radio on the Bosbaan during training, but not during racing, so that was OK.

Before we examine the thaw of the Cold War, let's briefly look over the evolution of international rowing, particularly the Olympics, the peak of the mountain. The story goes like this: FISA was founded in 1892 by The Netherlands, France, Switzerland, Italy and Trieste (then part of Austria), and began annual European championships in 1893, three years before Coubertin's International Olympic Committee's first modern Olympic Games, set in Athens. Until the Second World War, English-speaking countries won most of the Olympic medals, while FISA and its European Championships were predominantly Continental European. The hastily arranged Games in London in 1948 brought these worlds closer together. England had two national federations divided by different definitions of the word amateur. They were forced to merge and affiliate to FISA in order to be allowed to compete in the Olympic Regatta in Henley. Meanwhile, Olympic rowing as we know it was taking shape.

In 1920 entries per country per event were reduced to one. The five ring flag and motto 'Faster, Higher, Stronger' were introduced. The repêchage 'second chance' round was introduced in 1924. In 1936 came the torch relay and athletes' parade at the opening ceremony.

Through this period Britain and America vied for most of the medals. Britain won the eights in 1908 and 1912, after which it was the US at every Games. Jack Kelly (US) and Jack Beresford (GB) were the first great sculling duellists, followed in the 1960s by Stuart Mackenzie (Australia) and Vyasheslav Ivanov (USSR) and, in the 1980s, Peter-Michael Kolbe (West Germany) and Pertti Karppinen (Finland).

The Soviet Union entered the Olympic arena at Helsinki in 1952, where the organisers were forced to provide two villages for athletes, one for the East and one for the rest. A famous incident of ice-breaking was the invitation to the American eight – who were from the US Naval Academy – to take tea with the Soviet eight in their village. The US management was against the idea, but the crew defied officialdom and a great party was had by all.

During the Cold War the Olympic arena became a gladiatorial display of power politics on the lake as well as in the arena. Several battles were in progress, apart from boycotts and tit-for-tat disputes. The USA and the USSR eyeballed each other for world dominance. West Germany and East Germany were engaged in a private battle for national honour. And East Germany, desperate to convert its status and perception from a Soviet occupied military zone to a state, took on the Soviet Union and the other Eastern bloc countries in addition to the US and Federal Germany.

East Germany got its wish after the 1968 Olympics. It was recognised in its own right by the IOC, and no longer had to form joint Olympic teams with West Germany. While unlimited government resources were thrown at sports like rowing by Moscow and East Berlin, the rest bumbled on, passing the wisdom of amateur coaching forbears down the line.

This was certainly the case in Britain, the motherland of the sport. A handful of clubs formed crews in a variety of styles and put them forward for selection, and then wondered why they had not seen a gold medal since 1948. While the USSR and East Germany dominated the medal tables – particularly in women's rowing after the IOC admitted women's events in 1976 – other countries were starved of cash and knowledge. At best, the West could only nibble on the fringes of the honours.

Gradually, however, western countries gnawed their way in. The West Germans inadvertently laid much of the ground adopted by their eastern compatriots when Karl Adam began his work at Ratzeburg in the 1950s. Norway and Thor Nilsen found the Hansen brothers, world-dominating double scullers. Finland found Pertti Karppinen, three-times Olympic champion in single sculls. Italy found the Abbagnale brothers, champions in coxed pairs for more than a decade. Britain hired its first full-time professional coach, Bob Janousek, to regain the Olympic podium with an eight and a double scull in 1976. A sprinkling of coaches from the East turned up in North America and were at work adapting the programmes written for full-time athletes to the part-time culture of Western countries. These are, of course, among those who gather on Bullshit Point.

The examples above brought a number of strands to play on performance and preparation in the West. Karl Adam, a heavyweight boxer and hammer thrower in his time, taught physics, philosophy and physical education at a school in Ratzeburg. In 1948 he revived rowing there at the request of the school's director. He had no knowledge or experience of rowing, so he applied what he knew from athletics and boxing to develop a programme that included much 'steady state' work and eventually produced a gold medal for the German eight at the 1960 Olympics in Rome. Adam's oarsmen regarded themselves as anti-establishment upstarts, a view shared by the German rowing establishment. But they changed the world, and the maestro's influence showed up later when the East Germans had government funding to go on where Adam left off.

Thor Nilsen rowed for Norway in the 1952 Olympics and coached in 1960. Until the Second World War and after, Norwegian rowing was a summer sport based firmly on the teaching of Steve Fairbairn, an Australian who spent most of his life in England. Nilsen took his country into the international arena with help from Ivan Vanier, a Dutch Indonesian who knew physical education and psychology, and whose chief contribution was the 'international modern style' derived from Adam. Nilsen also cooperated with the fathers of exercise physiology, the Swede P. O. Astrand and the Norwegian K. Rodahl. In 1975, when the East Germans were well established in rowing's driving seat, Nilsen coached his first gold for the outstanding double-sculling Hansen brothers, Alf and Frank. He set up training centres in Spain and Italy and was the prime mover in FISA's development programme, of which more later.

The coach Bo Gammels brought the giant Finnish sculler Pertti Karppinen to the start line in 1976 when he won his first of three Olympic titles in the single scull. As a part-time village fireman and manager of a tiny bus company, Karppinen was ideally placed to be a sculling champion. His day job allowed flexible hours and he did not require the kind of resources that bigger boats required.

Giuseppe and Carmine Abbagnale were born at Pompeii into a family of gladioli growers, and are an example of outstanding athletes breaking into top level performance in a small boat – helped by the Italian federation that was one of the better resourced in the West. The Abbagnales also had great family support. For most of their career, that included two Olympic and seven world titles, they were coached by their uncle.

Britain's Amateur Rowing Association hired Bob Janousek in 1969, primarily to write a coaching education programme and secondly, to be chief coach of the men's senior team. Janousek came with an Olympic record as medallist and coach, and he possessed qualifications in sport science. His arrival began the long process of adapting East European methods, where athletes had two outings a day and an assured career path, to the British way of life where one outing was the norm and financial and technical back-up was minimal.

In the spring of 1976, Janousek requested the British Olympic Association (BOA) to ask employers to give his Olympic squad an hour off work each day to fit an early morning outing into their schedule. The BOA refused, arguing that it could not single out one sport for special treatment. Janousek then wrote the letters himself, and all employers readily agreed. Across the Atlantic, Olympic crews were mostly made up of students and recent graduates who were wealthy enough to postpone careers for a few years or to have employers willing to give them time off.

Although cards were generally kept close to the chest, the narrowing gap between medal winners and also-rans caused information exchange to open up. FISA began to organise international coaches conferences, conferences that play an important part in FISA's strategy to spread the gospel of rowing. Politically, it is essential that rowing remains an Olympic sport, for without the Olympics and its television rights, rowing would wither. Hence the continued emphasis on growing the number of member federations, and hence the importance of the FISA development programme in bringing coaching expertise, technical help, boat building and equipment maintenance tips to lesser developed rowing worlds – particularly in Asia, Central and South America and Africa.

Conferring and cooperating have transformed rowing despite its pathetic resources for development as compared with 'box office' sports. Ten years of debate during the 1980s resulted in the distance rowed by juniors and women to increase to 2000 metres, the same distance as men. In the case of women, the move from 1000 metres converted their competition from sprint to endurance. After the Barcelona Games in 1992, the Olympic programme was adjusted to bring in events for lightweights. One effect of the Olympic handle was that national federations – including those of the Eastern bloc – were able to attract funding for lightweight crews. Regatta entries from continents other than Europe and the English-speaking world are rare no longer. Funding has also increased career opportunities for professional coaches. Additionally, science came to the notice of a sport that traditionally considered itself an art. All these things fortified the excuses and justifications to be whispered among the growing crowd on Bullshit Point.

How things have moved on since my own illustrious career as a coach! This took place on one day in 1957 on the Bristol Avon. As the last member of the school boat club to get off the bus that afternoon, there was no seat for me in a boat, so I was given a bike and told to ride the towpath and shout at some novices. In time-honoured fashion I told them what I had heard a week beforehand. The classics teacher in charge of rowing had sat at the feet of men who had sat at the feet of Steve Fairbairn at Jesus College, Cambridge. He taught us that we should put pressure on the foot stretcher to keep the heavy old fixed-seat tub level, and that it was a good idea to drop blades into the water and get them out again at the same time.

Crucially, he demonstrated that we should sound a bell note each time we put the blade in at the 'catch'. On the Bristol Avon in the 1950s, the tolling of bells was the ultimate aim and achievement of future titans of the oar. Somehow the point of it – a quick catch – was lost in the salubrious waters that sludged past a paper mill, a tar works and a sewage farm as well as our boathouse. You should try ringing a bell note in that cocktail of effluent. Although such sonority is impossible these days when big blades are the norm.

When the Eastern bloc cracked apart in the early 1990s, rowing had talent spotting schemes for athlete selection, technical approaches to training and rowing style, and a plethora of support services and experts medical, psychological and physical. There were diets, fitness, weight training, cleavers and rowing machines.

People more qualified than me will take this story on under the blue sky of the 21st century. Some of Coubertin's remarks a century ago still apply today. Spectators often catch only a few quick glimpses of a spectacle that only the initiated can appreciate. But rowing remains a rigorous, tough cult, which is all about obedience and self-denial, the keys to its value and endurance.

And the only bell notes that you hear on Bullshit Point these days are on the Rotsee in Lucerne, where they dangle from the necks of cows.

About the Authors

Charles Simpson

Charles Simpson (PhD) is a Senior Lecturer in Sport and Exercise Science at Oxford Brookes University in the UK where he is also the course leader for the Master's programme in Applied Sport and Exercise Nutrition. He has degrees in sport science and human physiology from the Universities of Texas, Sydney and Aberdeen. Charles has 30 years of experience as a rower and coach. He currently works with various rowing teams in the UK to help enhance their training and nutrition approaches. He is also a past recipient of British Rowing's Coach of the Year award.

Previous publications:
The Complete Guide to Indoor Rowing (with Jim Flood), Bloomsbury, London, 2012
Various articles in rowing magazines and scientific publications

Jim Flood

Jim Flood is currently a Coach Educator for British Rowing and the Fédération Internationale des Sociétés d'Aviron (FISA, the World Rowing Federation). He has helped to develop rowing in Argentina, Chile, Kenya, Nigeria and Uganda. As a former design engineer, his interest is in developing basic rowing equipment that can be made using local skills and materials. See http://openergo.webs.com/http://openergo.webs.com/

Previous publications:
Know the Game: Rowing, A & C Black, London, 2007
The Complete Guide to Indoor Rowing (with Charles Simpson), Bloomsbury, London, 2012
Various articles in rowing magazines and websites such as https://www.rowperfect.co.uk/

Acknowledgements

Our thanks to our editors Charlotte Croft and Sarah Skipper for their insightful comments, encouragement, support and advice.

We also want to particularly thank Steve McArthur and Don Somner for their help in sourcing and providing photographs that support and illustrate the text.

Photo credits

All photos are credited as they appear throughout the book with the exception of the following: P.9 © Noel Donaldson; p.31 © Johan Flodin; p.47 © Simon Cox; p.79 © Ben Lewis; p.95 © Dave O'Neill; p.109 © Mark Fangen-Hall; p.127 © Robin Williams; p.148 photos curtesy of University of Agder; p.171 © Trent Lawson; p.186 curtesy of University of Agder; p.209 © Conny Draper; p.222 © Christopher Dodd; p.229 (top photo) curtest of University of Agder and bottom photo © Jim Flood

Index

Note: page numbers in *italic* indicate illustrations; those in **bold** indicate tables and figures